"If you want to continue to advance your skills and confidence as a therapist — but don't want to add yet another 'approach' or 'technique' to your already overstuffed toolkit — this is the book for you. Ellis works on the assumption that you already have the knowledge and resources you need to be an effective therapist, and she provides a treasure trove of useful tips and easy-to-practice exercises to help you strengthen your therapeutic muscles and further refine your therapeutic techniques. There's a reason we call what we do a 'therapy practice' — and although in our profession practice will never make perfect, it will certainly make you better — and Ellis's nuggets of wisdom will certainly help you get there."

Victor Yalom, PhD, *founder and CEO of Psychotherapy.net*

"I don't know how she did it, but Stephanie Ellis managed to cram half a graduate program's worth of foundational research on psychotherapy into a book that weighs less than a bag of coffee beans, and by some magic it reads more like an engaging mystery novel than a textbook! This book is everything you could hope for — knowledgeable and practical, challenging in the way that brings out your best, and lighthearted and endlessly entertaining."

Scott Barry Kaufman, **PhD**, *host of The Psychology Podcast, author of* Transcend: The New Science of Self-Actualization

"Stephanie Ellis provides a relational approach to help therapists better themselves. Up-to-date information. Engaging read. Easily incorporates methods to improve your practice regardless of preferred theory or level of experience."

Jeffrey K. Zeig, PhD, *director of the Milton H. Erickson Foundation*

"A valuable resource for new and experienced therapists alike, each chapter of *Five Minutes a Day to an Upgraded Practice* directs you to the foundational elements of effective psychotherapy, next-level nuances of theory and practice, and pragmatic ways to apply these concepts right away. If you want to improve as a therapist, use the advice we give to our clients and make small, consistent, and meaningful changes, and read one short chapter a day of this engaging, informative book."

Joel Minden, PhD, *psychologist, author of* Show Your Anxiety Who's Boss: A Three-Step CBT Program to Help You Reduce Anxious Thoughts and Worry

"Dr. Stephanie Ellis's masterfully written book is an excellent guide for therapists in all stages of their careers. In a fun and engaging manner, Dr. Ellis describes the bedrock concepts of the field and then transforms each principle into a practical tip. The wisdom throughout the book will be especially useful to novice therapists seeking powerful ways to enhance patient care."

Kathryn H. Gordon, PhD, *clinical psychologist, author of* The Suicidal Thoughts Workbook: Cognitive-Behavioral Therapy Skills to Reduce Emotional Pain, Increase Hope, and Prevent Suicide

Five Minutes a Day to an Upgraded Therapy Practice

Five Minutes a Day to an Upgraded Therapy Practice is a compilation of short, useful suggestions based on classic theory, current research, and wisdom gathered over fifteen years of clinical practice, supervision, and graduate teaching in psychology and counseling. Chapters include highly practical upgrades on standard therapy techniques and ideas for continual therapist development (that respect the busy life of the mental health professional!). The book is made up of ten sections, each with ten short chapters, each readable in under five minutes. It is an indispensable resource for practicing mental health clinicians, including counselors, clinical social workers, psychologists, and other helpers, as well as advanced students in counseling or similar graduate programs.

Stephanie Ellis, PhD, is a licensed psychologist with a doctorate in counseling psychology. For over fifteen years, she has been providing psychotherapy, teaching psychology and counseling, and delivering group and individual supervision.

Five Minutes a Day to an Upgraded Therapy Practice

Transtheoretical Tips to Help You Make the Most of Each Session

Stephanie Ellis

Routledge
Taylor & Francis Group

NEW YORK AND LONDON

First published 2022
by Routledge
605 Third Avenue, New York, NY 10158

and by Routledge
2 Park Square, Milton Park, Abingdon, Oxon, OX14 4RN

Routledge is an imprint of the Taylor & Francis Group, an informa business

Library of Congress Cataloging-in-Publication Data
Names: Ellis, Stephanie (Psychologist), author.
Title: Five minutes a day to an upgraded therapy practice :
    transtheoretical tips to help you make the most of each session /
    Stephanie Ellis.
Description: New York, NY : Routledge, 2021. | Includes
    bibliographical references and index.
Identifiers: LCCN 2020054479 (print) | LCCN 2020054480
    (ebook) | ISBN 9780367636135 (hardback) | ISBN
    9780367636142 (paperback) | ISBN 9781003125082 (ebook)
Subjects: LCSH: Psychotherapy.
Classification: LCC RC480 .E44 2021 (print) | LCC RC480
    (ebook) | DDC 616.89/14—dc23
LC record available at https://lccn.loc.gov/2020054479
LC ebook record available at https://lccn.loc.gov/2020054480

ISBN: 978-0-367-63613-5 (hbk)
ISBN: 978-0-367-63614-2 (pbk)
ISBN: 978-1-003-12508-2 (ebk)

DOI: 10.4324/9781003125082

Typeset in Helvetica
by Apex CoVantage, LLC

To my students and my clients – it takes a garden to grow a gardener.
Thank you.

Table of Contents

Acknowledgments

My deepest thanks and appreciation to …

… my family, without whom this never would have happened. Seth (my husband, and my never-ending encourager, my balance, my dreambuilder, and the rope that binds, who deserves a book's worth of acknowledgments), Ashlynn and Audrey (my wise and super cool daughters, my goddesses, my elves, my scientists, my blessings, my snugglers, my flowers, my bugs, my playmates, my delights, who make every day vibrant and allow me the honor of glimpsing into their amazing worlds), Mom and Dad (my parents, and my foundation-builders, possibility-makers, and support-givers, who helped me believe I could do something like this by never having a doubt in their minds that I would), Michelle (my sister, and my inspiration, my co-comedienne of this crazy life, my total-opposite-and-somehow-exact-match, who tolerates my weirdness and makes afternoons more fun) and the friends who are family, too (my whiskey-sharers, my late night conversationalists, my gaming buddies, and my mass meme-senders). Your support, in all its forms, has literally made this possible. Also, thank you for your encouragement, enthusiasm, acceptance of my occasional insanity, and for giving me the time and space when I needed it to write.

… my collaborators, without whom this would have been a complete mess. Carlos, my consultation partner and flaneuring companion, who can read it all in my voice. Thank you for the gentle, honest feedback, the occasional surprised delight that made the writing process so worthwhile, and for co-tending the garden that much of this book grew in. Grace and Stace, who guide my steps. Thank you for ushering me gently through the process. Monica, who guides my words. Thank you for your intervention in my quasi-addiction to hyphens. And Anna, my editor. I finally know why editors are always included in the acknowledgments. Thank you for your quick replies, unending encouragement, and – of course – for the chance to write this.

… my inspirations and my teachers, without whom there would have been nothing to write. My formative, real-life supervisors (Mike, Tony,

Dave, & Dave) and my "desktop supervisors" (Irv, Gene, Carl, Carl, Carl, Viktor, Alfred, Albert, Karen, Cloe, Bill, William, Wilhelm, Elizabeth, Abe, Sigmund, Virginia, Ken, Lev, BF, Rollo, Fritz, Dan, Dan, Dan, Søren, Marvin, Martin, Martin, Milton, John, Jay, Jacob, Joseph, Julian, Michael, Michael, Mihaly, Bessel, Eric, Erik, Erich, Frieda, Peter, Paul, Phil, Sue, Esther, Otto, Tem, Dick, & Harry). Thank you for every gift that you've given in your writing, research, practice, and teaching. I pray that I share them faithfully.

Introduction

Don't you love it, when you make a purchase at a little country store, and you discover that the owner has thrown in a few hard candies for your kids? That's a *lagniappe.* It's the extra ounce of wine you get in a pour for being a regular customer, or the free bunch of cilantro you get at the farmer's market. It's a Spanish–French–Louisianan word that means "a little something extra." This book is about how you can give that lagniappe to your clients. In five minutes a day, over the next few months, you can transform your clinical practice with quick and easy adjustments to your therapy that will pay off in client satisfaction, growth, and commitment. (And maybe some personal growth, too!)

Inside you'll find quick but powerful ideas about how to get the most out of techniques you already use, introductions to theories you may never have learned, ethical guidelines for real life, challenges to common cognitive distortions, suggestions for changes in therapeutic language, and more. Each chapter concludes with a brief and pragmatic practice tip. Chapters 1–5 are about things to know and things to do inside sessions to make sessions more effective. Chapters 6–10 are about ways-to-be; these are professional development ideas that, though they happen outside of session, also improve in-session work. It's all based in the primary sources (so don't be nervous when you see those old references!) and supplemented with current research (because there's nothing new under the sun ... except validated instruments and meta-analyses).

If you're reading this book as part of class in your training program, I expect it will be the easiest and most enjoyable "textbook" you ever have. My hope is that you'll treat it like you treat a good supervisor – let it inform you, certainly, but mostly let it spark interesting discussions and encourage you to be your best therapist self. If you're reading this book as a professional, I hope you'll treat it like a "bathroom book" – absorbing these short tidbits from over a decade and a half of psychotherapy and supervision and then taking the ones that fit you into your therapy room to get *a little something extra* from that 50-minute hour.

Just one more thing before you get started. Even though this book has a lot of practical ideas, it is not about "equipping your toolbox." Technicians are skilled professionals who *use tools to fix things.* We are skilled professionals who *use relationships to help people.* That's the bottom line. Please enjoy!

How Does the "Talking Cure" Cure? (The Infrastructure of Therapy)

Let's begin at the beginning. Since long before the birth of psychology and psychotherapy as we know it, some of the primary principles of healing the conditions of human life have been well established (Katz, 2017). Over time, theorists and researchers have tried to enumerate these principles as they pertain to the kind of healing that we practice now – when mental/emotional healing is largely separated from physical healing, when trauma is often a private rather than community event, when we choose strangers as our healers. This kind of research began almost a century ago, with identification of such common factors as "effective therapist personality" and "adherence to a system that is adapted to the client" (Rosenzweig, 1936). In this section, we'll look at some of the ways that these fundamental healing principles have been conceptualized and researched, and how we can bring them to bear in therapy for maximal effect.

CHAPTER 1
GETTING ROGERS RIGHT

Let's begin with the foundations of the foundational therapy – Person-Centered Therapy.

Rogers (1957) enumerated the six core conditions he believed to be necessary and sufficient to "inaugurate the process [of] constructive personality change."

Wait, wait, wait. SIX? Didn't we learn *three* of these in our Theories class?

Yes, don't worry. They're in here. And we'll give those three their due time in the next chapter.

Here we go, in summary form. (1) Client and therapist must be in psychological contact. (2) The client has to be incongruent. (3) The therapist has to be congruent. The therapist has to have (4) unconditional positive regard for the client and (5) empathic understanding of the client's internal experience. The therapist has to (6) communicate all of that and the client has to receive it. There you have it.

First, we should make a mental note that all of these conditions were described by Rogers as a continuum. We aren't expected to do all of this perfectly all the time (thank goodness!), so it should really read like this: Client and therapist must be in psychological contact. The client has to be (at least somewhat) incongruent and the therapist has to be (at least somewhat) congruent (at least during the therapy hour). The therapist has to have (at least some) unconditional positive regard for the client and (at least some) empathic understanding of the client's internal experience. The therapist has to communicate all of that (at least somewhat), and the client has to receive it (at least somewhat). Though the more we do it, the better therapy seems to go.

Second, we should notice that Rogers said doing all of this would *inaugurate* the process of therapeutic change, not complete it (so we don't need to argue the necessary-but-not-sufficient literature here).

OK, now we're ready to talk about these conditions more, starting with "being in psychological contact." This sounds really fancy, but it basically means that the two people notice each other's existence. Rogers believed that significant positive changes don't happen in a vacuum; there has to be a relationship of some kind. (Note: He makes a point to say that this might not be accurate and is just a theory. Maybe some people do plenty of

 DOI: 10.4324/9781003125082-2

personality change from reading excellent books. But if they do, they might be in the bookstore and not in therapy, so we can let that go for now.)

Rogers went on to describe the elements that make that relationship so helpful (which we'll tackle later, I promise) and he ends by saying that, no matter how perfectly we have mastered the intricate understanding of clients' experiences and how authentically we have accepted them, it's all for naught if it isn't communicated to the client. Here, *communicated* has its full meaning – not just that we intended for it to be communicated, or that we implied it or even said it out loud – but that the client has perceived it accurately. Unlike most every other conversation – in which the listener has an equal share of responsibility for interpreting – in therapy, the lion's share of that responsibility is ours.

PRACTICE TIP

How can you know that this magic has been achieved? That you have communicated unconditional positive regard and empathic understanding and the client has received it? Simple! You don't have to make uncanny judgments of clients' progress or just wait to see if they terminate therapy or even trust your "gut." You can just ask! There are two great ways to do this:

- All clarifying questions are either trying to get at this understanding, checking to see if it's been communicated, or both. So, littering your therapy with reflection and clarification is a great way to make sure this is happening. This should be a staple throughout therapy, not just in the beginning.

- Request client feedback directly. One strategy for this that is becoming somewhat popular is the use of brief outcome questionnaires that are filled out by clients after each session or each few sessions. Alternately, you can just ask clients how this is going every now and then. "How comfortable are you feeling?" "How am I doing at getting the sense of what you're saying?" "It seems like I was a little off in understanding you today; there were a few times I worry that I made the wrong assumption. How did that seem to you?"

CHAPTER 2
ROGERS' REAL DEFINITIONS

Ok, let's tackle the juicy parts of what Rogers (1957) said about the core conditions necessary to set the stage for therapeutic change. Just as I promised, we'll now talk about congruence, empathy, and unconditional positive regard.

The first thing Rogers said about congruence is actually about the state of the client, not us. He noted that the client must be in a state of *incongruence.* This means that there is some discrepancy between who the client actually is and who the client believes he is (or ought to be). His description of incongruence sounds surprisingly psychodynamic. He gives examples such as a student developing agoraphobia to cover an actual fear of failing exams or a mother developing an illness in order to keep her children close to home. Effectively, clients develop symptoms to bridge the gap between their actual experience of themselves and a more tolerable idea of themselves, and they do so with varying degrees of conscious awareness. Whoa! That's very different than the definition of congruence we usually hear, which is something like "don't be a robot; let your personality show."

For our part, Rogers is quite lenient with us, and suggests that we need only be congruent during the therapy hour. But he's not quite lenient enough to say "Just let your personality shine through." When Rogers said that congruence is the "absence of a façade" or "being freely and deeply ourselves," he meant that when we are in session, we need to be fully aware of all of our thoughts and feelings (even when they aren't particularly therapeutic). Ok, we can probably do that.

This gets a little more challenging when we begin to think about our other two tasks. The requirement for congruence means that if we are going to *show* unconditional positive regard to a client, we had better be *feeling* unconditional positive regard. This has been described in a few different ways: as "warm acceptance" of the client, as "prizing" the client as a complete and separate person, as "non-possessive caring," and as the opposite of evaluation. It means that clients are allowed to be fully themselves, with all of their thoughts, feelings, distortions, behaviors, habits, defenses, etc., and are accepted completely, warmly, and without judgment. Even the parts we don't like. Wait, isn't not liking a judgment? Yes, exactly. See? It's harder than it seems at first.

 DOI: 10.4324/9781003125082-3

This brings us to therapist empathy. Many of us are under the impression that empathy has something to do with our feelings. It doesn't. It certainly does not have anything to do with sharing the client's emotional pain, though this is a common misconception (and one that is even praised!). Empathy has to do with *sensing* the client's private world. This does include sensing their feelings (along with their thoughts, assumptions, biases, perceptions, bodily activations, etc.), but *without our own feelings getting in the way* (Rogers, 1961). It has been described as "thinking with" the client (Brammer et al., 2003) or "understanding what another person is experiencing or trying to express" (Elliott et al., 2018). Any feelings that we authentically have as therapists are more appropriately described as "feeling toward" the client or client's situation (as opposed to "feeling for" or "feeling with"), and that's part of congruence, not empathy.

PRACTICE TIP

Being fully congruent in session, as Rogers noted, means having your real experience and experiencing it fully. However, even he reminded us that *having* your full experience does not necessarily mean *sharing* your full experience. Care should be taken to expose only those facets of congruence that are therapeutically meaningful (e.g., probably it is not appropriate to say to the client, "I just got distracted thinking about how distracting squirrels can be.") or beneficial (e.g., probably it is not appropriate to say to the client, "I'm thinking about squirrels because I'm actually really bored listening to you right now."). Being *aware* of those congruent states can be useful, though. If you become aware that you are distracted, you can gently bring your attention back to the client. If you become aware that the client really is boring, you might realize something important – they are avoiding the real issue, they have a social skills deficit that needs to be addressed, or you have a less than totally conscious reason for not paying full attention!

CHAPTER 3
THE MYTH AND THE RITUAL: PART I

Let's talk about aspirin and email. Do you know how either of these actually works? Probably not. When we think about how things work, we usually are thinking about how they work *functionally*. This means that we know that we can take an aspirin and our fever goes down or that if we put in the address and hit send, the email appears where it should. We usually aren't thinking *mechanistically*. This is something more like how aspirin inhibits COX-1 and COX-2 activity through covalent modification of active site serine residues (Ornelas et al., 2017) and how email is composed of charges and non-charges of electrons that are stored on one capacitor and then encoded and transmitted as radio waves or light pulses to a different capacitor (Cass, 2007). And, let's be real, most people don't know that. Seriously, ask your regular family doctor or your IT guy about either of these and you'll see what I mean. And the few people who do know the mechanisms still don't know the whole story. Even a biochemist can't tell us exactly how and why molecules work the way they do and even a physicist can't tell us exactly how and why electrons work the way they do.

These are just examples to show that we don't need to be alarmed by this language of the "myth." This is an idea that underlies all sciences, though scientists prefer to call them "hypotheses" or "theories." The myth is "a rationale [or] conceptual scheme ... that provides a plausible explanation for the patient's symptoms" (Frank, 1982). And in the context of a healing setting and emotionally charged relationship with a helper, the myth (along with the ritual) is an indispensable part of psychotherapy.

An especially important factor in utilizing the myth in therapy is *co-creating* the myth with our clients. We may occasionally have a client who is completely baffled by themselves, ready to be fully compliant, and desperate for our expertise. In which case, we should probably provide a myth consistent with whichever kind of work we do best (and maybe check for dependent personality disorder!). But, typically, clients have some idea about why things are the way they are. Maybe they think they need to build resilience or that they've been looking at their world from the wrong perspective. Great – that makes it really easy! Or maybe they think their mother or their circumstances or their chemistry made them this way. Even if their myth isn't healthy or effective, accessing this belief system can help us to coordinate our thinking with the client's, and develop a working

DOI: 10.4324/9781003125082-4

theory (excuse me, a "myth") that at least partly fits with the client's already-established belief system. This should help with client comfort and willingness to engage with the work.

PRACTICE TIP

If you haven't previously thought about the idea of the therapeutic myth, start by identifying your primary theoretical orientation. This is probably intimately tied to the "myth" you most often subscribe to in your conceptualization and that you propose as an explanation for clients. So, the next time you teach a new client how "the way you think impacts the way you feel" or "patterns of relating that you learned in your early family are carried into current relationships," you can realize that you are cooperating to build a myth of the client's distress.

CHAPTER 4
THE MYTH AND THE RITUAL: PART II

Now let's explore the ritual part of the myth–ritual combo. A ritual is any procedure that "requires active participation of both patient and therapist and that is believed by both to be the means of restoring the patient's health" (Frank, 1982). We could create a ritual like "when you wake up in the morning, turn around three times to the left, and that will alleviate your depression." And it might work, especially if we have helped to build the myth that depression is caused by misalignment of neurotransmitters that occurs due to the northern hemispheric rotational patterns and needs to be compensated for. If we really maximize our placebo ingredients, we're likely to get a decent anti-depressant effect. You'll note, though, that the ritual has to be believed *by both client and therapist*! (So, we probably wouldn't go with that one.)

The real magic is that, with psychotherapy, we aren't creating a ritual to just maximize placebo. We are co-creating a ritual that includes research-supported mechanisms of change – restructuring inaccurate cognitions, strengthening neurological systems for parasympathetic activation, re-writing problem-oriented personal narratives, extinguishing unneeded associative reactions, re-patterning social interactions, etc. Many of these types of change, regardless of which one we emphasize, happen in tandem with several others. For example, behavioral interventions may induce cognitive dissonance that naturally creates change in negative thoughts.

When we help clients develop an internally consistent understanding of their distress and a pathway to reduce it – when we co-develop a myth and a ritual – we are also increasing their overall self-efficacy (i.e., the belief that they can produce the desired change by their actions). Most actions we choose to take are initially shaped in our thoughts (myth), and those thoughts guide the action forward (ritual), even for things like developing skills (Bandura, 1997). For example, I might really want to get in shape, but being set loose in the gym with a picture of a fitness model isn't going to take me nearly as far as a personal trainer with a plan would (and I'd be utterly hopeless on Wednesdays when my trainer isn't there if she hasn't explained to me what I need to do). When clients are able to clearly imagine or mentally construct the path forward toward desired outcomes, they will have higher self-efficacy for the work of therapy.

DOI: 10.4324/9781003125082-5

One other benefit of the ritual is that it may give clients permission to abandon maladaptive behaviors or symptoms that they have been ready to abandon but couldn't find an opportunity to let go of (Frank, 1982). The novelty of the therapy environment may be enough for some clients; the therapist's "permission" may be what another needs. For example, a long-time migraine sufferer who needed the quiet and dark to escape from maternal responsibility can't just abandon having migraines when her kids leave home – that might mean her migraines weren't "real!" (And, of course, they were. Just because a symptom is functional doesn't mean it's fake!) Or a husband who has long been ready to abandon his dependence, but couldn't bring himself to "rock the boat," can now point to his therapist as the reason he needs to act more assertively.

PRACTICE TIP

The "ritual" that you and a client choose to engage in doesn't necessarily have to match the myth that you co-created. While that might help, for continuity's sake, as long as you and they can connect the ritual to the myth in a plausible way, it will still be helpful! For example, you might both believe that the fundamental issue is the unmet, early-childhood needs and resulting interpersonal patterns. But, if the client doesn't have much memory of their childhood (or access to parents, or wants to move more quickly, or is more comfortable doing cognitive work, or any of many other reasons), you can simply establish that one of the outcomes of that kind of early-childhood experience is distorted, irrational core beliefs (myth) and that changing those beliefs will necessarily change the disordered interpersonal patterns (ritual). Voilà! You can both believe it and it gives you both the freedom to do cognitive work while maintaining the myth/ritual coherence.

CHAPTER 5
LAMBERT PIE PART I:
EXTRATHERAPEUTIC FACTORS (40%)

A discussion of common factors is woefully incomplete without a discussion of Lambert's (1992) publication that gave us the "Percentage of Improvement" pie chart. This study gave us the oft-repeated graphic describing how much of the variance in clients' positive change was attributable to which therapeutic factors: 30% therapeutic relationship/ alliance, 15% hope/placebo/expectation, 15% theory/technique, and 40% extratherapeutic change.

Extratherapeutic factors are everything the client "brings with them" when they come to therapy: their disorder(s) with their symptoms and severity, background/history, past traumas, interpersonal skills, ego strength, psychological mindedness, personality (e.g., openness, neuroticism), level of motivation, current stressors, social support, and all other internal and external risks and resources (Asay & Lambert, 2004). But, looking at that list, I can't help but wonder if that category is a little mis-named. At the very least, I don't love how this portion of the pie sometimes gets taught, with a shrug, as "things we can't use." There's plenty in here that we can use!

First, many of these extratherapeutic factors are positive factors that clients bring. If we're attentive to them, we can maximize the benefits. For example, highly motivated clients and those with secure attachments regularly have better outcomes (Bohart & Wade, 2013), and if we recognize these factors, we can pretty safely move headlong into the work. When factors like these aren't optimal, sometimes we can use the therapy to turn them from liabilities into strengths. If a client comes in with low motivation, but we recognize it early, we can move straight into a motivational-interviewing modality to shore up motivation before moving on to the "real" work. If they were brought unwillingly to therapy (e.g., by the justice system, a demanding partner, or an overwhelmed parent), we can prevent rapport-breakage (and save time) by deliberately aligning ourselves with the client and addressing their fear that we are in cahoots with the Awful Someone who made them do this. We might not attend to clients' attachment styles early (or ever!), but if we do recognize when clients have insecure attachments, we can pay extra attention to the therapeutic relationship and avoid some of the therapeutic "backsliding" that can happen when we push too much, too quickly.

 DOI: 10.4324/9781003125082-6

There are some other ways that we can intentionally modify our strategies to increase potential benefit or at least reduce potential loss of effectiveness based on client factors. For example, we can match our techniques to the client's coping style (externalizing to behavioral/skills work and internalizing to insight-oriented work; Beutler et al., 2011), but only if we assess that style early. If clients come in without a strong social support system (which helps with additional positive change outside of sessions), we can include that as a focus of therapy, even if they don't immediately suggest it as an important goal.

PRACTICE TIP

Another way to think about this is that clients have a tremendous capacity for self-healing, and that therapy simply uses natural change processes in a targeted, mindful way (Tallman & Bohart, 2013). Imagine your therapy office as a sandbox. Not *that* kind of messy sandbox used by kids! Imagine it the way that software developers think of a "sandbox." This is a specially created, virtual space where untested software can be run safely and securely, and all the bugs can get worked out. The more clients bring of their own natural worlds into the therapy space, the better they can "test out" new ways of looking at their lives, new thought patterns, and new behaviors in session. Bonus: Clients tend to like and understand this sandbox language, too.

CHAPTER 6
LAMBERT PIE PARTS II & III:
RELATIONSHIP (30%)
& PLACEBO (15%)

These two concepts are presented together because they are deeply related (not just to make this section ten chapters!). A large part of the placebo effect comes from the degree of confidence in, respect for, and trust of the therapist. There is strong agreement in the research literature that the therapeutic relationship (as described in Chapters 1 and 2) is critical to the process (e.g., Asay & Lambert, 2013; Norcross & Lambert, 2018). It even has a moderately strong positive impact on outcomes in medication-only treatments (Totora et al., 2018)!

The expectancy factor (sometimes also called placebo or hope) encompasses all of our clients' beliefs about the processes of therapy and how those processes may help (Asay & Lambert, 2013). When we are motivated to help clients, propose a means to help them, and share the goal of their improvement, and we and clients share the sincere belief that both parties bring important abilities for change to the table, clients can develop positive expectancies and hope for the process (Snyder et al., 2013).

The intersection of hope and relationship is this: Beyond client pre-therapy expectations of benefit, where do they get hope from? From us! As therapists, to maximize the placebo effect, we want to maximize our expert power (French & Raven, 1959). *Expert power* means that one person is believed to know more about a certain subject than the other person and is deserving of trust. For example, this could mean accepting the legal advice of an attorney or even accepting directions from a stranger when in an unfamiliar city.

Ostensibly, clients have come to therapy because therapists are considered the experts in the processes of change – we have sound, science-based information to give, as well as the ability to help clients apply that information. In the best case, clients will also believe us when we set the stage for their growth by expressing confidence in their abilities to do the work that will lead to improvement (hope/expectancy/placebo). We must balance our expert power to deliver appropriate, accurate information to clients *and* to promote clients' beliefs in their own self-efficacy for change. If we supply all of the ideas and energy for the work, we foster dependence

DOI: 10.4324/9781003125082-7

instead of hope; if we supply none of the ideas or energy for the work, we deplete clients' hope (Snyder et al., 2013).

For a client to benefit, they need to believe that our information (including our estimation of their own change power) is reliable. But make no mistake! They also need to believe that we are being honest, and that we have their best interests at heart. Hence, the connection to the importance of the therapeutic relationship.

PRACTICE TIP

The only other type of social power you might want to be using in therapy is *referent power.* This basically means that a client wants to be like you. Assuming that you are (at least in session!) demonstrating really excellent ways of being (e.g., healthy cognitions, good emotion regulation, openness to experience, willingness to engage with what you're afraid of), that's probably ok. You don't want to find yourself utilizing the power of praise (reward power; more about this in Chapter 49) or punishment (coercive power), or even legitimate power (which means the client believes they "should" listen to you because they've been taught to respect certain authority figures). All of these can undermine the therapeutic process.

CHAPTER 7
LAMBERT PIE PART IV:
THEORY/TECHNIQUE

Whenever this part of the Lambert Pie is mentioned, it seems to always have the word "only." For example, Ogles et al. (2013) say, "Specific techniques account for *only* 15% of the variation in outcomes" (emphasis mine). I have never seen a source say anything like "Specific theory and technique account for a whopping 15% of the variance in positive change in therapy!" Why is this? People take antipsychotic medication (with all of its side effects) for an average of less than a 10% reduction in their positive symptoms.[1] I say we should squeeze out every drop of therapeutic benefit that we can get for our clients!

It is essential to integrate specific, targeted procedures with the common factors (e.g., therapeutic alliance, positive expectancy) to make therapy optimally effective, because they create a pathway for the client to focus their meaningful, goal-oriented work (Wampold & Ulvenes, 2019). At the very least, we can present empirically supported treatments to clients, based in part on their symptoms and diagnoses, to help them to formulate their understanding of their distress and its remediation (their "myth and ritual"). At most, we can use empirically supported treatments to secure the maximum therapeutic benefit for clients (American Psychological Association [APA], 2006). For example, if we are treating a client with anorexia nervosa, we may do well to work with them using a cognitive-behavioral or family-based treatment. For borderline personality disorder, dialectical behavior therapy or mentalization-based treatment may be the best starting place. There is strong evidence that obsessive-compulsive disorder responds well to exposure and response prevention therapy. Under certain circumstances, the research shows that it really does matter (APA, 2006).

However, because the theory/technique accounts for *only* 15% of the variance in therapeutic progress, if we are going to capture all of that 15%, we need to make sure that we are really doing these therapies, not just incorporating a single technique or an idea from a theory. One piece of this is using empirically supported treatments correctly and effectively. This means that we probably need to invest in acquiring and learning from the treatment manuals that are used in research. The other piece is that we need to learn our theories and their main principles and techniques more fully than just what we were briefly exposed to during our training. For example, a razor-perfect

DOI: 10.4324/9781003125082-8

behavior modification plan that has been tailored to a client's internal and external situation, is firmly grounded in all of the principles of conditioning, and is modified as circumstances change should work stunningly well. A behavior modification plan that forgets to address internal antecedents or the negative reinforcements of a current problematic behavior dooms us (and clients!) to stuckness and frustration.

I suggest that, along with current treatment manuals and texts, we also read the classic authors on each theory that we want to use. For example, Joseph Wolpe's *Life Without Fear: Anxiety and Its Cure* (1988) is the ultimate text on the process of systematic desensitization; there is so much more depth and richness to this technique than we were taught. What did we learn (and remember) about Gestalt therapy? The empty chair technique. And guess what – we probably learned it wrong. Reading *Gestalt Therapy: Excitement and Growth in the Human Personality* by Fritz Perls (1951) will either scare us off from the immense power of Gestalt work or straighten us out to see it's a deeply cohesive theory and not just a set of interesting techniques. How many of us can really define Socratic dialogue? If we want to do cognitive therapy well, there is no substitute for Aaron Beck's *Cognitive Therapy of Depression* (1979).

PRACTICE TIP

So, I just said that you should read Beck if you want to learn to do cognitive therapy well. And I stand by that. I also want to give you this little gem. When Aaron Beck (2017) was asked "What book would you recommend to therapists who want to do cognitive therapy better?" His answer: "Read Carl Rogers."

NOTE

1   For example, the anti-psychotic Abilify's full prescribing information (FDA, 2002) reports the average placebo-subtracted change was 8.85 points on the Positive and Negative Syndrome Scale (PANSS), which has a range of 30–320. If it is calculated based on the starting average score of 93.5, it is – in the most generous estimation – about a 9.5% difference (not including the study that found no significant change).

CHAPTER 8
"TRUST THE PROCESS"

When I was in my training, I used to hate it when clinical professors would say "trust the process." Then, I became one of those professors, and I tried my best to never say it. (I did. But, in my defense, I only said it in my group therapy class.) But the point here is that there is another way of thinking about common factors, and it's more like "common processes."

What is it that happens during therapy? Across various theories and therapists, many similar things are going on as clients are growing. A couple of these are things that we've already been thinking about — creating and interacting in a solid therapeutic relationship and clients' positive expectations about what therapy can do. Some that we haven't yet considered include (1) building client awareness, (2) supporting corrective experiences, and (3) establishing better reality testing (Goldfried, 2019).

One of the things we can do as part of the therapy process is to help clients become more aware of what contributes to their difficulties and see the opportunities for change. This ability to "step outside oneself" has many iterations (Norcross, 2011). Sometimes it is called the observing ego, meaning a part of self that can observe all of the goings-on of the other parts, including when and how they run into trouble. We might say it is part of the executive functioning system, which is responsible for abilities like imagining the future consequences of actions and inhibiting impulsive behavior. We may even call it mindfulness — being non-judgmentally aware of our own thoughts, feelings, and internal processes in the moment so that we can better see the consequences. Regardless of what we call it, we say that strengthening it (observing ego, executive functioning, mindfulness skill, etc.) is a good thing. And we can probably help clients do this in a number of ways including modeling, noticing and reinforcing when they engage in it, direct psychoeducation, and in-session practice.

A large part of effective therapy involves clients *doing things differently*. Though it sounds like this is an exclusively behavioral statement, it isn't. There are versions of this principle that cross every theoretical domain. Psychodynamic therapists focus on the corrective emotional experience, experiential therapists create moments of change right in session, existential therapists encourage exploration into the areas of life that have previously felt terrifying, cognitive therapists build counterthoughts to make new behaviors more possible, and even solution-focused therapists (for all their emphasis

 DOI: 10.4324/9781003125082-9

on what *has worked*) are still looking for exceptions. Whether it happens in session or as homework, clients don't really change until they do something new.

Reality testing here means something a bit broader than the gross distinction between people who are psychotic or not. Rather, nuanced reality testing means being able to accurately evaluate the impact that one's behavior has on the outside world and the overall consequences. This is a bridge between increased awareness and experimenting with new behaviors that can create a useful "upward" cycle of change. When clients can see that their fears were unfounded, or recognize that a secure attachment is possible, or notice that they get better outcomes with their new behaviors, or see evidence that their schemas were inaccurate, etc., they are motivated to continue on the path forward. When they can evaluate correctly when things don't go as well, that's important, too. We can help them improve their reality testing with behavioral homework, experiential in-session activities, or even within the therapeutic relationship, and we can maximize the improvement in reality testing if we process those events overtly.

PRACTICE TIP

When a client seems stuck during therapy, it can be useful to conceptualize their "stuck place" on this upward spiral. If they're stuck at reality testing, they might need a different kind of "proof" that their changes are useful. If they haven't been experimenting with new behaviors, you may need to address barriers – fear, motivation, or not knowing how. If you both feel stuck, it might be because there's a missing piece; in that case you may need to go back to the awareness step. And there's no reason to keep it a mystery – you might even want to explain this and ask them about it explicitly.

CHAPTER 9
MISSING PIECES

We began this section of the book by noting that there have been healers and healing practices for as long as there have been people. There is much to be learned about "psychological treatment and health" from people groups who have been healing mental and emotional disturbance since before psychology as a discipline was born, and those who haven't been exposed to psychology as we think of it – indigenous peoples.

Various indigenous cultures have many similarities in healing practices despite distance and lack of exposure to each other; we might say they have their own "common factors." Just a few of these are concepts like the pervasiveness of spirituality in health and the daily practices of life, a view of development that is more circular than linear, and the fundamental importance of social/community interconnectedness (Katz, 2017).

Mainstream psychology doesn't handle these concepts in the same way. For example, we may reduce concepts like spirituality into measurable or observable phenomena (e.g., a set of behaviors that are associated with increased optimism). But part of indigenous healing is knowing that every aspect of life – individual and collective, mundane and exceptional – is spiritually imbued, and therefore healing is available in many ways through many people and experiences, especially through the involvement of the community. Another tendency of Western science is the preoccupation with prediction, control, and generalizability; the tendency of indigenous healers is to emphasize understanding and meaning-making on an individual level. A core belief of many indigenous groups is that there is no one right way to know, understand, and heal – each journey is unique. We might agree with that in principle, but then our next sentence is usually something like "so I will use this empirically supported treatment with this client instead of that one." Perhaps development, growth, and progress don't need to be understood as movement toward a known, achievable goal. But they do if we are writing a treatment plan that has goals that must be evaluated for progress every six weeks using a validated instrument. What about the idea that there can be power and value in every developmental stage, and that the process can be more important than rushing to the end? Most therapies are literally designed to raise awareness of the discrepancy between a client's current functioning and their goals, and to make as straight a path as possible to that end. Yet, with all of these differences between effective Western

    DOI: 10.4324/9781003125082-10

psychologies and indigenous healing, there is no doubt that the principles of indigenous healing do, in fact, heal.

There's no way to simply incorporate all of the wonderful gifts (these and many more) of indigenous healing practices into what we do. It's neither appropriate (in fact, it's *cultural appropriation*!) nor possible, because it is the culture itself that is healing (Katz, 2017). In addition, there are pragmatic factors associated with the general practice of mental health treatment in most of our settings that we may not want to or be able to change, like receiving payment for our services and maintaining professional boundaries. But there may still be lessons for us and our therapy practices. We can broaden our minds to see growth as an upward spiral, rather than something linear. We can make the cultivation of community and a healthful support system a goal for any client. We can remember that healing takes place out in the world where clients are living, in addition to our office spaces.

PRACTICE TIP

One specific thing that I think is often missing in therapy is the opportunity for clients to have spiritual *experiences* and incorporate them into their work. It's common to at least touch on spiritual health as one of the major areas of life (e.g., physical health, social health), and you may already attend somewhat to client spirituality. But, even if you are a faith-based counselor and your client has indicated wanting to incorporate faith issues or practices, you're still a *counselor.*

What might it be like to encourage clients to interact with the healers in their faith traditions? To go on a prayer walk, a meditation retreat, or a vision quest, as fits their experience? Or to encourage clients who don't subscribe to a particular religion or who are atheists to give themselves an opportunity to have a deep reflective experience, like a solo hike or group trip to breathe in synchrony with the ocean? It's not part of our job to offer these kinds of experiences, but we don't have to be afraid of them; we can honor them. And when clients have these experiences, it's critical to allow them to bring their experiences of change – slight or profound – back into the therapy room, *accept them at face value,* and incorporate these personal changes into therapy.

CHAPTER 10
YOUR "RECIPE"

What makes a cake a cake? We've pretty much got to have flour, sugar, eggs, and something like butter. We usually need to also have something like water and a leavening agent. Heat it up awhile and you have cake. Drop any one main ingredient and we might still have cake – flourless chocolate cake or pound cake or angel food cake. Add a few ingredients and we have tres leches or devil's food cake.

It may be that the common factors can stand alone as an approach to therapy (vis-à-vis the empirically supported therapies like cognitive-behavioral therapy; Bailey & Ogles, 2019; Higginson et al., 2011; Laska et al., 2014). Certainly, almost a century's worth of clinical experience and research evidence suggests that the main ingredients we've been discussing are central to the experience of therapy (Wampold, 2015). That fits nicely with the American Psychological Association's definition of *evidence-based practice* – which advises using the best research evidence, plus clinical expertise, as well as client characteristics, culture, and preferences (APA, 2006).

That means we need to balance these fundamental elements along with tailoring the therapy experience to each client. One client may be able to digest an elaborate wedding cake – deep therapy with multiple tiers of theory, multiple flavors of technique, and intricate icing of advanced between-session homework. Another client may only be able to tolerate cupcakes – solution-oriented sessions every now and then to help navigate situational challenges. Clients will have preferences for different flavors of cake, certainly. Some will want more emphasis on family and community connectedness while others prefer to focus on individual growth and mastery. Some will want to stay in the realm of behavior and cognition; some will prefer to emphasize existential issues or spirituality. Some clients might just want cake mix and a tutorial on baking!

What if a client has special dietary needs like allergies or intolerances? Psychotherapy proper isn't the right or best form of help for every person. What might be the equivalent of banana bread, scones, or biscotti in the realm of mental health? We need to always consider whether the right fit is something like a referral to a great psychiatrist, support from an indigenous helper, a physical health resource like a physician or dietician, or something else.

                                        DOI: 10.4324/9781003125082-11

PRACTICE TIP

Taking all of this into account, how can you decide just what to do with each client? A relatively easy decision-guide, grounded in evidence-based practice (APA, 2006), is something like this:

- First, does this client want/need cake? If so, research indicates the importance of the use of the common factors in therapy (and this is what clinical expertise is, fundamentally, along with things like self-reflection and consultation).

- Second, what kind of cake does the client want? Does the client already have an idea about what their distress is about? Can you use that to help formulate the recipe for treatment?

- Third, are there any elements that can help that specific kind of cake to bake well? That is, does reliable research evidence exist about any specific treatment for the client's diagnosis/symptoms? Can you incorporate that into the course of treatment?

Last, *if there isn't enough guidance in the answer to questions two and three, then offer them your favorite cake.* Do what you do best. Formulate the client according to the theory you like most and are most familiar with, help them to build a narrative of the therapy process from that orientation, and proceed with the rituals of your preferred theoretical orientation.

REFERENCES

American Psychological Association, Presidential Task Force on Evidence-Based Practice. (2006). Evidence-based practice in psychology. *American Psychologist, 61*(4), 271–285. https://doi.org/10.1037/0003-066X.61.4.271

Asay, T. P., & Lambert, M. J. (1999). *The empirical case for the common factors in therapy: Quantitative findings.* In M. A. Hubble, B. L. Duncan, & S. D. Miller (Eds.), *The heart and soul of change: What works in therapy* (pp. 23–55). American Psychological Association. https://doi.org/10.1037/11132-001

Bailey, R. J., & Ogles, B. M. (2019). Common factors as a therapeutic approach: What is required? *Practice Innovations, 4*(4), 241–254.

Bandura, A. (1997). *Self-efficacy: The exercise of control.* W H Freeman/Times Books/ Henry Holt & Co.

Beutler, L. E., Harwood, M. T., Kimpara, S., Verdirame, D., & Blau, K. (2011). Coping style. In J. C. Norcross (Ed.), *Psychotherapy relationships that work: Evidence-based responsiveness.* (2nd ed., pp. 336–353). Oxford University Press.

Beck, A. T., & Beck, J. (2017, December). *New breakthroughs in cognitive therapy: Applications to the severely mentally ill.* Keynote presented at the Evolution of Psychotherapy Conference, Anaheim, CA.

Beck, A. T., Rush, A. J., Shaw, B. F., & Emery, G. (1979). *Cognitive therapy of depression.* Guilford Press.

Bohart, A. C., & Greaves Wade, A. (2013). The client in psychotherapy. In M. J. Lambert (Ed.), *Bergin and Garfield's Handbook of Psychotherapy and Behavior Change* (5th ed., pp. 219–257). Wiley.

Brammer, L. M., & MacDonald, G. (2003). *The helping relationship: Process and skills* (8th ed.). Allyn & Bacon.

Cass, S. (2007). How much does the internet weigh? *Discover Magazine.* Retrieved from https://www.discovermagazine.com/technology/how-much-does-the-internet-weigh

Elliott, R., Bohart, A. C., Watson, J. C., & Murphy, D. (2018). Therapist empathy and client outcome: An updated meta-analysis. *Psychotherapy, 55*(4), 399–410. https://doi.org/10.1037/pst0000175

Food and Drug Administration. (2002). *Highlights of prescribing information: Abilify (aripiprazole).* Retrieved from https://www.accessdata.fda.gov/

Frank, J. D. (1982). *Therapeutic components shared by all psychotherapies.* In J. H. Harvey & M. M. Parks (Eds.), *Master lecture series, Vol. 1. Psychotherapy research and behavior change* (pp. 9–37). American Psychological Association. https://doi.org/10.1037/10083-001

French, J. R. P., Jr., & Raven, B. (1959). *The bases of social power.* In D. Cartwright (Ed.), *Studies in social power* (pp. 150–167). University of Michigan.

Goldfried, M. R. (2019). Obtaining consensus in psychotherapy: What holds us back? *American Psychologist, 74*(4), 484–496. https://doi.org/10.1037/amp0000365

Higginson, S., Mansell, W., & Wood, A. M. (2011). An integrative mechanistic account of psychological distress, therapeutic change and recovery: The perceptual control theory approach. *Clinical Psychology Review, 31*(2), 249–259. https://doi.org/10.1016/j.cpr.2010.01.005

Katz, R. (2017). *Indigenous healing psychology: Honoring the wisdom of the first peoples.* Healing Arts Press.

Lambert, M. J. (1992). Psychotherapy outcome research. In J. C. Norcross & M. R. Goldfried (Eds.), *Handbook of psychotherapy integration* (pp. 94–129). Basic Books.

Laska, K. M., Gurman, A. S., & Wampold, B. E. (2014). Expanding the lens of evidence-based practice in psychotherapy: A common factors perspective. *Psychotherapy, 51*(4), 467–481. https://doi.org/10.1037/a0034332

Norcross, J. C. (Ed.). (2011). *Psychotherapeutic relationships that work: Evidence-based responsiveness* (2nd ed.). http://dx.doi.org/10.1093/acprof:oso/9780199737208.001.0001

Norcross, J. C., & Lambert, M. J. (2018). Psychotherapy relationships that work III. *Psychotherapy, 55*(4), 303–315. https://doi.org/10.1037/pst0000193

Ogles, B. M., Anderson, T., & Lunnen, K. M. (2013). The contribution of models and techniques to therapeutic efficacy: Contradictions between professional trends and clinical research. In M. A. Hubble, B. L. Duncan, & S. D. Miller (Eds.), *The heart and soul of change: What works in therapy* (pp. 201–226). American Psychological Association. https://doi.org/10.1037/11132-001

Ornelas, A., Zacharias-Millward, N., Menter, D. G., Davis, J. S., Lichtenberger, L., Hawke, D., Hawk, E., Vilar, E., Bhattacharya, P., & Millward, S. (2017). Beyond COX-1: The effects of aspirin on platelet biology and potential mechanisms of chemoprevention. *Cancer Metastasis Review, 36,* 289–303. doi: 10.1007/s10555–017–9675-z

Perls, F. (1951). *Gestalt therapy: Excitement and growth in the human personality.* The Gestalt Journal Press.

Rogers, C. R. (1957). The necessary and sufficient conditions of therapeutic personality change. *Journal of Consulting Psychology, 21*(2), 95–103. https://doi.org/10.1037/h0045357

Rogers, C.R. (1961). *On becoming a person.* Houghton Mifflin.

Rosenzweig, S. (1936). Some implicit common factors in diverse methods of psychotherapy. *American Journal of Orthopsychiatry, 6*(3), 412–415. https://doi.org/10.1111/j.1939-0025.1936.tb05248.x

Snyder, C. R., Michael, S. T., & Cheavens, J. S. (2013). Hope as a psychotherapeutic foundation of common factors, placebos, and expectancies. In M. A. Hubble, B. L. Duncan, & S. D. Miller (Eds.), *The heart and soul of change: What works in therapy* (pp. 179–200). American Psychological Association. https://doi.org/10.1037/11132-001

Society of Clinical Psychology. (2016). *Psychological diagnoses and other targets of treatment.* Retrieved from https://www.div12.org/diagnoses/.

Tallman, K., & Bohart, A. C. (2013). The client as a common factor: Clients as self-healers. In M. A. Hubble, B. L. Duncan, & S. D. Miller (Eds.), *The heart and soul of change: What works in therapy* (pp. 91–132). American Psychological Association. https://doi.org/10.1037/11132-001

Totura, C. M. W., Fields, S. A., & Karver, M. S. (2018). The role of the therapeutic relationship in psychopharmacological treatment outcomes: A meta-analytic review. *Psychiatric Services, 69*(1), 41–47. https://doi.org/10.1176/appi.ps.201700114

Wampold. B. (2015). How important are the common factors in psychotherapy? An update. *World Psychiatry, 14*(3), 270–277.

Wampold, B., & Ulvenes, P. G. (2019). Integration of common factors and specific ingredients. In J. C. Norcross & M. R. Goldfried (Eds.) *Handbook of Psychotherapy Integration* (pp. 69–87). Oxford University Press.

Wolpe, J., & Wolpe, D. (1988). *Life without fear.* New Harbinger Publications.

We've Got to Walk Before We Dance (Revisiting and Revamping Basic Skills)

Virtually every profession – certainly every performance profession – has not only a long period of basic skills development, but places value on the repetition of basic skills throughout the career. Ballet dancers never stop doing barre work; vocalists never stop warming up with scales; football players never stop running drills in practice. This is true no matter how long their careers persist.

For one thing, there is too much risk in over- or under-developing certain "muscles." For example, we may become masters at cognitive work or intricate behavior modification plans, only to find that we lose clients because we've lost our finesse in rapport building. Second, small slips can take on a life of their own over months or years of going unnoticed. What was once a purposeful three-second silence for contemplation may become a well-intentioned (but hurried) half-second check-in.

Another risk is in developing automaticity (Bargh, 1994) of the basic counseling skills. While automaticity reduces cognitive load and may allow us to attend to more complex information in the interaction, automatic behavior is more useful in situations where the behavior can be performed in the same way each time. Because it is the opposite of mindfulness, it is less effective in situations that require moment-to-moment adjustments, such as tailoring the therapy experience to each unique client in the here and now.

Hopefully, these next chapters can refresh us on the value of attending to basic skills and give us a few ideas to breathe new life into old classics.

CHAPTER 11
ALWAYS ASK FOR THEIR EXPECTATIONS

One of the cardinal rules of therapy is that if clients don't stay, they don't get any work done. Unfortunately, the modal number of sessions (that is, the most common number of sessions that clients attend) is one (Connelly Gibbons et al., 2011). A single session. And one of the quickest routes to a second-session no-show is failure to find out what the client's expectations are (Schwartz & Flowers, 2010).

We always have one of two kinds of clients: those who are new to therapy and those who are veterans of varying degrees. Both kinds of clients come to the first session with ideas about what will happen, whether it is hopeful anticipation or anxious trepidation. The more aware we are of these expectations, the better able we will be to tailor the therapy experience to fit their personalities and desires. The more clients feel understood, respected, important, and comfortable, the more likely they are to stay.

New therapy clients will often have developed their ideas about therapy from popular media sources: the harrowing scenes played for shock value (pun intended) in *One Flew over the Cuckoo's Nest*, the casually psychoanalytic sessions played for laughs on the sitcom *Frasier*, the sensationalized confrontations of *Dr. Phil*, the disregard for boundaries in *Good Will Hunting*, the dramatic entanglements of Dr. Melfi in *The Sopranos*, etc. We know those aren't anywhere near reality, and so one of our jobs in this situation is to dispel those myths, whatever they are. In addition, it's very common for clients to have fears about starting therapy such as being labeled as crazy or otherwise stigmatized, believing that their problems are too severe to be helped or not severe enough to warrant help, having concerns about confidentiality, and worrying that the treatment will be terribly unpleasant or that they won't have any say in the process (Chekroud et al., 2018; Gulliver et al., 2010). So, if we're lucky enough to have brave clients who have made it to the first session, we owe it to them to address those fears. We also have to watch out for the outlandishly optimistic expectations: that two sessions are all it takes, that wisdom will be delivered in a gift-wrapped package, or even just that treatment always progresses linearly!

Veteran therapy clients (or those who have gotten information from family or friends who have been in therapy) pose different challenges. Their expectations, based in experience, will almost certainly be more reality-based.

DOI: 10.4324/9781003125082-13

At first blush, that seems like a good thing, but it may not be. These clients may have had quite negative experiences. In that case, we need to applaud their bravery at trying again and find out what went badly. No need to repeat another therapist's mistakes! Alternately, they may have had really positive experiences, which is a bit trickier. If they have idealized a previous therapist, we might not be able to compete. In this case, it is worthwhile to find out what they liked about the therapy process with an emphasis on the client's involvement, stressing that the client is the primary factor in whether therapy is enjoyable and productive.

Finally, we need to remember that clients don't have a perfectly accurate memory of their therapy and their report of the experience will be distorted to some degree. We should keep an ear to the ground for personality disorders, but otherwise we can take our lead from Adler (1931/2014) – how the client has integrated the experience into their memory is often more important than what actually happened. Regardless of our new client's predictions, it takes just a moment to establish more realistic expectations, and this will reduce frustration on our part and theirs.

PRACTICE TIP

If you have the luxury, add an expectations question to your pre-intake paperwork. This lets clients have a bit more time to consider the question, and you may find it takes less time in the actual intake to address it. If not, add it onto your own list of in-person intake questions; it doesn't end up taking too long. Clients may know exactly what they are expecting (hoping for, afraid of) and they'll be able to tell you in a few sentences. They may not know right away, and you don't need to spend ten minutes trying to dig it out of them. Just the fact that you ask will let them know that you intend to honor their wishes and experience in therapy, and that it's open for discussion later. Specifically, I like to ask, "Have you ever done anything like this before?" It gives them permission to include any relevant experiences even if they weren't specifically *psychotherapy* and opens the door easily for what they did and didn't like.

CHAPTER 12
SILENCE: IT'S FOR THEM

One of the things we like to say about therapy is that it gives clients "space." What do we really mean by that? It might be that we give them a literal chair in which to sit and a door to close between them and the rest of the world; in this way we give them a space that belongs to them and no one else.

Except it doesn't. That space also belongs to us.

So, what about giving clients space in session? In session, space means time. Welcoming silence – room to speak – is one of the things that makes therapy unlike any other experience (Hill et al., 2003; Rogers, 1942; Tindall & Robinson, 1947). Conversations with partners, bosses, children, teachers, colleagues, customers, and even friends are rarely punctuated with measured silences in which to gather thoughts, make connections, or search out feelings. Welcoming silence is a three-fold gift that we can give to clients that they rarely get anywhere else:

- Silence honors clients. It says, "Your voice is the most important voice right now."
- Silence encourages the development of their own wisdom. It says, "You know yourself and your life better than anyone else, including me."
- Silence provides them with processing time that they often don't give themselves, and encourages them not to avoid. It says, "What you're struggling with matters, and deserves your attention, even in the midst of your busy/chaotic/stressed life."

Silence used inappropriately can lead to therapeutic ruptures (Ackerman & Hilsenroth, 2001). A welcoming silence isn't a bored, fidgety, or exasperated silence. It's not a silence during which we're planning the next thing to say or the next question to ask. It's not a time for us to try to predict what the client is going to say next, mentally write our treatment plan, or (gasp!) prepare for our next client.

When we are practicing welcoming silence, we are comfortable, unhurried, and curious. We keep gentle, non-penetrative eye contact (don't worry; they generally aren't looking at us while they're processing). We allow our minds to relax in a state of readiness to hear what's coming next. We simply wait.

29   DOI: 10.4324/9781003125082-14

> ## PRACTICE TIP
>
> Most of us aren't used to waiting in a way that's unhurried. So, practice this outside of the therapy room first. Start by finding (or creating) some 30–60 second moments of peace in your world and begin to mindfully listen to anything that's present – the air conditioner, the traffic nearby, etc. When you become distracted by your internal dialogue, as you inevitably will, gently remind yourself to just listen. After you're able to listen to ambient sounds for half a minute without planning your grocery store trip, wondering when the time will be over, or judging your own listening performance, move on to listening to human conversation. Listening to other people presents a new challenge, as now there are two voices competing for your attention – the person you're listening to and your own. The purpose is to quiet your own mind when you have both your grocery list trying to break in as well as your own reactions to what they are saying. As they speak, wait. Wait without planning the next thing you're going to say. You may notice that it takes you a few extra seconds to respond to them. That's good!

CHAPTER 13
SILENCE: IT'S FOR US

I know how precious the therapy minutes are. It's true even if we work in a setting where we get 50 whole minutes and so much more so in a setting like an inpatient hospital, where we're lucky to get 20 minutes and we know the client will be discharged within the week. So, the pressure to use every second for something worthwhile creates a tension against even giving clients time for silence; it can seem like the height of indulgence to ask for time to process something for ourselves.

Or we might worry about how it might sound to a client if we say, "Give me just a moment, please. You've said a lot that's important and I'd like to take a minute to sit with it before we move forward." We might worry that it damages our credibility – wouldn't a true expert always have the right thing to say on the tip of their tongue?

Let's imagine a few scenarios and this may become clearer. What if your primary care physician said, "Let me think about this so that I can compile all the symptoms you've described, taking into account your personal medical history and your current life circumstances, and consider the best information that research has to offer about potential treatments." Wouldn't you be willing to wait a moment (or a week!) for a treatment plan? What if a politician in a presidential debate took a moment to think about their answer to a question, rather than reciting whatever half-related policy their staff had already drafted? What if a teacher paused to really consider your child's strengths and needs before tailoring a project to their areas of growth, instead of whatever the curriculum template said was good for a generic seven-year-old?

When we take time to process a client's information, that means that we were really listening to them, that we're unwilling to jump to conclusions, that we experience them as a real individual and not just as "one more case of depression." And those are just the benefits on the clients' ends.

Silence benefits us, as well. Despite how much we wish it might be possible in our time-constrained sessions, multitasking in therapy simply is not possible. Listening actively, reflecting on clients' communication, formulating responses, and responding intentionally are each a *controlled process* (i.e., they take attention and conscious effort, compared to an *automatic process*, like walking on a flat surface; Schneider & Shiffrin, 1977). Part of what it means to be "fully present" in therapy is that we reduce distractions

 DOI: 10.4324/9781003125082-15

and allow the therapeutic experience to be all that we are paying attention to (our *perceptual load*; Lavie, 1995) and all that we are responding to (our *cognitive load*; Sweller, 1998) during session. The kicker is that we can only effectively do one controlled process at a time, especially with a high perceptual or cognitive load, so we need to do one therapeutic task at a time.

Silence relieves us of the responsibility to always have the right quick answer. It permits in-the-moment conceptualizations and adjustments to our therapeutic hypotheses. It allows us to remember the ultimate therapy goal and direct our next statement or question in that direction, so that we don't get to the end of session and wonder, "What just happened?" As a bonus, silence gives us an opportunity to model thoughtfulness in the here and now.

PRACTICE TIP

If you're still unsure about asking clients for time to process in session, set aside one to two minutes before and after each session to at least give the gift of silence to yourself. Re-read their latest progress note and remind yourself of the overall goals before each session. After session, don't launch straight into the progress note. Use the restroom, stare out the window, or heat water for tea. (You do have a single-serve water heater, don't you? If not, consider that a bonus practice tip!) Just give your brain a solid 60 seconds to sit with what happened before you start your summary. That will improve the quality of your notes (and how quickly you write them) and may even streamline your course of treatment.

CHAPTER 14
THE POWER OF REFLECTION
(PART I): FEELING HEARD

When is the last time you talked to a little kid, under four years old? If it hasn't been this week, then let me remind you what it's like.

> Child: I found a pretty rock!
> Adult: mm-hmmm.
> Child (louder): I found a pretty rock!
> Adult: Yes, baby.
> Child (pulling on adult's shirt): I found a pretty rock!
> Adult: I see.
> Child (frustrated): NANA, I found a pretty rock!
> Adult: Oh. Is it for me?
> Child: No! (walks away)

Sometimes, we can do much better. See if you can tell the difference:

> Child: I found a pretty rock!
> Adult: Oh, wow! You found a pretty rock!
> Child: It's for you.
> Adult: Oh, it's for me? Thank you so much!
> Child: It's a purple rock! That's my favorite.
> Adult: Oh, it looks purple to you? I know that's your favorite color. It looks sort of brown to me. I like it.

We would never have developed our capacity for relational connection or even for language if grown-ups didn't pay attention to us and engage with us when we were little (e.g., Tomasello, 2010; Vygotsky, 1962/2012). When adults engaged with us, how did we know they were paying attention and understood us? *They repeated what we said.* That's how we knew that it was safe to move on to the next pieces of information.

At what point in our interpersonal or cognitive development did we lose the need for others to give our words back to us to show that they are really listening? *We didn't.*

Think about talking with your partner or your child. Do you ever find yourself saying the same thing over and over (maybe louder and louder)? Do they ever say the same thing, as if they weren't even listening to what you had just said? Clients do this, too. We experience it with boredom or

DOI: 10.4324/9781003125082-16

frustration, but clients (and partners and kids!) will keep saying the same thing over and over until they are sure we have heard it.

Saying "I hear you" or "I understand" or "I can imagine" isn't half as powerful (and it's often not entirely true). If we want clients to feel heard and understood, we have to reflect. And that means giving their words back to them. We can get fancy and reflect their emotion, use our therapeutic vocabulary, summarize, identify themes, make connections, or give spot-on interpretations. But none of that takes the place of reflecting back, *repeating back*, the content of what they've said in terms of creating and displaying accurate empathy. (Not like robots, of course! It helps if we are attuned to our clients and make our tone and other non-verbals consistent with theirs when we reflect. Remember, we are reflecting the *message*, not only the words.)

PRACTICE TIP

Don't let clients say more than you can reflect at one time. For most of us, that's not more than about four sentences (or small ideas) at a time. So, don't be afraid to *gently* interrupt to make sure you're staying on the same page. It's important for us but it's also ok for them to go slowly – they don't usually have the opportunity. If they are finding that's difficult for them, or they do get frustrated with it, process that – I can almost guarantee it's relevant to what they're working on therapeutically!

CHAPTER 15
THE POWER OF REFLECTION (PART II): CREATING THERAPEUTIC MOVEMENT

We all have had this thought at some point, haven't we? "All I'm doing is listening, nodding, and reflecting. How can this possibly do anything therapeutic?" Maybe you haven't become convinced that it does. I won't attempt to argue the "necessary but not sufficient" literature, because I don't rely entirely on person-centered strategies myself and wouldn't advise anyone to do so exclusively. However, Rogers (1961) has clearly seen reflection (and its cousins, paraphrasing and summarizing) lead to tremendous, almost magical, changes. There's a large body of evidence that the core conditions of therapy (Rogers, 1957) do evoke positive change, even without the influence of other techniques (Norcross & Lambert, 2019). Many of us have experienced it, even if it seemed mysterious.

The answer to this therapeutic mystery might lie in the realm of working memory. The working (sometimes called short-term) memory holds information while you are manipulating it (Diamond, 2013). For example, when we hear a math problem and solve it "in our head," we are using working memory. Working memory has a limited capacity; the most commonly cited limit is five to nine objects (or "chunks") at a time (e.g., Baddeley, 1986). Think about it like this: most of us can add 43 and 28 in our heads, but most of us can't add 17,445 and 32,692 without having it written down.

What this means for therapy is unexpectedly simple. When clients are ruminating over their concerns, it's no surprise that they think the same few negative thoughts over and over, or get a few steps into a decision-making process only to feel stuck, or consider only one salient emotion with its attendant concerns. That's all their working memory will allow, especially when they are alone. Even with friends, who tend to follow normal conversation patterns, the sense of "stuckness" often remains, or is bypassed by well-intentioned but often unhelpful advice.

Therapy, however, follows a communication pattern that isn't found much elsewhere. The skills of reflecting, paraphrasing, and summarizing allow clients to trust you to hold their content while they make room in their working memories for new information (e.g., thoughts, emotions, plans,

 DOI: 10.4324/9781003125082-17

perspectives). At times, your paraphrasing or summarizing allows them to "chunk" previously isolated bits of content, making even more room. This may account for that peculiar phenomenon of unexpected insight, when you're sitting back thinking, "But I didn't do anything!"

PRACTICE TIP

Think of your office space as a mental/emotional work-desk. Imagine, as clients disclose information, that these bits of content are bits of paper. Once you've accurately reflected content back to clients, they will trust you to hold each sticky note, paper napkin, and old receipt. You can set them all out metaphorically on the desk and begin to organize. As you notice similar content, you paraphrase, and that's like stacking up five bits of paper and binding them with a paperclip. Voilà! More desk space. As connections are made or themes are uncovered, you summarize. This is like replacing a messy stack of thoughts or a wild flurry of emotions with a neatly penned index card. Clients can now see beyond the first five to nine sticky notes that will fit on their mental desk, and they get space for more insight, creativity, and emotional awareness to flow.

CHAPTER 16
TELL ME MORE ABOUT THAT

Sometimes we want to get clear, specific information from clients –
during intake when we need to cover all of our questions, during a suicide
assessment, or anytime we're working with a rambler, right? To do this, we
use closed-ended questions, which direct clients toward specific information,
are often answered with yes or no, and discourage clients from giving
additional information (Sommers-Flanagan & Sommers-Flanagan, 2017).
Although, I might challenge the necessity and usefulness of closed questions,
even in these circumstances. Encouraging clients not to say more than
they would like to in the first session often elicits more disclosure (Zeig &
Lankton, 1988); welcoming, compassionate, less diagnostically focused
questioning in suicide assessment fosters more honesty (Sommers-Flanagan &
Shaw, 2017); here-and-now processing of a rambler or monopolizer has much
more utility in reducing the behavior and stimulating a different interaction
(Yalom & Leszcz, 2005).

The virtue of open-ended questions is that they facilitate more disclosure
than just one-word answers (Cormier et al., 2017). And the best open-
ended question isn't even a question; it's an invitation: "Tell me more about
that." (If that's a cliché, so be it. It may be the most useful sentence in the
therapeutic vocabulary.)

What makes "Tell me more about that" exceptional is that it's so open
that it takes our biases out of play. We know it's impossible for us to come
into a therapy session as a blank slate. We are all influenced by our own
background, history, culture, experiences – our "worldview … certain beliefs
and ideas about how everything in life fits together [which] orients us in
the world, defines our attitudes towards it, and allows us to create meaning"
(van Deurzen & Adams, 2016). Moreover, our perceptions and thoughts are
influenced by any number of things unrelated to the person sitting in front
of us – our own personal current stressors, the client who just left the office,
maybe even the new billboard we didn't consciously notice on the way in to
work. But this perfectly open-ended inquiry can protect us from artificially
narrowing clients' experiences and allow us to be surprised by clients. That
can be a good sign that we are following them into their own stories, rather
than choosing the path for them.

The only assumptions that it makes are that clients are the experts on
their own lives, that they have access to their own internal experiencing, and

DOI: 10.4324/9781003125082-18

that there is more to be discovered. It offers them space to really think and check in with themselves. It empowers them to develop trust in their ability to become self-aware and listen to their internal voice. (Even if their internal voice isn't adaptive and healthy, if we don't hear it, we can't help clients to change it!) It offers a clear demonstration that they are valued for their comments, beliefs, experiences, and opinions.

PRACTICE TIP

Of course, over-using any one phrase will get tiresome for clients. And if you say, "Tell me more about that" in a gruff, demanding voice, you're not likely to get the response you hope for. If you need some variety in language, but want to say the same thing, try these:

- What else do you know about it?

- What other thoughts or emotions are there?

- What more can you tell me?

- Keep going; I'm enjoying hearing about your experience.

- This helps me to understand you (or your situation) better, so tell me everything you can.

- Take a moment. Look (or listen, or feel) inside and tell me what you find.

CHAPTER 17
THERAPY IS NOT A CRISIS

Some clients come in weeping, shouting, or otherwise overwhelmed for the first session and we perceive them to be in crisis. If they come in the following three weeks in a row weeping, shouting, or otherwise overwhelmed, we begin to reclassify them. Some clients' lives are so stressful and their environments so out of control that there is a new legitimate catastrophe every week. This may be an indicator of a personality disorder, or it might be an indicator of a genuinely overwhelming system in which they don't have the internal and external resources to be able to function well.

A lot can happen in the long seven days they may have between sessions, and what is most salient to them might really change. The no-win situation looks like this: If we always focus on what's most present for them right now, we may go on indefinitely with no progress. If we don't focus on the immediate concerns, they may not like what they're getting in therapy and simply fire us. We need to balance rapport maintenance with therapeutic goals that include restructuring cognitions, behaviors, and/or relationships that serve to maintain the current (out-of-control) system and developing skills to better manage distressing situations and difficult emotions outside of therapy (Fusco & Freeman, 2012).

What options do we have for keeping this balance?

- If possible, we can set expectations early. We need to respect the client's need to "vent" while keeping an eye on the clock. If emotions have taken over the first 40 minutes of the intake session, we can use the "stop hand," thank them for their honesty and disclosure, and directly express the need to also set some goals for therapy to be helpful.
- We may need to explain that therapeutic goals are intended to help reduce overall stress and improve the client's ability to handle these kinds of stressors outside of session, rather than becoming dependent on us to help them handle them in session. Once goals are established, we may need to check on them every session, to help clients keep that larger picture in mind.
- Although this can feel counterproductive, we need to reflect, paraphrase, and summarize as often as possible. This actually ends up reducing the amount of repetition and time that is needed for the client to feel heard and validated.

DOI: 10.4324/9781003125082-19

- We might need to check that we aren't jumping into "solutions mode" in response to the client's level of distress. Although it may seem like that is what they are asking for (and they may even directly ask!), it's also often counterproductive. We can be sure it's counterproductive if we suggest solutions and are met with "yes, but ..."
- In the case that we didn't realize this was happening until several sessions have passed, or if we've tried goal setting and time management and it hasn't been working, it may be time for a process comment about it.
- If we need to, we can explain our ethical dilemma explicitly. The American Psychological Association (APA, 2017), American Counseling Association (ACA, 2014), American Association of Marriage and Family Therapists (AAMFT, 2015), the National Association for Social Workers (NASW, 2017), and many state laws require that we not keep clients in therapy when it's no longer benefitting them. Though they may say they feel better "just having a place to vent," we can add a goal of increasing their social support and skills so that they can have relationships in which to "vent" without continuing to pay us. (Note: this may require a little honest check-in with ourselves!)
- We can also recommend group therapy as a place where they can tell their stories and have a wider audience (of course, we need to make sure we have an appropriate group to put them in). The group, if it's functioning well, won't allow them to monopolize.

PRACTICE TIP

When all else fails, set a timer. Yes, an honest-to-goodness timer that will audibly ring halfway through the session. Have an explicit conversation with your client that you both are struggling to make time for the necessary work. Then contract with your client that you'll focus on the past week for half of the session and over-arching goals for the other half. There really is something a bit magical about the timer – if the client has unpleasant emotions about the time limit (e.g., frustration, resentment), somehow some of that emotional intensity gets transferred off of you and onto the timer, as if it is actually the passage of time that offends, rather than your request for structure.

CHAPTER 18
BUT SOMETIMES IT IS A CRISIS

Sometimes it's a client who has been dragged in by a best friend who didn't know what else to do. She's weeping and disheveled; she can't string a complete sentence together. After 25 minutes, all we can piece together is that it was a sexual assault, and it was recent. Or it might be our last client of the day, a walk-in. He seems really out of it, and he might be high. He's saying things like "last resort" and "out of options." It could be a family we visit in the city's civic center in the aftermath of the storm of the century, all sitting on the floor amidst a hundred other dazed families, while the whimpers of children too young to understand fill the space.

Now it's time to put a halt to all of our treatment plans, therapeutic techniques, and clinical wisdom. It's time to just be a human person meeting the most basic needs of another human person. The primary concerns aren't goals and accurate psychosocial histories; they're immediate safety and access to basic resources (Maslow, 1962).

Of course, we don't abandon all of our training. We still speak gently and reflect often. We are still mindful of cultural considerations and we avoid non-therapeutic touch. We don't actually take clients home with us. But the first questions aren't "What brings you in?" and "What would you like to get out of our time together?" In times like these, the questions are "Is it all right if I talk with you for a few minutes?" and "Is there anything you need right now, like water or to make a telephone call?"

During crisis, the steps we need to take for *psychological first aid* follow a different sequence than regular services (Vernberg et al., 2008). We start with making calm non-intrusive contact and prioritize the client's physical safety. Then, we make sure they are stabilized (i.e., oriented to the environment, not dissociated or completely overwhelmed). After that, we can move on to crisis-specific information gathering about their current experience, immediate needs, and additional risk and resilience factors. During crisis, we may also actually provide assistance with immediate needs that we wouldn't under other circumstances. For example, we may need to help clients get access to emergency medical services or assist them with making contact with a family member they have been separated from. After the initial aid is provided and the immediate crisis is managed, our job may become something more like referrals to additional supports/resources or more like traditional therapy, depending on the situation.

    DOI: 10.4324/9781003125082-20

PRACTICE TIP

Of course, you've heard all of the adages about self-care: "You can't help anyone if you don't take care of yourself." "Caring for yourself is not a luxury, it's an ethical mandate." "You can't pour from an empty cup." They're true, and they also just don't feel that pressing in the middle of a crisis. I want to encourage you that, during a crisis, it's ok to push yourself. Just not so far that you don't eat, sleep, or process what's going on.

If you're working with a group of other mental health professionals during a crisis, consider designating one person from your group whose job is to manage the basic needs *for the other providers* in the group. That one person can help make sure that everyone stays hydrated and takes breaks, watch for signs of overwhelm and fatigue, gather information or do needed "errands" so you can stay with your client, and be available to step in for additional support. This can increase the group's overall effectiveness of providing help to clients.

CHAPTER 19
THE NEW RULE FOR
SELF-DISCLOSURE

First, let's talk about the old rule for self-disclosure. We can probably all say it by heart: "Is the self-disclosure for you, or for the client? If it's for you, don't say it. If it's for the client, go ahead."

Allow me to challenge this. What kind of self-disclosure is *really* for the client? Let's consider the kinds there are. For the moment, let's exclude the low-intimacy, conversational self-disclosure that we often give while walking a client back to the office, in response to their inevitable polite queries (e.g., "Oh, a little tired, but good. Thanks." "Went to the beach, what did you do this weekend?" "Oh, no, I just don't wear these shoes very often"). These disclosures tend to be mild, brief, unrelated to therapy, mostly about following prescribed social roles, and can be beneficial (Danzer et al., 2019).

The rest of self-disclosure we can break into two main kinds: There-and-then and Here-and-now.

THERE-AND-THEN

This is usually the disclosure of some kind of life experience of ours. It may be that we went through something similar and want to let the client know that we have that in common. We may also have coped with a certain situation in a way that we think might be helpful for clients because it worked for us. Sometimes, clients initially or outwardly respond positively to this kind of disclosure. Focusing on similarity or sharing our stories may be a quick, easy way to enhance the relationship or show we're "human" (Hill et al., 2018). However, I believe we should be careful with it. We are very much at risk for saying to clients, "Your experience is the same as my experience," and that's not true. No matter how similar we and a client are, we aren't the same. We can rob clients of telling and writing their own stories when we interject ourselves. We're lucky if clients notice and call us out on it, but they usually don't. That's a little scary, because it might mean we're trampling on their experiences and they either expect us to do that or don't notice that we are. Frankly, we have other tools for building rapport that aren't so risky.

DOI: 10.4324/9781003125082-21

HERE-AND-NOW

These are disclosures that are related to the actual interpersonal experience
that's occurring in session (this is also called *immediacy*). They are things we
notice in the session — that the client is quiet today, that they seem more
put together and calmer than usual, or that they are fidgety and distracted
when they typically aren't. They are thoughts we have in session — wondering
about a possible connection, remembering something relevant from the
intake, or checking out a sudden insight. They are how we feel about the
client's situation — sad for their loss, angry at their abuser, or frustrated by
how circumstances seem to fall against them. They are how we feel about the
client — close to them after an important disclosure, overwhelmed by their
pressured monologue, or irritated by their resistance. These are much more
likely to be useful to clients' process (Danzer et al., 2019).

Here-and-now disclosures still ought to be treated with care. Just
because we are feeling, noticing, or thinking something in session doesn't
necessarily mean we should blurt it out. It still needs to meet the criteria
of being for the client. So how do we do that? First, we need to make sure
it's really happening, and that it's not countertransference. If we're not sure,
we can make a mental note and check on it with ourselves, a colleague, or
a supervisor. We can always bring it up next session. Second, here-and-now
disclosures tend to be pretty powerful, so we want to be sure to use gentle
language and a curious tone (Yalom, 2002).

PRACTICE TIP

Regardless of the type of disclosure – conversational, there-and-then,
here-and-now – it is more helpful when it returns *immediately* to the
client's thoughts, feelings, and reactions (Danzer et al., 2019). We can
structure even there-and-then disclosure to facilitate this; for example,
we can say something like, "When I've been in a similar situation,
I felt angry and powerless. How are you feeling about this situation?"
Remember that even when clients ask specifically if you've had a
certain experience (like when your teen asks you if you ever did drugs),
it's usually because they are thinking about it in their own lives, not pure
curiosity!

CHAPTER 20
BECOME A "BUTT–HEAD" THERAPIST

Before you skip this chapter, let me explain! As therapists, we have two jobs, each of which is plenty of work on its own. One job is bringing all of our training to bear – theories, techniques, the change process – on the goals of clients. We keep up with empirically supported treatments and apply them correctly, balance evidence-based practice with clients' cultural and personal variables and preferences, and constantly revise our hypotheses about clients' distress and trajectory as we learn new information. We have to discover clients' goals early and then constantly monitor their progress, in each session and over the course of therapy, even when they get distracted from the goal by immediate crises, overwhelming emotions, or the events of the week. While they are deep in the thrall of session work, we have to stay above the tumult and constantly choose our moments to redirect, reframe, and educate clients, keeping them headed toward their goals and sometimes making treatment-plan adjustments on the fly. That's the "head" part of being a therapist.

Our other job is to be with clients in the here-and-now. Fully in the moment, completely invested, pouring our energy into the development of the "I–Thou" therapeutic relationship (Buber, 1937) – a deeply human encounter during which we never treat the other person as someone to be acted on or even interacted with, but as someone to *stand in relation* with, to *be* with. We can't derive the full benefit from the facilitative conditions of therapy (accurate empathy, congruence, and unconditional positive regard; Rogers, 1957) if we aren't prioritizing the development of the relationship, which requires being mindfully present with clients.

Training in mindfulness – being aware of your moment-to-moment experience – often focuses on your breath, because your breath is always fully in the "now" (e.g., Segal et al., 2018). The last breath is gone, the next not yet arrived. It is used as an anchor when we notice we are not being mindful – remembering the past, worrying about the future, any distraction from what's happening in us and with us right now. But it can be difficult to focus on the breath in therapy, because we're often using our breath while interacting with clients. Another common target for anchoring in mindfulness training is the body, because the body is also always in the present moment. And there's one part of our body that's always there, but never really involved in therapy – our butt. It's always in the present

DOI: 10.4324/9781003125082-22

moment, but it's not like our heart (beating slower or faster, prompting us to evaluate it), or our left foot (which has a tendency to bounce, even when we're not anxious), or our stomach (which seems to be in the business of reminding us that we haven't eaten for three … four … five clients now). So that's the "butt" part – being fully present.

Doesn't it sound impossible to do both of those things at once?

A "butt–head" therapist works toward the synergy of being able to be both completely, mindfully in the moment with clients and tracking client movement and negotiating the treatment process at the same time. Whew! Sound exhausting? It can be. It's also worth it.

PRACTICE TIP

This takes time. Usually, therapists have a natural tendency to do one or the other. Early in career, it's often being a "head" therapist, working hard to say the right thing and do the right thing. As you practice this concept, the next stage is like a pendulum – swinging back and forth between being "in your head" and "in your butt" multiple times each session. And that is often good enough. With time and practice, you'll notice the change gets faster and easier, until – instead of finding a middle ground – you find that you begin to be able to do both simultaneously. But, of course, as soon as you notice you've done it, you're out of it!

REFERENCES

Ackerman, S. J., & Hilsenroth, M. J. (2001). A review of therapist characteristics and techniques negatively impacting the therapeutic alliance. *Psychotherapy: Theory, Research, Practice, Training, 38*(2), 171–185. https://doi.org/10.1037/0033-3204.38.2.171

Adler, A. (1931/2014). *What life could mean to you (3rd ed)*. Oneworld Publications.

American Association of Marriage and Family Therapists. (2015). *Code of ethics.* Retrieved from https://www.aamft.org/Legal_Ethics/Code_of_Ethics.aspx

American Counseling Association. (2014). 2014 ACA code of ethics. https://www.counseling.org/docs/default-source/default-document-library/2014-code-of-ethics-finaladdress.pdf

American Psychological Association. (2017). Ethical principles of psychologists and code of conduct (2002, amended effective June 1, 2010, and January 1, 2017). https://www.apa.org/ethics/code/

Baddeley, A. D. (1986). *Working memory*. Clarendon Press.

Bargh, J. A. (1994). The four horsemen of automaticity: Awareness, intention, efficiency, and control in social cognition. In R. S. Wyer, Jr. & T. K. Srull (Eds.), *Handbook of social cognition: Basic processes; Applications* (p. 1–40). Lawrence Erlbaum Associates, Inc.

Buber, M. (1937). *I and Thou.* Translated by Smith, R. G.. T. & T. Clark.

Chekroud, A. M., Foster, D., Zheutlin, A. B., Gerhard, D. M., Roy, B., Koutsouleris, N., Chandra, A., Esposti, M. D., Subramanyan, G., Gueorguieva, R., Paulus, M., & Krystal, J. H. (2018). Predicting barriers to treatment for depression in a U.S. national sample: A cross-sectional, proof-of-concept study. *Psychiatric Services, 69*(8), 927–934. https://doi.org/10.1176/appi.ps.201800094

Connolly Gibbons, M. B., Rothbard, A., Farris, K. D., Wiltsey Stirman, S., Thompson, S. M., Scott, K., Heintz, L. E., Gallop, R., & Crits-Christoph, P. (2011). Changes in psychotherapy utilization among consumers of services for major depressive disorder in the community mental health system. *Administration and Policy in Mental Health, 38*(6), 495–503. https://doi.org/10.1007/s10488-011-0336-1

Cormier, S., Nurius, P. S., & Osborn, C. J. (2009). *Interviewing and change strategies for helpers: Fundamental skills and cognitive-behavioral interventions* (Instructor's ed., 6th ed.). Brooks/Cole.

Danzer, G. S., Andresen, K., & Sugarbaker, D. (Aug 2019). *Therapist Self-Disclosure: What Does the Research Tell Us?* [Conference session]. 127th American Psychological Association Annual Convention, Chicago, IL. https://doi.org/10.1037/e509992019-001

Diamond, A. (2013). Executive functions. *Annual Review of Psychology, 64*, 135–168. https://doi.org/10.1146/annurev-psych-113011-143750

Fusco, G. M., & Freeman, A. (2007). The crisis-prone patient: The high-arousal cluster B personality disorders. In F. M. Dattilio, A. Freeman (Eds.), *Cognitive-behavioral strategies in crisis intervention* (3rd ed.) (pp. 122–148). New York, NY, US: Guilford Press.

Gulliver, A., Griffiths, K. M., & Christensen, H. (2010). Perceived barriers and facilitators to mental health help-seeking in young people: A systematic review. *BMC psychiatry, 10*, 113. https://doi.org/10.1186/1471-244X-10-113

Hill, C. E., Knox, S., & Pinto-Coelho, K. G. (2018). Therapist self-disclosure and immediacy: A qualitative meta-analysis. *Psychotherapy, 55*(4), 445–460. https://doi.org/10.1037/pst0000182

Hill, C. E., Thompson, B. J., & Ladany, N. (2003). Therapist use of silence in therapy. *Journal of Clinical Psychology, 59*(4), 513–524. https://doi.org/10.1002/jclp.10155

Lavie, N. (1995). Perceptual load as a necessary condition for selective attention. *Journal of Experimental Psychology: Human Perception and Performance, 21*(3), 451–468. https://doi.org/10.1037/0096-1523.21.3.451

Levinson, W., Roter, D. L., Mullooly, J. P., Dull, V. T., & Frankel, R. M. (1997). Physician-patient communication: The relationship with malpractice claims among primary care physicians and surgeons. *JAMA: Journal of the American Medical Association, 277*(7), 553–559. https://doi.org/10.1001/jama.277.7.553

Maslow, A. (1962*). Toward a psychology of being*. D Van Nostrand. https://doi.org/10.1037/10793-000

National Association for Social Workers. (2017). *Code of ethics*. Retrieved from https://www.socialworkers.org/about/ethics/code-of-ethics

Norcross, J., & Lambert, M. J. (2019). *Psychotherapy relationships that work: Volume 1: Evidence based therapist contributions* (3rd ed). Oxford University Press.

Rogers, C. (1942). *Counseling and psychotherapy: Newer concepts in practice*. Houghton Mifflin Company.

Rogers, C. (1957). The necessary and sufficient conditions of therapeutic change. *The Journal of Consulting Psychology, 21*, 95–103.

Rogers, C. (1961). *On becoming a person*. Houghton Mifflin.

Schneider, W., & Chein, J. M. (2003). Controlled and automatic processing: Behavior, theory, and biological mechanisms. *Cognitive Science, 27*(3), 525–559. doi: http://dx.doi.org.ezaccess.libraries.psu.edu/10.1016/S0364-0213(03)00011-9

Schneider, W., & Shiffrin, R. M. (1977). Controlled and automatic human information processing: I. Detection, search, and attention. *Psychological Review, 84*(1), 1–66. https://doi.org/10.1037/0033-295X.84.1.1

Schwartz, B., & Flowers, J. (2010). *How to fail as a therapist* (2nd ed.). New Harbinger.

Segal, Z. V., Williams, J. M. G., & Teasdale, J. D. (2013). *Mindfulness-based cognitive therapy for depression* (2nd ed.). The Guilford Press.

Sommers-Flanagan, J., & Shaw, S. L. (2017). Suicide risk assessment: What psychologists should know. *Professional Psychology: Research and Practice, 48*(2), 98–106. https://doi.org/10.1037/pro0000106

Sommers-Flanagan, J., & Sommers-Flanagan, R. (2017). *Clinical Interviewing* (6th ed.). Wiley.

Sweller, J. (1988). Cognitive load during problem solving: Effects on learning. *Cognitive Science, 12*, 257–285.

Tindall, R. H., & Robinson, F. P. (1947). The use of silence as a technique in counseling. *Journal of Clinical Psychology, 3*, 136–141. https://doi.org/10.1002/1097-4679(194704)3:2<136::AID-JCLP2270030205>3.0.CO;2-E

Tomasello, M. (2010). *Origins of human communication*. MIT Press.

van Deurzen, E., & Adams, M. (2016). *Skills in existential counselling and psychotherapy* (2nd ed.) Sage Publications.

Vernberg, E. M., Steinberg, A. M., Jacobs, A. K., Brymer, M. J., Watson, P. J., Osofsky, J. D., Layne, C. M., Pynoos, R. S., & Ruzek, J. I. (2008). Innovations in disaster mental health: Psychological first aid. *Professional Psychology: Research and Practice, 39*(4), 381–388. https://doi.org/10.1037/a0012663

Vygotsky, L. (1962/2012). *Thought and language*. MIT Press.

Yalom, I. D. (2002). *The gift of therapy: An open letter to a new generation of therapists and their patients*. HarperCollins Publishers.

Yalom, I. D., & Leszcz, M. (Collaborator). (2005). *The theory and practice of group psychotherapy* (5th ed.). Basic Books.

Zeig, J. K., & Lankton, S. R. (Eds.). (1988). *Developing Ericksonian therapy: State of the art*. Brunner/Mazel.

Watch Your Mouth! (Therapeutic Language)

Therapists know better than most people how important language is; it's an incredibly powerful tool that helps us to structure our world and internal experiences. Even linguists agree that "natural language is not only a social, but also a psychological phenomenon" (Dik, 1980). We know the literature on how language can change our perceptions – the word "crash" leads us to overestimate a car's speed (Loftus & Palmer, 1974) and the mere verbal suggestion of pain relief reduces pain perception (e.g., Craggs, Price, & Robinson, 2014). We have emotion lists and wheels at our disposal in every session because we know how accurate emotional vocabulary helps clients to process (e.g., Wotschack & Klann-Delius, 2013). We see firsthand the difference that well-considered words can make in a marriage conflict (Gottman & Silver, 1999) or in a parent's discipline (Gottman & DeClaire, 1997). We see even more clearly how much damage can be done with ill-considered words.

Thankfully, much of our training and experience focused on learning to speak therapeutically. It is likely we are already the best models for healthy language in our clients' lives. These next ten chapters will explore some of the sneaky language traps that even the best of us might miss, and how to outsmart them using insights from current and classic research and theory.

CHAPTER 21
"MAKE YOU FEEL"

Let's start with a big one. It's an unfortunate cliché, the therapist's refrain of "How does that make you feel?" When we ask it, with only good intentions, we don't realize that it may contribute to clients developing an external locus of control. *External locus of control* is the belief that life is controlled by outside factors that a person cannot influence (such as other people, situations, chance, or fate); *internal locus of control* is the belief that one has power to control one's own life (Rotter, 1966). In general, a strong internal locus of control is associated with a host of positive outcomes, including higher resilience, lower depression, and more effective health behaviors. We want to honor and support the development of clients' internal locus of control by emphasizing that circumstances alone, while an important part of the equation, do not *determine* clients' feelings.

Yes, emotions are somewhat predictable. If we perceive an injustice, we feel anger. If we perceive a loss, we feel sadness. If we perceive a danger, we feel fear. That's good for therapists to know; for example, it can help us recognize when we're dealing with secondary emotions (e.g., a client who says they feel angry, but the cognitions are more about pain or shame). When, for example, a partner utters harsh words, certain perceptions may be activated, but the feelings are not *caused.*

It's beyond the scope of this little chapter to talk through how to teach clients to recognize their own cognitions and cognitive distortions, but it may be enough to say that the external situation is never the sole determinant of a client's emotional experience. (That is, it's never only the proverbial spouse – no matter how carelessly they speak – who "makes me mad.") Every emotion is felt in part because of the external environment (including insensitive partners!), but also through the filters of clients' histories, their particular vulnerabilities and conditions of worth, their own cognitive biases, their level of motivation and investment, their current levels of ego strength, their physiological states, anything that has primed them subconsciously, etc.

Most clients come to therapy with a sense that they don't have much control. When we use "make you feel" language, we may accidentally confirm to them that they don't have control over one of the few things they actually have some control over. We say to them, "Yes, you are a victim of circumstance, so there's not much to be done." Of course, that's not the message we intend.

DOI: 10.4324/9781003125082-24

We want to practice validating their emotions and experiences, without diminishing them or casting blame. So, we also don't want to say, "You choose how you feel, it's no one's fault but yours – so just feel differently!" We know that blaming isn't a good way to empower. So, we can practice replacing this language in our vocabularies when we find it there. The easiest option, and the one that almost certainly asks what we want to know, is: "How did you feel when …?" This conveys genuine interest, without blaming or disempowering. This is a small change, but it's very impactful.

PRACTICE TIP

Here's a metaphor I sometimes use with clients: If someone throws a baseball at a house, what determines if a window gets broken? (Hint: The client is the house!) Three kinds of things. One, the thrower (the other person or circumstance). What did they throw, how hard, with what kind of aim? Was it an insult? A particularly nasty insult? Was it targeted at the client's vulnerable spots? Two, the actual house. How many windows (i.e., vulnerable spots, conditions of worth) does it have? How big are they? What are they made of? Are there walls, fences, or trees blocking the vulnerable areas (i.e., defenses)? Three, the intervening space (how accurately does the listener perceive the speaker's intention?). Is it windy that day? Does/can someone else catch the ball? A baseball thrown does not a broken window make.

CHAPTER 22
"BUT"

We need to be careful with this little word! While it has many formal and old-fashioned linguistic uses, the primary way it is used in conversation is as a conjunction – it connects two thoughts together. Specifically, the word "but" is an *adversative conjunction* – it connects in a way that disqualifies what comes before it. It is meant to express opposition or exception, not mere contrast (Garner, 2016; Saitō, 1899). For example, we could say, "My theoretical orientation is existential, but his is behavioral." However, it's likely we mean something closer to "My theoretical orientation is existential and his is behavioral" or "My theoretical orientation is existential; his orientation is behavioral." (Unless, of course, we're making a referral for behavior therapy and *want* to disqualify ourselves!)

In another example, if I say, "I'm glad you bought this book, but you really should have gotten it on sale," the take-away message is that you overpaid. If I say, "You really should have gotten it on sale, but I'm glad you bought this book," the message is that I'm happy you have it, regardless.

Here are a few therapy examples when we might use "but" (but probably shouldn't):

- "I hear that you want to connect with me outside of session, but I have to hold that boundary to protect us both."
- "I know you were really angry, but that sounds like an ineffective way to show it."
- "I care about you and want you to be successful, but I see you getting in your own way."

All that great work we might have just done reflecting the client's content and emotions, working the perfect paraphrase, or making a spot-on interpretation – poof! Everything we say before the word "but" effectively disappears.

To make matters worse, the better we did crafting the first part of the sentence (clarifying, reflecting, etc.), the more invalidating it might be after the little eraser does its work. The client thinks, "They really, really get me … but it doesn't matter." How likely are they to hear the important message we have for them in the second half, if they're busy feeling diminished or disqualified?

 DOI: 10.4324/9781003125082-25

PRACTICE TIP

If you simply attempt to reduce your use of "but," you may find yourself accidentally just using synonyms such as "however," "yet," and "though." (Clients do this all the time when they are first learning this skill!) There are a few useful options that can help you clearly express your intent and save "but" for when you really mean it. Experiment with these and when they might fit better:

- Use "and." (This is a *copulative* conjunction that emphasizes joining or accumulation. The words "too" and "also" have a similar effect and may fit a particular sentence better.)

  "I hear that you want to connect with me outside of session, and I have to hold that boundary to protect us both."

- Use a period. (This allows you to offer both thoughts without determining the specific connection between them. A semi-colon serves almost the same function.)

  "I know you were really angry. It sounds like you used an ineffective way to show it."

- Use "so." ("So" is an *illative* conjunction which implies inference or consequence. Its cousins are "then" and "therefore.")

  "I care about you and want you to be successful, so I want to let you know when I see you getting in your own way."

CHAPTER 23
"OR ..."

We know the value of open-ended questions (as discussed in Chapter 16). They give us rich, detailed pictures of the most salient parts of our clients' worlds. They help us avoid sounding like interrogators or attempting to guess our way into understanding our clients' perspectives.

We also have experiences in therapy when, despite our best efforts, it just doesn't work. It may be because clients are depressed, and don't have enough internal energy to drag out a clear explanation of their experiences. Clients may have a limited vocabulary for explaining their internal worlds, perhaps because it's something they've never done in their families or cultures. It may even just be because clients are young – children or teens – and haven't had much practice.

In these cases, closed-ended questions may get a little more response, but the danger of using them remains. Closed-ended questions like "Did you feel such-and-such?" and "Was it like thus-and-so?" open the door for yes-or-no answers that don't get us much further with clients who are already having trouble disclosing. An additional risk of questions like these, especially when we're not just repeating back what clients have said, is that we might put words into their mouths (and thus, into their experiences) that may not really belong there. When we do that, most clients either don't want to correct us, or (worse!) don't even realize that they should.

We may want clients to hear us use some emotion words to help increase their vocabularies or model an insight-focused summary because they don't yet have those skills. But we don't want to lock them into our choice of words and take away their power and opportunity for growth. Effectively, we want to harness Vygotsky's concept of the *zone of proximal development* (1978). This is the space between what a client (in Vygotsky's writing, a child) can already do alone and what they can do with our help. Here is a delightfully simple option for balancing in that space: We can ask an "or" question, but not in the traditional way (between two choices). We use it at the end. Like this:

Imagine a social anxiety client has said, "I wish I were just different," and we've said, "Tell me more about it" and gotten nothing else, and we've asked "Different how?" and gotten nothing else, and we're at a loss. The next thing we might say is, "Do you wish you were different like less anxious or different like you wish you looked physically different?" Instead, we might

 DOI: 10.4324/9781003125082-26

get a richer or more accurate response if we said something like, "Hmmm ... different like less anxious or like physically different *or ...?*" Bonus points when we say that final "or" with an inviting tilt of the head and let it linger in the air.

PRACTICE TIP

A really profitable use of this technique is when asking about client emotions. When clients have a limited emotional vocabulary, you'll hear a lot of answers like "I just feel bad" or "I was so upset." After you've tried your open-ended follow-ups, you may want to start giving them some emotion vocabulary.

"You said you feel bad. There are lots of ways of feeling bad, and I'd like to get a good picture of your kind of feeling bad. When you think about that bad feeling, is it a little more like bad-angry, or like bad-scared, or ..." (let it linger!) If clients are silent, remember to give them time. If they're silent for a long while, consider following up in the silence with a quiet invitation like "Maybe more than one of those? Or something different? Or ...?"

CHAPTER 24
"WHAT" (INSTEAD OF "WHY")

Have you ever accidentally bitten a fingernail too far and had the soft tissue beneath become exposed? It is painfully vulnerable and sensitive to even a breath of air. Clients come into therapy similarly vulnerable. It is rare for a person to utilize therapy as their first-choice coping strategy, which means many people come to us after having tried "everything else." They're vulnerable from their distress, or maybe from being "forced" into therapy by a loved one or the court system. They're vulnerable because they've been working hard for a long time, in a lot of ways, and nothing has helped enough yet. They often feel they have exhausted their own resources and they weren't enough – not strong enough, or smart enough, or just enough – to do it on their own.

When your fingernail has been torn off, you protect it, right? So, in addition to being vulnerable, clients are also guarded, often against two very profound fears: "This is all my fault" and "It won't ever get better." Considering these fears, even the highest functioning clients are primed to take things the wrong way, to be bruised or offended by even carefully chosen words. Without delving too far into Aristotelean ethics, a "why" question asks, "to which purpose?" or "in service to what?" (Sloan, 2010). These questions imply *intention*, and that often hits too close to home for someone who (reasonably!) doesn't want to take full responsibility for their current, painful situation. Remember our discussion about locus of control (from Chapter 21)? While it is important to emphasize internal locus of control, we don't want to dismiss external sources of control completely. So, we can reduce the risk of unintentionally hurting a vulnerable client, and we can get a less defensive and more complete answer if we structure our questions with "what" instead of "why."

For example:

Instead of "Why did you do that?":

- "What led you to that?"
- "What factors were at play there?"

Instead of "Why didn't you do that?":

- "What has kept you from doing that?"
- "What barriers have there been?"

DOI: 10.4324/9781003125082-27

When clients ask "why" questions (e.g., "Why did she have to die?" "Why do bad things always happen to me?" "Why did I lose that job?"), it's important for us to determine the intention behind their question.

- They may actually be looking for reasons or causes. For example, "Why did I lose that job?" In this case, we may want to switch them to "what" questions, such as "What factors were involved?" because it's unusual for there to be a single, knowable cause for anything.
- They may be expressing their perception of external locus of control. For example, "Why do bad things always happen to me?" In most cases, there will be some aspects of difficult situations that are external and some that are internal, and we'll want to explore both. We could initiate this discussion by saying something like, "What parts of this seem out of your control?"
- They may simply be expressing their distress at the uncontrollability of genuinely uncontrollable circumstances. For example, "Why did she have to die?" At these times, supportive listening and reflection is probably the safest bet.

PRACTICE TIP

This is another one of those techniques that is entirely about practice, just building your therapeutic vocabulary. Make this a little game with a colleague: The two of you can practice catching each other asking "why" questions and then rewinding to say it a different way. This is much easier than working on it in session. Although, as you change your vocabulary in this way, you're bound to accidentally drop a "why" into session and notice right away. No problem – just say, "oops, I meant to ask ..." Clients will benefit from your modeling!

CHAPTER 25
"FEEL LIKE"

This phrase is a trap! And it's a sneaky trap because we usually don't notice it. It goes like this: First, we ask something like, "How do you feel about that?" Then, the client answers. Suddenly, it's 11:49 and we don't know how they feel!

This is what happened: See, we asked, "How do you feel about that?" and the client (probably unknowingly!) slid the trap closed with, "I feel like ..." and then the session disappeared while we were searching for the feelings. But what clients are usually telling us when they say "I feel like ... " is actually "I think ..." or "I believe ...." Let me give some examples:

* "I feel like this is all my fault."
* "I feel like there's nothing else I can do."
* "I feel like he hates me, but just won't say it."

In English, "I feel like..." has become a softer way of saying what we are thinking (which is not necessarily a bad thing). When we hear what a client thinks or believes in those statements, it could be very rich and powerful information. Absolutely, we want to honor that and move toward it therapeutically – *with cognitive work, recognizing that it is a thought*. We have well-established strategies for working specifically with cognitions (e.g., Beck, 1979) and for working specifically with emotions (e.g., Greenberg, 2009). And while the two are definitely interconnected (e.g., Storebeck & Clore, 2007), they are separate enough that they both deserve attention.

So, we just want to be careful that we don't confuse clients' thoughts with their emotions. That's how we lose track of the session – believing we're doing emotion-based work when the client is working in the sphere of cognitions. Paying attention to this misused phrase can help us stay on the same page. And it might just remind us not to let them "get away with" not telling us the emotion!

If we want to do emotion work, we may have to go so far as to explain this concept to our clients and demonstrate the difference. Sometimes clients will get this right away, and we can simply give a quick correction (e.g., "Oops! That wasn't an emotion...") or corrected-reflection-with-follow-up (e.g., "I hear that you believe you're responsible for what happened. And what are the feelings that are going along with that belief?"). Sometimes clients will really struggle because they aren't used to attending to or

DOI: 10.4324/9781003125082-28

expressing their emotions. In this case, it might be time for us to pull out our trusty emotion-words wheel.

(As a side note, this is also a problem in couple's work, when clients will avoid exposing their own emotions and slyly accuse their partner at the same time. For example, "I feel like he doesn't take me seriously" instead of "I feel sad and worthless when I think my opinion has been dismissed." More about this in Chapter 27.)

PRACTICE TIP

There's an exception to this rule, and it's when a client says, "I feel like …" and then gives you a simile or analogy. For example, "I feel like a bear who has been hibernating and just awakened to the first beautiful spring day" or "I feel like I am a rope that has just been fraying and fraying from overuse." If they give you a metaphor like these – first, count your lucky stars for this client. Then, just say, "Tell me more about that."

CHAPTER 26
THE GENERIC "YOU"

Linguistically, the "Generic You" is the use of the pronoun "you" that is meant to refer to an unspecific or indefinite person. It is a less formal way of stating something universal, a more casual thing to say than "one" (Huddleston & Pullum, 2002). For example, "You know how it's really hard to find great therapy books that you actually have time to read?" That sounds so much more natural than "One may know how difficult it is for one to find a great therapy book that one actually has time to read." Clients use this often, and we rarely realize it, because it is so pervasive in our speech. But we want to listen for it very carefully, because clients are often using it to avoid saying "I" and "owning" their thought, feeling, experience, etc.

The Generic You is a deeper issue than it may seem up front; it deals with existential aloneness and personal responsibility. As Viktor Frankl says, "Each man is questioned by life; and he can only answer to life by answering for his own life; to life he can only respond by being responsible" (Frankl, 1959).

Clients pull the Generic You into service primarily in two ways – one in group therapy and one in individual. In group therapy, when clients use the Generic You, they're often seeking the approval or understanding of the group members by phrasing their experiences as universal truths. For example, they may say, "When your boss is so demanding, you just get burnt out." They usually don't realize it, but this can be an attempt to get other members to normalize their feelings, to create a sense of "we" in the group, where it might not actually exist. They especially do this in the beginning stages of group and if we allow that to happen, we never get to the "storming" phase and beyond. Everyone will feel artificially connected, rather than experiencing the real cohesion that happens only after they've recognized and appreciated their differences. Dangerously, this may also isolate and silence any group member who feels differently!

In individual therapy, clients often use the Generic You when they're transitioning into something that's difficult for them that they don't want to internalize. This is also typically outside of their awareness. Here's an example:

> "It's hard being a mom now. I don't have as much time as I used to. I'm tired a lot, mostly. I don't know what I'm doing all the time. You know, you feel inadequate when you're a new parent."

DOI: 10.4324/9781003125082-29

In this example, we want to go to the feeling of inadequacy. That's where the work is. This client showed it by transitioning to the Generic You because that content was uncomfortable, and we know clients can't work on what they aren't holding, what they aren't owning.

PRACTICE TIP

When clients begin using the Generic You, it is often necessary to stop and ask them if they mean "I." Perhaps they don't, and they really are explaining what they see as a universal experience. (Not likely, though.) Be prepared to gently explain why you've asked, and then develop a shorthand with clients who do it often so that you don't have to interrupt sessions multiple times to talk about it. If need be, you can always say, "Can you repeat that, and say 'I'?"

The most important thing is that you are noticing it when it happens. If a client says "you" in session, they should be referencing the very specific, completely un-generic, identifiable You – the person they are speaking to. If they aren't, it's worth some extra attention.

CHAPTER 27
"I" STATEMENTS

We all know the beauty of the traditional "I" statement, popularized by couples' therapists (e.g., Gottman & Silver, 1999) and family therapists (e.g., Ginott, 1965). It's a classic for a good reason! Instead of the client saying, "You make me so angry" or "My boss drives me crazy," we artfully get them to say, "I feel angry when you _____" and "I feel a little crazy when my boss _____." This technique reduces the listener's defensiveness. We can power up this formula with this extra step:

> "I feel (emotion) when (situation) because I (personal experience/ vulnerability)."

Here are a few examples:

- "I feel sad when you come home late because I worry that I'm not fun to be with."
- "I feel angry when my boss says I have to work late because I think the people without kids should be the ones who work late."

Yes, this can feel very artificial at first. That's ok. It's basically a completely new way of communicating, which means a completely new skill set. Any time we begin practicing something new, it's stilted and feels awkward. It's useful to let clients know this, and to have them practice correctly anyway. Once the skill is mastered, that's when we can play around with it. We have to practice scales, then practice songs, before we write our own music.

There are two main reasons it's important to follow the script at first. One, it makes it easier to hear. If the situation includes the word "you" (e.g., "I feel sad when *you* come home late"), the personal vulnerability that follows can really help the offending "you" (the listener) get into the speaker's phenomenological world. It keeps the focus on the speaker's experience and gives the listener less fuel for gearing up to be defensive.

Two, it gives the speaker more power. If they are able to link their feelings to their personal experiences and vulnerabilities, it means they don't have to rely on the (highly unreliable but ever popular) strategy of attempting to change other people or the world. They give themselves the opportunity to realize, as we discussed previously, that they have some power in how they experience things and that circumstances don't simply "make them feel."

DOI: 10.4324/9781003125082-30

PRACTICE TIP

Remember "Mad Libs?" (This is the game where you're asked to give a random noun, then a number, then an adjective, and so forth, and after you're done, the other person reads a story that uses your silly words to fill in the blanks and it's suddenly hilarious.) This technique is a therapeutic game of Mad Libs, so be sure to follow the rules. The most important rule of Mad Libs is that you fill in the blank with the right kind of word. It really messes up the whole thing when the story goes: "and the _____ went back to work and showed off his new top hat" and you accidentally said "yellow" when you should have said "squirrel."

When we ask clients to engage in this kind of activity, we need to listen very carefully – it's easier to hear mistakes in Mad Libs than in therapy. Make sure clients are using emotions (not cognitions), situations (not character traits), and vulnerabilities (not excuses) to fill in the blanks of the formula. It works like magic when they do.

CHAPTER 28
THE PARROT

The art of "parroting" (that is, tracking clients verbally by repeating the important words they say in a low, un-interrupting voice) seems largely left untaught these days, replaced with the non-verbal skills of head-nodding and therapeutic mumbling (i.e., minimal verbal followers, or "mmm-hmmm'ing") and the more sophisticated skills of reflection and paraphrase.

Often, when therapists are taught the skills of reflection and paraphrasing, we are taught not to repeat back clients' words verbatim, but to use synonyms. (In a textbook world, clients give a rambling, alexithymic monologue and then we brilliantly summarize with the "perfect" emotion word or phrase, building trust by our almost mythical levels of understanding. And if you're Carl Rogers, possibly you can do this.)

But here's the thing about synonyms. They don't really mean the same thing. Discomfort, pain, and agony aren't the same thing. Sad, depressed, and miserable aren't the same thing. Neither are difficult/problematic, angry/irritated, guilty/ashamed, or upset/bothered. Language wouldn't have developed these fine-grained synonyms if they didn't have different meanings. Moreover, clients may not have the same internal definitions as we do, and we cloud those issues further when we add new words. Our textbooks also rarely discuss what happens when we reflect, paraphrase, or summarize *badly*. These kinds of misunderstandings lead to therapeutic ruptures, and they are dependent on the client mentioning that it happened, which they typically do not do (Rhodes et al., 1994). When in doubt, use the language clients have already used. When we repeat a client's most important word every couple of sentences, not only can they be sure we're tracking them, but they know we're paying close enough attention to pick out what's most important, without changing it.

We need to be careful with the head-nodding and therapeutic mumbling, too. We intend it to show that we are paying close attention and following the client reliably. Actually, these non-verbal behaviors are very easy to over-use and then we risk signaling to the client: "I hear you, I hear you, hurry up; it's my turn to talk." (If you haven't noticed this, ask a therapist friend to demonstrate it to you – you'll be shocked!) Another risk of the chronic head-nodding is that some clients interpret it as agreement or reinforcement (e.g., Verplanck, 1955). When using the parroting technique, we don't have to worry about that.

     DOI: 10.4324/9781003125082-31

There are two times that parroting works well. First, you can do this as the client is speaking, if they're monologuing quite freely. For example:

> C: When I was young, she was really hard on me. She used to smack me in the back of my head. It didn't really hurt, but it was like she was telling me all the time that I was stupid. (T, quietly: stupid) She was annoyed with me all of the time, with my homework and the way I cleaned up the kitchen and even the way I played football! She doesn't even know anything about that! She just criticized everything I did. It was just like I was a bother to her (T, quietly: a bother), nothing I did was ever right, ever good enough.
>
> T: She was really critical, about everything, and you got the impression that you were a bother to her, that she thought you were stupid.

The other time that this technique works especially well is when the client has ended a sentence or taken a pause. In this case, using a slight question tone can make the parrot function as a clarification and help the client take their thought farther.

> C: When I was young, she was really hard on me. She used to smack me in the back of my head. It didn't really hurt, but it was like she was telling me all the time that I was stupid …
>
> T: Stupid?
>
> C: Yeah, she was annoyed with me all of the time, with my homework and the way I cleaned up the kitchen and even the way I played football! She doesn't know anything about that! She just criticized everything I did. It was just like I was a bother to her …
>
> T: A bother.
>
> C: Yeah, nothing I did was ever right, ever good enough.

PRACTICE TIP

Parroting feels strange in the same way that standing with your arms at your sides feels strange – only to you. It seems natural to others and gets easier with practice. You're probably already mentally holding on to those important words and emotions, so that you can paraphrase or summarize, so you know what they are. Experiment with it, adding it to your current active listening skills (not replacing them!). Do this with a colleague or partner first, if that's more comfortable.

CHAPTER 29
"DON'T"

One of the most problematic little words in a client's vocabulary is the word "can't." What a disempowering, distorted, irrational word! And sometimes they *can't* seem to give it up!

First, let me be clear that I'm not talking about those clients who are recognizing legitimate limitations. For these clients, sometimes learning to use the word "can't" is a powerful, healthy departure from the early learning that they can do anything, should be able to be anything, and must be all things to be deserving of love.

I'm thinking here about the clients (and this is most of those who use the word) who actually mean "it would be uncomfortable to" or "I would feel scared" or "some important person would be upset" or "a long time ago someone told me that I couldn't." When they use the word "can't," they aren't addressing legitimate limitations, but have often made something seem impossible in their minds that is really quite attainable.

What options do we have? One option is to change the language to "won't:" "It's not that you can't talk to your mother or ask your boss or use the new behavior or sit quietly with an emotion – it's that you won't." But … ouch! Clients who have disavowed personal power and responsibility by using the word "can't" often respond poorly to the word "won't." It feels harsh and blaming and far from their personal experience. We want to find the balance (or the tension, perhaps) between two of the primary therapeutic factors: Instillation of hope and existential factors (i.e., personal responsibility; Yalom, 1995). With "can't" and "won't" language, the balance is all tipped in the direction of responsibility – if they can't, they have no responsibility and if they won't, it's completely their responsibility. There is little emphasis on hope, and therefore, less room for therapeutic movement.

I'd like to offer an alternative that may help to balance all of these out. How about the word "don't?" It carries a connotation that is about midway between the helplessness of can't and the willfulness of won't. When we offer it gently, and pair it with a solid reflection of clients' content and emotion, it doesn't come off harshly. Then, we can follow it up with some open-ended questions to get more information about the disempowerment and the legitimate obstacles, and clients' abilities, resources, and strengths – that brings in both internal locus of control as well as hope.

DOI: 10.4324/9781003125082-32

A close cousin of the word "don't" is the word "haven't." It captures a similar balance of responsibility and hope, and carries a connotation that there are understandable reasons that change isn't yet apparent. An especially nice thing about "haven't" is that it adds the explicit implication that it will or may change in the future, without adding a lot of demand.

PRACTICE TIP

You don't need to beat them over the head with it. You don't even need to make the change explicit, though some clients will benefit from an overt appraisal of the (in)effectiveness of their language. But you can just drop it in, casually.

C: I just can't bring it up! I'd be mortified!
T: You don't bring it up, to protect yourself. What's scary about it?

Or

C: I can't do it; it's too hard. It'll never work out.
T: You haven't done it, because you don't feel up to it. Tell me about what seems difficult.

CHAPTER 30
"TRY"

This one is a secret from the hypnosis literature. During hypnosis, clients take everything quite literally. Here's an example: If you tell a class full of students to "raise your hand," they'll all do exactly what you expect – some students will have hands high in the air, some will have elbows on the desk with hands lifted, and everything in between. But if you tell a client during hypnosis to "raise your hand," they will lift just the hand, at the wrist. It's a very concrete understanding.

This is why, when using hypnosis, therapists either refrain from using the word "try" or use it in a very specific way (Hammond, 1990). Like this: "Now that you are very relaxed, *try* to open your eyes, and realize you just can't. And enjoy how complete the relaxation feels." Or, after suggesting that a client's hands are locked together, as if by a magnet: "Now *try* to pull your hands apart and find that you cannot." The word "try" is only ever used in hypnosis to confirm that a client *cannot* do something. This is because failure at the attempt is implied in the word "try."

Are you thinking of Yoda's famous quote right now? "Do or do not; there is no try." It's a good example of this idea when it's taken in context, because Yoda is likewise suggesting that *trying* is acceptance of failure from the start. While he is – in his mysterious way – demonstrating his confidence in Luke's ability, it's also a good example of what we as therapists *don't* want to do, because he wants Luke to map his experience lifting a rock to his experience lifting a spaceship with no intermediate building of strength, skills, etc.

If we want to demonstrate our confidence in a client's ability, we – like Yoda – should not ask them to try. If we ask a client to try to do their homework, we may be implicitly suggesting that it won't get done. If we ask them to try to relax their body or take a deep breath when they are panicking, we imply that they won't be able to – and they're already quite invested in the fear that they can't.

Instead, we can use language like "when you complete the homework …" and "next time you feel anxious, you can apply these techniques and notice an increase in your relaxation." See? It can sound natural and easy. Don't believe me? Re-read this section of the book. It's full of things for you to "try," right? See if you can find that word.

Spoiler alert: You won't. When I write about something that I know you can do, I encourage you to do it. I'm not asking you to *attempt* things. When

DOI: 10.4324/9781003125082-33

I want you to play around with something *that has no criteria for success or failure* just to explore what happens, I ask you to "experiment with" it, which takes away the potential evaluative component of asking you to "try" (more on the scientist mindset in Chapter 77).

PRACTICE TIP

Clients will make more progress when they take the steps they know they can take (at least, more progress than not taking steps they believe they'll fail!) When clients express concern about their ability, competence, motivation, etc. – that is, when they hedge by saying, "well, I'll try ..." – just change the assignment to something so small and manageable that they really can't not comply. Then neither you nor the client needs to really worry about "trying." As the solution-focused (e.g., de Shazer et al., 2007) and strategic theorists (e.g., Haley, 1963) agree – small changes lead to big changes.

REFERENCES

Beck, A. T. (1979). *Cognitive therapy of depression.* Guilford Press.

Craggs, J. G., Price, D.D., & Robinson, M. E. (2014). Enhancing the placebo response: functional magnetic resonance imaging evidence of memory and semantic processing in placebo analgesia. *The Journal of Pain, 15*(4):435–446. doi: 10.1016/j.jpain.2013.12.009.

de Shazer, S., Dolan, Y., Korman, H., McCollum, E., Trepper, T., & Berg, I. K. (2007). *More than miracles: The state of the art of solution-focused brief therapy.* Haworth Press.

Dik, S. (1980). Seventeen sentences: Basic principles and application of functional grammar. *Syntax and Semantics,13*, 45–75.

Frankl, V. (1959). *Man's search for meaning.* (Original title: From death-camp to existentialism). Beacon Press.

Garner, B. (2016). *Garner's modern English usage (4th ed.).* Oxford University Press.

Ginott, H. (1965). *Between parent and child: New solutions to old problems.* Macmillan.

Gottman, J. M. & Silver, N. (1999). *The seven principles for making marriage work.* Crown Publishing.

Gottman, J. M., & DeClaire, J. (1997). *Raising an emotionally intelligent child: The heart of Parenting.* Simon and Schuster.

Greenberg, L. (2009). *Emotion focused therapy.* American Psychological Association.

Hammond, C. D. (1990). *Handbook of hypnotic suggestions and metaphors.* Norton & Company, Ltd.

Haley, J. (1963). *Strategies of psychotherapy.* Grune & Stratton.

Huddleston, R., & Pullum, G. (2002). *The Cambridge grammar of the English language.* Cambridge University Press.

Loftus, E. F., Palmer, J. C. (1974) Reconstruction of automobile destruction: An example of the interaction between language and memory. *Journal of Verbal Learning & Verbal Behavior, 13*(5), 585–589. https://doi.org/10.1016/S0022-5371(74)80011-3

Rhodes, R. H., Hill, C. E., Thompson, B. J., & Elliot, R. (1994). Client retrospective recall of resolved and unresolved misunderstanding events. *Journal of Counseling Psychology, 41*, 473–483.

Rotter, J. B. (1966). Generalized expectancies for internal versus external control of reinforcement, *Psychological Monographs: General and Applied.* 80: 1–28. doi:10.1037/h0092976.

Saitō, H. (1899). *Practical English grammar: Adverbs, prepositions, conjunctions.* Kobunsha.

Sloan, M. C. (2010). Aristotle's Nicomachean ethics as the original locus for the septem circumstantiae, *Classical Philology, 105*, 236–251. doi:10.1086/656196

Verplanck, W. S. (1955). The control of the content of conversation: Reinforcement of statements of opinion. *The Journal of Abnormal and Social Psychology, 51*(3), 668–676 https://doi.org/10.1037/h0046514

Vygotsky, L.S. (1978). *Mind in society.* Harvard University Press.

Wotschack, C., & Klann-Delius, G. (2013). Alexithymia and the conceptualization of emotions: A study of language use and semantic knowledge. *Journal of Research in Personality, 47*(5), 514–523. https://doi.org/10.1016/j.jrp.2013.01.011

Yalom, I. D. (1995). *The theory and practice of group psychotherapy. 4th ed.* Basic Books.

It's Actually Not Magic (Exploration of Change Processes)

By and large, there are some good reasons for us to choose an overall theoretical orientation to work from, or at least to establish the theoretical orientation from which we plan to work with each client (based on factors like diagnosis, client preference, and our experience). For example, having a structure can help to determine the steps involved in clients' "work" and contribute to their adherence and positive change (Wampold & Ulvenes, 2019).

However, there are some particular concepts and skills that are emphasized by multiple different theories that can be used to supplement our work, based on the situation at hand (e.g., client personality, current stressors, certain kinds of "stuckness"), regardless of the kind of therapy we are doing at the moment. These are some of the "magical ingredients" in therapy that supply a lot of clients' positive growth, but there's really nothing magical about them. This section will introduce several of these concepts (a few were mentioned briefly in Chapter 8), discuss how they are used in various theoretical systems, and address some of the situations for which they might be beneficial.

Hopefully, in this section, I'll also introduce you to some theories you aren't familiar with. If you want to learn more, you'll be able to use the references from this chapter to find good learning sources for each of these kinds of therapy.

CHAPTER 31
STAGES OF CHANGE

Before getting into some of the specific techniques and concepts that cross multiple schools of therapy, it's worthwhile to review a model that gives some "shape" to the therapy process and can help us to determine when to introduce various techniques.

The Transtheoretical Approach to change (including but not limited to therapeutic change), offers a straightforward platform for conceptualizing change processes (Prochaska & DiClemente, 2005; DiClemente et al., 1991). The parts of this model that we tend to be most familiar with are the "stages of change." *Precontemplation* is the time during which clients have low motivation for using change processes because they have not identified any need for change and/or have identified reasons to maintain the status quo; this is marked by unwillingness to change (these clients have often been coerced into therapy by parents, partners, or judges). The *contemplation* stage may follow next, as clients become aware of the possibility of change and navigate through the potential risks and rewards of change; this stage is marked by ambivalence and uncertainty. If clients move forward, they move on to the *preparation* stage, during which they have determined that change is necessary and/or desirable and focus on seeing the path forward; this stage is about planning and commitment. The *action* stage will follow next (if things are going well!), and clients will enact the steps toward change that they enumerated in the previous stage and possibly do any troubleshooting that is needed; the main focus is on implementation and movement. Finally, clients may reach the *maintenance* stage, during which they establish new systems and skills to maintain their progress; this stage is about solidifying and preserving.

The part of this change model that we tend to be less familiar with is *how* clients can be helped to move through these stages. Certain processes and techniques can help to facilitate movement within and through each stage and on to the next one (Prochaska & DiClemente, 2005). For example, when clients are precontemplative, they won't be able to plan changes effectively or jump into making progress, and this will just frustrate us both. Instead, they may need information to raise their awareness about the negative effects of their current behaviors (e.g., psychoeducation or interpersonal feedback) or tasks that will help them to increase their emotional investment in the issue (e.g., experiential activities or feelings-centered conversation). Much of the

75

DOI: 10.4324/9781003125082-35

work in the contemplation and preparation stages is affective and cognitive work. It's not until the action and maintenance stages that some of the more overt and behavioral techniques can be effective.

One form of therapy that integrates the "stages of change" model is Motivational Interviewing (Miller & Rollnick, 2013). It is a relatively directive kind of therapy, though still client-centered, and its focus is on helping clients move through these stages, especially through contemplation, while emphasizing clients' autonomy and building their self-efficacy, to elicit behavior change. It is most often used for treatment of alcohol and other substance-related or addictive problems, though it is helpful as a framework for any kind of therapy, once clients' goals are established.

We can think back to Chapter 20 and being a "butt–head therapist" – using this model is part of being a "head" therapist. We need to be operating at something of a meta-level, thinking in terms of the overall sequence of therapeutic progress and the processes that help that progress move forward. Then, we can use specific techniques, like those discussed in the rest of this section, tailored to clients' level of readiness, to propel the therapy process.

PRACTICE TIP

Put this on your progress note. It's helpful for you, in reminding you to think when you first meet a client about where in the process they are starting (because this can be different!), and for keeping track of how therapy is going. It's also remarkably helpful for anyone who might read your notes in the future. For example, this is incredibly valuable information for your client's next therapist, should they move on for any reason. Second, it's worthwhile for showing progress during any kind of case review (e.g., legal review, supervision).

This will more than pay off for the amount of work it is (which is basically none). One item that allows you to checkbox or circle the client's current stage of change is all it takes! Also, it allows you to handle that "head" part of things outside of the actual session, if that's more comfortable for you.

CHAPTER 32
AWARENESS

Awareness is a difficult word to define; it takes on different shades of meaning in various contexts. We can think about it in terms of what it means to be conscious or have consciousness (Damasio, 1999) or we can think about it in a socio-political way, meaning how broad, deep, and current our knowledge is about certain issues (Jones, 2019). We can talk about awareness of self and others in the sense of being culturally competent (Sue & Torino, 2005). But for this discussion, we need a relatively broad working definition: something like "accurate, conscious recognition of some aspect of internal or external reality" (Gorlin, 2020) or even just "coming to know things that weren't previously known."

Virtually every type of therapy has some level of emphasis on raising clients' awareness; what makes each one different is what they want the client to be aware of. For example, in the transtheoretical model just described, consciousness raising (i.e., raising clients' awareness of the negative effects of their current situation/behavior) is an important part of entering into the change process (Prochaska & DiClemente, 2005). Psychoanalysis underscores the importance of gaining insight regarding previously unconscious material or drives (e.g., Freud, 1923/1949) and even the brief psychodynamic therapies focus on becoming aware of relational patterns, unmet needs, etc. (Charman, 2003). Humanistic and client-centered therapies value awareness of one's feelings, needs, values, and other internal aspects of self (e.g., Rogers, 1957), while experiential therapies focus on what the client is aware of in the present moment (e.g., Gendlin, 1969; Perls, 1969). Existential therapies attempt to bring awareness to the basic existential conditions, such as the finiteness of life, death anxiety, and personal responsibility (e.g., Frankl, 1955; Yalom, 1980). Cognitive and cognitive-behavioral therapies rely on the ability to become aware of automatic thoughts and schemas, as well as patterns of behavior and consequences (e.g., Beck et al., 1979). The core condition for mindfulness-based therapies is non-judgmental awareness of internal stimuli, including feelings and thoughts (Segal et al., 2002) and much of the power of solution-focused brief therapy comes from being aware of exceptions (de Shazer & Dolan, 2007).

One way to amplify the power of client awareness in our sessions is to determine our underlying philosophy about those things that clients become aware of. While we are probably all working to help clients build awareness,

DOI: 10.4324/9781003125082-36

we may differ in how we treat that material once it arises. Primarily, do we accept and incorporate things that clients have become aware of or do we manage and modify those things? We might base this decision on our professional or ethical philosophy (e.g., prioritizing autonomy as the highest ethical value may lean us in the direction of accept and incorporate), our theoretical orientation (e.g., following strict cognitive therapy may push us the other way), or whether clients prefer a more directive or non-directive approach.

If we do both, under which circumstances is each method appropriate? (Do we overtly address this with clients early and then follow their preferences? Do we choose to modify the products of awareness based on their convergence with our idea of what is healthy? Have we established what that is with our clients?) Having this kind of directional focus can help us ensure that we are providing a consistent and coherent experience for clients. When they know what to expect from us, they can invest more easily and fully in the process.

PRACTICE TIP

Whatever your theoretical orientation, experiment with applying this awareness to *yourself* in session. Are you a hard-core CBT therapist? Begin by noticing your own automatic thoughts during session. You can share these as here-and-now examples with clients. Solution focused? Which moments in the last few sessions have you felt exceptional rapport? Do you have an existential bent? Allow yourself to get in touch with not just the finiteness of life, but the finiteness of this session. (Bonus: You might gain a new appreciation for "doorknob disclosures" if you do this!)

CHAPTER 33
WISE MIND

The outside world seems to think that thoughts and feelings are at odds with each other. We can hear it in misguided colloquialisms like "I'm a left brain/right brain thinker" and in the protestations of partners: "She's just over emotional!" and "He's such a robot; he has no feelings at all!" Of course, we know, as mental health professionals, that thoughts and feelings are deeply connected. They each co-create and sustain the experience of the other.

The "wise mind" concept in Dialectical Behavior Therapy (Linehan, 1993) is the intersection of one's rational/thoughts-oriented mind with their emotional/feelings-oriented mind. It's not a simple balance or compromise concept; the idea is that the full cooperation of these two parts can combine dynamically into something greater – "wise mind," which integrates these two parts and synergizes them into intuitive knowing. In "wise mind," the full value of facts, logic, and pragmatics is welcomed. Likewise, the full experience of moods, emotions, and urges are honored. It is the *integration* of both that tempers and reforms into something more like "inner knowing" or wisdom.

A similar concept is found in Transgenerational (Bowenian) Family Therapy. *Differentiation* is typically taught in family therapy as the ability of a person to disentangle themselves from their family of origin, in terms of values, emotions, cognitions, rules, systems, or structures; it is the ability to stay reasonably connected with a group or family system, but to identify as an individual with separateness. *Differentiation of self,* however, is considered to be the intrapersonal foundation for being able to create this interpersonal balance – it is the ability of an individual to differentiate their own thoughts from their own feelings (Kerr & Bowen, 1988). When this is fully exercised, the result is a person with a strong sense of self, firmly held convictions, resistance to coercion, and manageable anxiety. It is marked by a consistent way of thinking that has robust ties to the inner experience as well as the reality of the outer world and an ability to connect emotionally with others without fear of being overwhelmed. (Doesn't that sound like something we want for all of our clients?!)

We can bring this concept of cognition–emotion synergy into session, even if it's not a regular part of our brand of therapy, first by making sure that we're keeping thoughts and feelings straight ourselves. Remember in

DOI: 10.4324/9781003125082-37

Chapter 25, the caution about clients using the term "feels like?" We won't be able to help manage the balance of the two if we can't separate them!

Second, we can balance following the client's lead toward thoughts or feelings (this is often in the direction they're more comfortable in) and intentionally bringing up the other way of experiencing. For example:

- "It sounds like you have a really detailed plan for going about that. How do you feel when you imagine it going just as you have planned?"
- "I hear you're feeling really disappointed and a bit hopeless about this situation. What do you think are some of the factors that you do and don't have control over?"

Over time, keeping that balance makes it more likely the synergy will be possible, and helps clients to have a more comprehensive therapy experience, especially for those clients who seem to get easily stuck in one modality or the other.

PRACTICE TIP

It's true that you may have some clients who are more likely to go in head-direction or heart-direction automatically, but that doesn't mean that's what is most therapeutic just because it's most comfortable. But when you bring in this balance, clients may resist. Instead of just thinking to yourself, "Oh, this is just a really cognitive client" and going with it, lean into the resistance a bit and consider exploring it with a process comment. For example, "I've noticed that whenever I ask about your feelings, you seem to spin it into a question about your thoughts. Has that ever come up for you before? What do you make of that?"

CHAPTER 34
FELT SENSE

The idea that our bodies are intricately involved in our mental and emotional functioning isn't new. It's at least as old as the concept of *character armor:* muscular tensions, postural misalignments, and rigid facial expressions that develop into long-term conditions of the body as a result of inner, psychological defenses (Reich, 1933). Focusing-oriented experiential psychotherapy (Gendlin et al., 1968; Krycka & Ikemi, 2016) attends to the feeling in the body as the primary way of recognizing progress in therapy, and the sensations and movements of the body hold a vaulted place in Gestalt Therapy (Perls, 1969). The body is beginning to have a recognized place in relational and interpersonal psychotherapy (e.g., Carroll, 2014) and several trauma-related therapies include elements of somatic experiencing (e.g., Levine, 2015; van der Kolk, 2015). Attention to the sensations and signals of the body are important in many treatments for anxiety (e.g., panic control therapy; Hoffman et al., 2010).

Even if our primary orientation isn't humanistic or experiential, I'd like to suggest that we can all benefit from listening to clients' bodies (and teaching clients to listen to their own bodies) as a way of making sure that we're headed in the right direction. This way of "checking in with the body" is most meticulously described as the process of *focusing* (Gendlin, 1969; 1978; 1996). This involves tuning into the body by first making a space to consider what the most important thing is, right at the moment. Then, rather than trying to put words to it right away, we wait to get a bodily feeling or sensing of the whole issue altogether. Most people will find that they can get this "felt sense" somewhere in the middle part of their bodies. After getting a sense of the whole thing, we can then try out different language until something really resonates. This requires a little bit of time; generally anything that comes up in the first few seconds is just something we've been telling ourselves, and it's not the real thing. The magic happens at the end, when there is a shift in the "felt sense." This is a feeling in the body that is often described as the feeling of a knot coming undone or a key in a lock clicking open; it is a feeling of *just exactly right*. When this happens in session, we both leave with that awesome feeling of something really important happening.

This doesn't have to be quite so specific for it to be helpful for us and our clients. Rogers (1961) describes doing this with clients in a less formal

DOI: 10.4324/9781003125082-38

way (with much fancier language!), suggesting that one of the fundamental change processes in therapy is the "free experiencing of the actual sensory and visceral reactions" that allow a client to "formulate himself out of his experience, instead of trying to impose a formulation of self on his experience." For us, though, this might be as simple as asking a client something like, "Are you feeling that we're heading in the right direction?" or "How is this 'sitting with' you so far?" This kind of wording implies the congruence of the feeling in the body with the more cognitive appraisal of their progress. (Bonus if you gesture to the center of your torso when you ask either of those questions!)

This won't "sit right" for some clients (especially those who are more "in their heads") and they might look at us like we're crazy. That's ok, we don't have to push it. But it's worth trying it out with everyone, because with clients who do resonate with the practice of "checking in," it will be invaluable for our therapy progress and it's a skill they can take with them after therapy as well!

PRACTICE TIP

How does your client's body *look*? You don't need to get certified in Somatic Experiencing or take a course in Anatomy and Physiology to incorporate this information. It's one of the reasons that there are so many observational items on the typical mental status exam. When you are on the right track, clients will look open, loose, and free to move, while still having a dignified posture and a sense of structure and strength in their bodies. If they appear tight, tense, closed, or rigid, check in with them (e.g., they may be feeling anxious or resistant). If they appear limp, wilted, or unsteady, check in with them (e.g., they may be feeling overwhelmed, exhausted, or out of control). Also, any body-posture or non-verbal behavior that is uncharacteristic of the client is worth attending to.

CHAPTER 35
OLD PATTERNS

It's a cliché that people so often talk about the "inner child' when they're talking about (or making fun of!) psychotherapy. Don't be alarmed – I'm not suggesting that we all abandon our allegiance to brief or empirically supported therapies and jump into psychoanalytic training. In fact, many of the kinds of therapies that are most popular today are based in the experiences that clients had as children and the patterns they developed. Where do those schemas that we address in cognitive therapy come from, anyway? The inner child is what the outer adult is made from. Let me give a few examples:

Emotionally Focused Therapy (EFT; Johnson, 2004; 2019), which is often used with couples, emphasizes the relational "dance" that we engage in with partners. This is a pattern of recurring sequences of interactions that perpetuate cycles of distress. The music we dance to (the emotional tone and experiences of our lives) and the attendant dance steps (the cognitions and behaviors that follow that music) are often learned early, from interactions with our family systems, and so our repertoire is necessarily limited. (We probably won't learn the Cha-cha from our family of origin if our parents were champions in the Viennese Waltz!) One of the main pieces of work in emotionally focused therapy is recognizing these patterns of interaction and then teaching new ways of interacting, with increased engagement and authenticity. For example, a client's early relationships may have left them unfamiliar with or afraid of certain emotional experiences with a pattern of relational skills that is focused on avoiding those uncomfortable emotions. EFT changes the old patterns of emotional avoidance to emotional engagement, and then helps the client to rewrite their old patterns of thinking and behavior accordingly.

The interpersonal process approach to therapy (Teyber, 2000; which is based on interpersonal theory, object relations theory, and family systems theory) describes several kinds of patterns that clients can become stuck in because of early learning experiences. We usually get to see just the tips of these icebergs, unless we're looking beneath the surface. For example, clients may be drinking too much (but it's really a self-punishment coping style), or feel lonely (but it's really a deeply buried abandonment terror), or be uncomfortable crying in session (but it's really an intolerance of vulnerability). The interpersonal process approach helps clients to make

DOI: 10.4324/9781003125082-39

realistic assessments of the strengths and problems that existed in their families of origin, tie them to their current behavior, and (here's the magic!) identify those maladaptive patterns as they are being acted out in the therapy relationship (because they are). Then, we can process those conflicts in real time, allowing clients to try out new thoughts and behaviors, and build new, healthier ways of relating, in the safe context of the therapeutic relationship.

Old patterns, recognized or not, are present in the here-and-now. What we might give a diagnostic label (e.g., anxiety or depression) or a symptom label (e.g., lack of self-care, rumination) may actually be part of a long-term, maladaptive pattern. It can be easier to notice with clients who have personality disorders or other chronic or prolonged issues of a similar nature. But, often, even the clients who are having panic attacks for the first time or who have just developed their first depressive episode may be acting out part of a pattern that has been triggered by a certain life circumstance. For example, finally getting treatment for migraine headaches may precipitate the onset of panic attacks, if those migraines were part of a pattern of needing to be an under-adequate relationship partner. Or the depressive episode might have begun when the client's last child left for college. Maybe that's a simple transitional issue related to being an empty nester; possibly it's a consequence of a lengthier pattern that began with the schema that "being good means taking care of others." Sometimes, changing to a longer-term perspective that includes clients' childhoods can be beneficial, even if we don't choose to interact with the childhood material.

PRACTICE TIP

Whether we are aware of it or not, clients tend to enact their old patterns with us. And they're good at it – they usually get us to fall into our role right away (e.g., nurturing mom, tough-love coach, a partner for philosophical banter) from the first session or two. Once we recognize that, we can choose how to use it. In a brief, solution-oriented therapy, you could choose to just go with it, because that's what's comfortable for them. In a process-oriented therapy, you could call it to the client's attention and see where that goes. In a relationally based therapy, you could begin to shift your role slowly but intentionally in directions that stretch the client's relational capacities.

CHAPTER 36
PURPOSEFUL SYMPTOMS

Why do we have symptoms, anyway? (I know, that's way too big of a question!) Various schools of psychotherapy have tried to tackle that question in the sense of "How do symptoms come to be?" For example, Freud (1923) suggested that we have symptoms as a result of underdeveloped egos that can't manage the balance of libidinal tension between id and superego, while Rogers (1957) assumed that some symptoms are manifestations of trying to create a congruent self-image.

Another way of answering the question "Why do we have symptoms?" is to consider what *purpose symptoms serve*. This form of the question is preferred by the various forms of strategic therapy (e.g., Haley, 1963; Haley, 1993; Madanes, 1981), which are based on using direct strategies in order to solve specific problems (i.e., remove specific symptoms) typically by targeting a symptom's function in the present situation. For example, symptoms are often seen as a form of communication or as a way of gaining or keeping a certain kind of power in a relationship. When the *function* of the symptom is determined, a strategic therapist will offer a behavioral directive that will eliminate the need for the symptom, make the symptom ineffective, change the dynamic of the relationship, etc. For example, the therapist may create an elaborate ordeal that the client must undergo whenever they perform the unwanted behavior (e.g., waxing the floors all night if they aren't asleep by 11pm) or create a paradox in which the unwanted behavior is modified and then prescribed to rob it of its purpose (e.g., requesting that a client with social anxiety blush whenever leaving the house, requiring a discordant couple to argue each night for exactly 20 minutes, even if they have to make up something to argue about). Some of us are a bit uncomfortable with the very directive nature of strategic therapy and get a feeling that it's not quite how we want to use our therapeutic power. (And for strategic therapy to be effective, we definitely have to be secure in our therapeutic power!)

Another kind of therapy that attends to the function of symptoms (but in a gentler, more collaborative way) is Coherence Therapy (previously known as Depth-Oriented Brief Therapy; Ecker et al., 2012; Ecker & Hulley, 1995). It suggests that symptoms are typically the result of patterns of implicit knowledge that got encoded (sometimes long ago) during emotional experiences. For example, we may have learned that "I have to be a good girl and conform in order to be safe" from an early family pattern or that

                    DOI: 10.4324/9781003125082-40

"People will inevitably reject me" from a traumatic bullying experience in grade school. The symptoms that clients display in the present are often responses to these kinds of emotional learning but may not be useful anymore for their original purpose (e.g., the social isolation that saved me from rejection is now keeping me from getting a job). Coherence Therapy works to determine the necessity of the symptom for managing life in the face of those maladaptive emotional learnings – the *function* of the symptom is to keep the client safe, acceptable, powerful, etc. A common technique that exemplifies this is *symptom deprivation* – when a client imagines the situation without the symptom, it will often unveil some specific problem or distress (real or imagined) that the client is able to avoid with the "protection" of the symptom. Unlike Strategic Therapy, which utilizes behavioral strategies to remove symptoms, Coherence Therapy suggests re-activating and re-encoding the original problematic learning in an experiential way to remove the necessity for the symptom.

If we have a working "myth and ritual" (see Chapters 3 & 4) and clients are making good progress, there may be no need to look further. But this concept is especially useful when we and our clients have been doing everything "right," and yet still feel stuck or have made no progress. And we don't need to use either of these specific techniques. Just engaging in a conceptualizing process (alone, with a consultation partner, or even with the client) that allows for the possibility that the distressing symptom serves a purpose can be enough to modify the direction or target of therapy to something more valuable.

PRACTICE TIP

Remember, just because a symptom is functional, doesn't mean it's not "real." Symptoms are real, painful, distressing solutions; they are not being faked. Approach these carefully. By this I mean, if you want to directly explain the situation as you see it, you'll probably need to do it very gently to get client buy-in (rather than defensiveness). Or you might choose to approach it indirectly (for example, setting up homework that makes the functional behavior incompatible) rather than attempting to target the symptom function outright.

CHAPTER 37
PSYCHODIVERSITY

The world is a complex and varied place. It doesn't require the same things from us all of the time. Luckily, we are also multifaceted creatures, and have the ability to adapt to many different environments. However, how often do clients come in complaining that they feel "stuck?" All the time! Whether that means stuck in an external situation (like a job or relationship) or stuck in an intrapersonal kind of way (such as in a negative thought pattern or unpleasant emotions that don't seem to change), we can often help clients by emphasizing the dynamism (i.e., the natural changeability) of the human condition.

Reversal Theory (Apter, 2001; 2007) gives us one way to think about this; it suggests that "We are more like dancers than statues." It is a state theory of personality (that emphasizes how we are different across time and situations) rather than a trait theory (which emphasizes how we are the same across time and situations). Specifically, it suggests that sometimes we are future- and goal-oriented, while other times we are present- and process-oriented. Likewise, sometimes we are more focused on fitting in vs. freedom to be, power/control vs. care/nurturance, self focus vs. other focus. These various ways of approaching and experiencing can be developed in service to *psychodiversity*, which is the ability to access whichever states are most effective for a given time and situation.

Another theory that speaks to flexibility in approaching life is Acceptance and Commitment Therapy (ACT; Luoma et al., 2017). Specifically, one of the aims is the development of *psychological flexibility*, which means being fully present and conscious in each moment, so that we can interact with each new situation as it is and choose to persist with or change our behavior in order to best serve our needs or valued ends. One of the main tasks to accomplish this is *self-as-context.* Building "self-as-context" is a way of loosening clients' fusion with their inflexible stories about who they are (e.g., I am a professional, I am a victim, I am a caring person) and instead viewing the self as part of a continually changing flow of experience. This increases their ability to tolerate the present, as well as to be flexible in how they approach their current (and future) situations.

We can help clients to access their potential for psychological flexibility or psychodiversity in a few ways. We can begin by educating them and abandoning language related to traits and fixedness. Second, we can help

                    DOI: 10.4324/9781003125082-41

them to identify possibilities according to a certain model, like Reversal Theory, or in any way that makes sense to them. For example, many clients respond well to discussing different "parts of self" (we might call them "ego states"), and that can be a fruitful avenue for increasing their options for interacting with the world. Third, we can broaden their cognitive, emotional, behavioral, and interpersonal repertoires using whatever theory we are already using.

PRACTICE TIP

Each client needs a slightly different version of you. If you have time between sessions to do a little meditation and get yourself in the right state, that's wonderful! If you need to write your note and refill your coffee, though, you might want to use a Reversal Theory technique to help. Some "tricks" for changing states are to use a short mantra, recall a state-based visualization, or look at/hold a state-specific object. For example, if you are in an other-mastery state with one client (i.e., encouraging, promoting change, think "personal trainer") and you need to be in an other-sympathy state for your next client (i.e., caring, nurturing, think "grandma with ice cream"), that can be a hard but necessary transition. But with some practice, adding a pillow to your chair and changing your posture may be all you need to facilitate that change.

CHAPTER 38
METACOGNITION

Take a deep breath. Now, exhale. As you read this next sentence, slowly, allow yourself to become aware of the feeling of your eyes moving, the "sound" of your mental voice, and maybe even how you find yourself wondering what the purpose of this exercise is. And feel free to be a little amazed at how easy it is for you to think about your own thoughts this way. That's metacognition.

Metacognition is narrowly defined as cognition about cognition (or thinking about thinking), but is sometimes defined more broadly, encompassing awareness of one's mental processes and knowledge about how and when to use those processes. This awareness of our own consciousness and the ability to reflect on our own mental states is actually so fundamental to the process of most therapies that I think we take it for granted.

For example, mindfulness involves cultivating the moment-by-moment awareness of what we are experiencing, including sensations, emotions, and cognitions, which makes it a kind of metacognitive therapy (Hussain, 2015). The mindfulness literature emphasizes that metacognitive awareness should be *nonjudgmental*, for example, simply noticing thoughts without evaluating those thoughts (Kabat-Zinn, 2003). But we also use this capacity for metacognition in traditional therapies, like Cognitive Therapy, specifically to recognize, evaluate, and change distorted thoughts (Beck et al., 1979).

This will probably not be surprising, but a great example of the use of metacognition in therapy is in Metacognitive Therapy (Wells, 2011). It is based on the idea that, instead of experiencing our thoughts as our*selves*, which we usually do, we learn to experience our thoughts as objects. Then, thoughts can be observed but so can the processes that we are using as we interact with our thoughts. Unlike traditional Cognitive Therapy, Metacognitive Therapy is focused on modifying metacognitive *processes* that perpetuate distress (rather than the distressing or dysfunctional thoughts themselves). For example, one target of metacognitive therapy is the *cognitive appraisal system*, a thinking style that combines rumination with emphasis on threat and coping attempts that perpetuate the rumination (e.g., the meta-belief that "I have to worry; that's what keeps me safe" and the unhelpful attempt at coping by trying to suppress additional worry).

Another therapy that uses metacognition in a similar way is Acceptance and Commitment Therapy (ACT; Luoma et al., 2017). The ACT concept of

 DOI: 10.4324/9781003125082-42

cognitive defusion is a process in which clients are taught how to "watch what the mind says, rather than be a slave to it." The intention is to help clients begin to break the imaginary causal tie between thoughts and emotions or thoughts and behaviors. For example, a client may believe that the thought "I will embarrass myself" will necessarily lead to social withdrawal, but when it is recognized as "just a thought," the emotions and behaviors that follow do not need to be automatic.

One way that we can use the power of metacognition as part of any therapy is through the concept of *cognitive integrity*, which means engaging with our mental processes in an active, conscious, intentional way (Gorlin & Schuur, 2017). It can also be described as exercising agency (our "will") to direct our attention in a way that serves our goals and is reality-oriented. For example, intentionally turning our thoughts toward self-efficacy rather than allowing ourselves to be "dragged around" by rumination or purposefully "calling ourselves out" rather than engaging in self-deception. Though various theoretical orientations take different views on how much genetics, environment, family, and other factors determine one's experience, all psychotherapies emphasize the intentional, active participation of the client in helping to create their own growth, so developing clients' capacity for cognitive integrity will probably be useful in any session. (To be fair, I suppose this isn't compatible with the psychoanalytic technique of free association. So, it's not perfectly transtheoretical. But how many of our sessions are fully psychoanalytic?)

PRACTICE TIP

Once special type of metacognition I want you to know about is the *feeling of knowing judgment*. It is exactly what it sounds like – the degree to which you believe you know something and could recall it when needed. This is what happened when (instead of actually studying) you flipped through a textbook before an exam, saw the highlighted words, got a feeling of recognition, felt really confident, and then were completely shocked when you got a C. Turns out, people are really bad at making accurate feeling of knowing judgments. Bad at it in math, bad at it in reading, and even equally bad at it when we get to choose the topics we're most familiar with (Campbell & Gaudagnoli, 2004)! So, the lesson is, when you're about to teach a client something you're "totally sure" you remember, consider looking it up with them, instead. And keep a healthy skepticism about what they "remember perfectly," too.

CHAPTER 39
DRAMA

What is the difference between acting and behaving? Sometimes, we use those words interchangeably. For example, we'll say "cognitions, emotions, and behaviors" when we're with other therapists, but we'll call them "thoughts, feelings, and actions" with clients. But the word *acting* has a second connotation that implies something like "pretending for an audience." Well, there's always an audience, even when we're alone (ask a sociologist about this![1]). So, it makes a lot of sense to converge these definitions. If we are going to target behavior as part of therapy (and we do, all the time), we may want to consider the use of a true strategy of behaving... drama.

Some forms of psychotherapy overtly use drama as an important element in the healing process. Psychodrama, the most obvious version, is a type of group therapy in which clients use spontaneous dramatization, dramatic self-presentation, and other forms of role play therapeutically to gain insight as well as practice new behaviors (Moreno, 2014). A Psychodrama therapy group reenacts current, past, or future situations – including inner mental processes, new avenues of behavior, various parts of self – acting them out in the present. Participants and audience members then evaluate the "scene" and reflect on the behavior (as well as cognitions and emotions displayed and their own responses). This helps the primary actor (as well as auxiliary actors and audience members) more deeply understand themselves, their internal conflicts, their patterns of thinking and behaving, and potential avenues for growth.

Another example is Gestalt Therapy, which is a highly active, experiential type of therapy, known for its use of here-and-now behavior and emphasis on authenticity (Perls, 1969). It includes a close attention to all client behavior (including non-verbal behavior, expression changes, etc.) and invites direct experiencing through the acting out of dreams, imaginations, parts of self, emotions, etc. in order to increase insight, work through unfinished business, create honest and effective contact between clients and their environment (including other people), and move clients forward through actual change in the session.

Some other forms of psychotherapy use drama but do it in secret, calling it something slightly less (dare I say it?) dramatic. For example, Trial-Based Cognitive Therapy uses a simulated judicial process, casting client and therapist as members of the court (e.g., defendant, prosecutor, judge) in

DOI: 10.4324/9781003125082-43

order to identify and challenge clients' irrational core beliefs (de Oliveira, 2016). Likewise, even traditional Cognitive Behavioral Therapy (CBT) often includes role play and skills practice and using these more active behavioral strategies in session can make CBT more effective (Padesky, 2017).

I'm not sure why, but many of us are afraid of "drama." But it's just "acting." It's just "behaving." On the other hand, it's not *just* anything. It is drama; it is acting; it is behaving. That's a huge part of us living in the world and if we can help clients to engage with that part of their lives in a real, experiential, and healthy way – let's do it! We can challenge ourselves to take advantage of the power of behavior in every therapy session, by attending to here-and-now behavior of the client, by inviting a bit of psychodrama, or by setting up a role play.

PRACTICE TIP

I have a confession. I really hate it when people say, "Fake it 'til you make it." First, it implies that clients are not capable. Second, if they are capable of "faking it" (whatever *it* is), they are actually already doing *it*! If they can sit with dignity and speak assertively, they aren't pretending to be confident just because they don't feel very confident. They are acting with confidence, doing confidence, possibly even being confident. And feelings actually do change as a result of experiencing oneself behaving differently. So, clients don't need to fake the emotion either. They may just need to allow it to develop.

I know it doesn't rhyme,[2] but could I ask you to say something like, "Practice until it's more comfortable," instead?

NOTES

1   E.g., The "looking-glass self" (Cooley, 1902) is a definition of self-concept that relies on our assumptions about the way that other people see us – I am not who I think I am; I am who I think you think I am. It has been demonstrated to be active, even when not in the presence of others (Yeung & Martin, 2003).

2   Here's a ridiculous, but well-established research finding – we believe sayings that rhyme more and more easily than ones that don't (McGlone & Tofighbakhsh, 2000)! Let's make an effort to resist that particular cognitive bias, yes?

CHAPTER 40
STORIES

Once upon a time, in a village very near where you are now, there lived a child. The child grew up, restless and uneasy, in a world full of dangers both visible and hidden. As time went by, her attempts to escape that world were thwarted at every turn. Until one day, she befriended a kind traveler, who listened to her concerns rather than dismissing them and met her always with encouragement and a belief in the girl's destiny to grow in strength. With time, and trial, and adventure, she did grow. Until she grew strong and clever enough to escape her world of danger, and she went out into the wide, wide world, as a friendly traveler who would come to befriend many restless souls.

I dare you to say you don't resonate with that story of the therapeutic process. Stories are timeless and transcendent. The use of stories for developing wisdom and nurturing wellness is way older than psychotherapy; it's at least as old as the oldest civilizations, and stories are found in moral teaching in virtually every faith tradition.

Narrative Therapy, on the other hand, has been around for only a few decades (White, 2007; White & Epston, 1990). The aim of this kind of therapy is for clients to re-author their problem-saturated storylines. In the process, concepts like main characters, setting, plot events, obstacles, and character growth are emphasized (Madigan, 2019). It can be done in as practical or as imaginative a way as the client and therapist are comfortable with. One of the main benefits of narrative therapy (besides being terribly interesting!) is how perfectly each client's phenomenological world can be honored (it is literally their own story), and so it has wonderful potential for clients across all cultural dimensions.

The use of a narrative account (a recollection of events in which the client is the central figure) is also common in other types of therapy, because we think in stories. For example, emotion-focused therapy has adopted the exploration of client narratives (both *micronarratives*, or stories of discrete events, and *macronarratives*, which are continually developing life stories) as a method for understanding clients' sense of self, unpacking emotional themes, and helping clients to create meaning (Angus & Greenberg, 2011). Another example is Narrative Exposure Therapy, which aims to change the structure and meaning of traumatic experiences by integrating the trauma into a

DOI: 10.4324/9781003125082-44

cohesive life story that includes all of the major emotional memories of the client (Neuner et al., 2020).

One of the most useful techniques that comes from Narrative Therapy, that can translate quite easily into other types of therapy, is the notion of *externalizing the problem* (White & Epston, 1990). In this technique, the problems that clients experience (even if they are "internal" problems, like depression or rumination) are objectified or personified. For example, depression may be cast as the stormy weather that won't let up, that's keeping the traveler (the client) holed up in a cave. Or the persistent urges to drink can be personified as the "party goblin" who nags and begs and even disparages the well-meaning socialite (the client) to get her to drink and then always ruins things, leaving the socialite to pick up the pieces of her broken furniture and relationships. Externalizing helps clients to reduce the kind of self-blame that tends to perpetuate rather than relieve problems and to examine their resources and potential courses of action differently. For example, a traveler in stormy weather might need to stay in a cave, but can they build a fire? Or does it turn out they have rain boots in their pack?

PRACTICE TIP

How did you come to be who you are, as a therapist? Most of us have a 30-second narrative about why we're in this profession; after all, we had to prep that response just to get through grad school interviews! But, have you considered pulling all the threads together to really see how you came to be here? What about how you have grown and changed since you started? It's almost certain to surprise you. Writing or sharing your story can help you experience yourself with integrity, define your values, recognize new possibilities, and even make better future choices.

REFERENCES

Angus, L. E., & Greenberg, L. S. (2011). An introduction to working with narrative and emotion processes in emotion-focused therapy. In L. E. Angus & L. S. Greenberg, *Working with narrative in emotion-focused therapy: Changing stories, healing lives* (pp. 3–17). American Psychological Association. https://doi.org/10.1037/12325-001

Apter, M. J. (2001). *Motivational styles in everyday life: A guide to reversal theory.* American Psychological Association.

Apter, M. J. (2007). *Reversal theory: The dynamics of motivation, emotion, and personality.* Oneworld Publications.

Beck, A. T., Rush, A. J., Shaw, B. F., & Emery, G. (1979). *Cognitive therapy of depression.* Guilford Press.

Campbell, B. D., & Gaudagnoli, M. A. (Nov 18 - Nov 21, 2004*). Stability in Metacognitive Judgments: A Pilot Study* [Conference session abstract]. 45th Annual Meeting of the Psychonomic Society, Minneapolis, MN. https://doi.org/10.1037/e537052012-375

Carroll, R. (2014). Four relational modes of attending to the body in psychotherapy. In K. White (Ed.), *The John Bowlby Memorial Conference monographs series. Talking bodies: How do we integrate working with the body in psychotherapy from an attachment and relational perspective?* (pp. 11–39). Karnac Books.

Charman, D. P. (2003). *Core processes in brief psychodynamic therapies: Advancing effective practice.* Taylor & Francis.

Cooley, C. H. (1902). *Human nature and the social order.* C. Scribner's Sons.

Damasio, A. R. (1999). *The feeling of what happens.* Harcourt, Brace, & Company.

de Oliveira, I. R. (2016). *The CBT distinctive features series. Trial-based cognitive therapy.* Routledge/Taylor & Francis Group.

De Shazer, S., & Dolan, Y. (2007). *More than miracles: The state of the art of Solution-Focused Brief Therapy.* Routledge Mental Health Classic Editions.

DiClemente, C. C., Prochaska, J. O., Fairhurst, S. K., Velicer, W. F., Velasquez, M. M., & Rossi, J. S. (1991). The process of smoking cessation: An analysis of precontemplation, contemplation, and preparation stages of change. *Journal of Consulting and Clinical Psychology, 59*(2), 295–304. https://doi.org/10.1037/0022-006X.59.2.295

Ecker, B., & Hulley, L. (1995). *Depth oriented brief therapy: How to be brief when you were trained to be deep and vice versa.* Jossey & Bass.

Ecker, B., Ticic, R., & Hulley, L. (2012). *Unlocking the emotional brain: Eliminating symptoms at their roots by using memory reconsolidation.* Routledge.

Frankl, V. E. (1955). *The doctor and the soul. An introduction to logotherapy.* A. A. Knopf.

Freud, S. (1923/1949). *The ego and the id.* (Das Ich und das Es.) Hogarth Press.

Gendlin, E. T. (1969). Focusing. *Psychotherapy: Theory, Research & Practice, 6*(1), 4–15. https://doi.org/10.1037/h0088716

Gendlin, E. T. (1978). *Focusing.* Bantam.

Gendlin, E. T. (1996). *The practicing professional. Focusing-oriented psychotherapy: A manual of the experiential method.* Guilford Press.

Gendlin, E. T., Beebe, J. III, Cassens, J., Klein, M., & Oberlander, M. (1968). Focusing ability in psychotherapy personality, and creativity. In J. M. Shlien (Ed.), *Research in psychotherapy* (pp. 217–241). American Psychological Association. https://doi.org/10.1037/10546-012

Gorlin, E., I., Bekes, V., & Kansas, M. (2020). *Agency through awareness: A unifying meta-process across schools of psychotherapy.* Poster presented at annual (virtual) meeting of Society for Exploration of Psychotherapy Integration (SEPI). Retrieved from https://psychology. unt.edu/sites/psychology.unt.edu/files/Gorlin.png

Gorlin, E. I., & Schurr, R. (2017). Nurturing our better nature: A proposal for cognitive integrity as a foundation for autonomous living. *Behavior Genetics, 49*, 154–167. doi: 10.1007/s10519-018-9919-x

Haley, J. (1963). *Strategies of psychotherapy.* Grune and Stratton, Inc.

Haley, J. (1993). *Uncommon Therapy: The psychiatric techniques of Milton H. Erickson, M.D.* W.W. Norton & Company.

Hofmann, S. G., Rief, W., & Spiegel, D. A. (2010). Psychotherapy for panic disorder. In D. J. Stein, E. Hollander, & B. O. Rothbaum (Eds.), *Textbook of anxiety disorders* (pp. 417–433). American Psychiatric Publishing, Inc.

Hussain, D. (2015). Meta-cognition in mindfulness: A conceptual analysis. *Psychological Thought, 8*(2), 132–141. doi: 10.5964/psyct.v8i2.139

Johnson, S. (2004). *The practice of emotionally focused couple therapy* (2nd ed.). Brunner-Routledge.

Johnson, S. (2019). *Attachment theory in practice: Emotionally focused therapy (EFT) with individuals, couples, and families.* Guilford Publications.

Jones, P. E. (2019). Partisanship, political awareness, and retrospective evaluations, 1956–2016. *Political Behavior.* Advance online publication. https://doi.org/10.1007/s11109-019-09543-y

Kabat-Zinn, J. (2003). Mindfulness-based interventions in context: Past, present, and future. Clinical Psychology: *Science and Practice, 10*(2), 144–156. doi:10.1093/clipsy.bpg016

Kerr, M. E., & Bowen, M. (1988). *Family evaluation: An approach based on Bowen theory.* Norton & Company.

Krycka, K. C., & Ikemi, A. (2016). Focusing-oriented–experiential psychotherapy: From research to practice. In D. J. Cain, K. Keenan, & S. Rubin (Eds.), *Humanistic psychotherapies: Handbook of research and practice* (pp. 251–282). American Psychological Association. https://doi.org/10.1037/14775-009

Levine, P. A. (2015). *Trauma and memory: Brain and body in a search for the living past: A practical guide for understanding and working with traumatic memory.* North Atlantic Books.

Linehan, M. M. (1993). *Diagnosis and treatment of mental disorders. Cognitive-behavioral treatment of borderline personality disorder.* Guilford Press.

Luoma, J. B., Hayes, S. C., & Walser, R. D. (2017). *Learning ACT: An acceptance and commitment therapy skills training manual for therapists* (2nd ed.) Context Press.

Madanes, C. (1981). *Strategic family therapy.* Jossey-Bass.

Madigan, S. (2019). *Theories of psychotherapy. Narrative therapy* (2nd ed.). American Psychological Association. https://doi.org/10.1037/0000131-000

McGlone, M. S., & Tofighbakhsh, J. (2000). Birds of a feather flock conjointly (?): Rhyme as reason in aphorisms. *Psychological Science, 11*(5), 424–428. doi:10.1111/1467-9280.00282

Miller, W. R., & Rollnick, S. (2013). *Applications of motivational interviewing. Motivational interviewing: Helping people change* (3rd edition). Guilford Press.

Moreno, J. D. (2014). *Impromptu man: J. L. Moreno and the origins of psychodrama, encounter culture, and the social network.* Bellevue Literary Press.

Padesky, C. (2017, December). *Mind over mood: Practical applications for therapists.* Evolution of Psychotherapy Conference, Anaheim, CA.

Perls, F. S. (1969). *Gestalt therapy verbatim.* Real People Press.

Prochaska, J. O., & DiClemente, C. C. (2005). The transtheoretical approach. In J. C. Norcross & M. R. Goldfried (Eds.), *Oxford series in clinical psychology. Handbook of psychotherapy integration* (pp. 147–171). Oxford University Press.

Reich, W. (1933). *Character-analysis*. Orgone Institute Press.

Rogers, C. R. (1957). The necessary and sufficient conditions of therapeutic personality change. *Journal of Consulting Psychology, 21*(2), 95–103. https://doi.org/10.1037/h0045357

Segal, Z. V., Williams, J. M. G., & Teasdale, J. D. (2002). *Mindfulness-based cognitive therapy for depression: A new approach to preventing relapse*. Guilford Press.

Sue, D. W., & Torino, G. C. (2005). Racial-cultural competence: Awareness, knowledge, and skills. In R. T. Carter (Ed.) *Handbook of Racial-Cultural Psychology and Counseling, Training and Practice, 2*, 3–18. John Wiley & Sons.

Teyber, E. (2000). *Interpersonal process in psychotherapy*: A relational approach (4th ed.). Brooks/Cole.

van der Kolk, B. A. (2014). *The body keeps the score: Brain, mind, and body in the healing of trauma*. Viking.

Wampold, B., & Ulvenes, P. G. (2019). Integration of common factors and specific ingredients. In J. C. Norcross & M. R. Goldfried (Eds.) *Handbook of Psychotherapy Integration* (pp. 69–87). Oxford University Press.

Wells, A. (2011). *Metacognitive therapy for anxiety and depression*. Guilford Publications.

White, M. (2007). *Maps of narrative practice*. W.W. Norton & Co.

White, M. K., & Epston, D. (1990). *Narrative means to therapeutic ends*. W.W. Norton & Company.

Yalom, I. D. (1980). *Existential psychotherapy*. Basic Books.

Yeung, K.-T., & Martin, J. L. (2003). The Looking Glass Self: An empirical test and elaboration. *Social Forces, 81*(3), 843–879. https://doi.org/10.1353/sof.2003.0048

What We Can Get Away With (And What We Can Get Away With, But Shouldn't)

This section is largely about therapeutic power. Remember in Chapter 6, when we talked about *expert power* (this is when one person is believed to know more about a certain subject than the other person and is perceived to be deserving of trust; French & Raven, 1959), we noted that this is the kind of power that really helps any kind of therapy to work especially well. In these next ten chapters, we'll explore how to make the most of your therapeutic power, while working to keep our heads straight about how not to go overboard. In true therapeutic fashion, all of these concepts are about holding this power in tension – so, every "Do" will have a "Don't" and every "Don't" will have an exception!

CHAPTER 41
DO REMEMBER YOUR POWER
(DON'T ABUSE IT)

Expert power is about knowledge and trust (French & Raven, 1959); clients need to believe that we have more information than they do and that we are working in their best interest. The therapeutic relationship, well-built and maintained, should hopefully take care of the trust part. (Although there are some factors there that aren't entirely in our control, such as snap judgements about trustworthiness made by clients based on our facial features; Zebrowitz & Montepare, 2015.) But what about the knowledge part?

Unfortunately, there are a few factors that lead to quick judgments of competence that are largely out of our control as well, such as being tall (Judge & Cable, 2004) and being attractive (Jackson et al., 1995). Though, there are some we can impact, like hanging our diplomas in our offices (Devlin et al., 2009). But we can demonstrate our knowledge and competence to clients more authentically by first *being* competent and then displaying our competence through the therapy work. When we have a solid training and experience base, especially in the common factors of therapy (see Section One), and when we genuinely engage in the helping relationship, we will have the expert power to utilize in session and know how to use it – to create an atmosphere of safety, to instill hope, to co-create the path forward, and to help clients move through the work.

We don't abuse our power in obvious ways, because none of us actually wants or means to do that. But it is still possible to abuse our power unintentionally. Here are some examples:

- We abuse it when we teach things we don't really know or only partially know. (That's why Section Six is so important.) It's so easy to let this get away from us without noticing. We just say what seems like the next right thing in session, and it seems true at the time, but we may not realize that in fact it's: a) a misinterpretation of a research finding (like that your brain responds to sex and shopping the same way – it doesn't; e.g., Berridge & Robinson, 2016), or b) inaccurate folk wisdom (like "flattery gets you nowhere" – it does (Chan & Sengupta, 2010) or "letting your anger out helps" – it doesn't (Bushman, 2002)), or c) something that really seems like it fits with the other things we know (like that spanking is effective if it's normative in a person's culture – it isn't; Grogan-Kaylor,

 DOI: 10.4324/9781003125082-46

2018). It might even be something we've said many times before and we're just quoting ourselves without remembering that we're the source!

- We accidentally sometimes use coercive power without realizing it. *Coercive power* is when we hold punishments over the client (French & Raven, 1959). These punishments may not be anything we intend but may be inferred by the client – things like our admonishment (which reminds them of their childhoods) or our disappointment (which they really care about because they care about us). Like all forms of punishment, the use of coercive power only leads to conformity (and only in the presence of the coercer), often leads to decreased interest and increased resistance, and isn't helpful in building more effective behaviors that clients can use in the future.

PRACTICE TIP

Having a very solid knowledge base and knowing that you are using it well (i.e., "being an expert") does not mean that you should lose your professional humility. In fact, therapists who continue to have significant professional self-doubt have better therapy outcomes (Nissen-Lie et al., 2017). So, keep on being curious and approaching each client with a sense of not being totally sure. We work best with clients when we're highly competent without being overly confident.

CHAPTER 42
DO ASK PERMISSION TO PUSH
(DON'T PUSH TOO FAR)

We do need to "push" clients, sometimes, but let's talk about what that means. Demanding, coercing, and domineering are definitely not therapeutic; persuasion, structuring, and encouragement are probably more what we want to do. But we can overstep our bounds even with these gentle techniques. Persuading means offering sound reasoning and relevant information to a client in order to change their views; we might want to do this when clients are operating on false information (for example, maladaptive learning from the early family environment or too much Googling!). Structuring is needed when clients have a desire to change, but an amorphous idea about how to make changes (or clear but ineffective ideas!) and difficulty in seeing a workable, healthy path forward to change. Encouragement is usually defined as giving support or showing confidence in the client, and we might do this when the client is on the right track (though moving slowly or hesitantly). I personally really like the Adlerian definition of encouragement – *instilling courage* to change, which includes a whole host of therapeutic activities including validation, reframing, facilitating use of resources, and the like (Wong, 2015).

What does it mean to push clients too far, and how can we avoid this? One thing it might mean is that we don't want clients to think we're being pushy or to feel too pushed. Luckily, the answer to that is pretty simple – we can ask their permission to push them. It's magic. I really mean it. It turns out that when we ask someone's permission to impose on them, we don't even need a real reason, and they pretty much always say yes (Langer et al., 1978; Key et al., 2009). They're even more likely to say yes to us, because of the therapeutic relationship and environment. Asking their permission and receiving that yes also begins to put them in a "yes set," which makes it more likely that they will continue agreeing (de Shazer, 1985; Erickson, 1959/2009).

The other definition of pushing clients too far is asking them to do something that is too challenging for where they are right now. And considering that they're almost certainly going to say yes, we need to be especially careful. When thinking about how far to (ethically and effectively) push clients, we can think about the *zone of proximal development* (the area between what a client can already do alone and what they can do with our

     DOI: 10.4324/9781003125082-47

help; Vygotsky, 1978). We can also consider the concept of *flow,* which is a mental state in which the client can be fully immersed in a feeling of energized focus and enjoyment (Csikszentmihalyi, 2008). Sounds amazing, right? It is, and it's great for therapeutic work. Flow is based on finding activities that are centered in the right level of challenge compared to their level of skill. If an activity is too easy, the client will be bored and unmotivated. If the level is too difficult, the client will be overstressed or anxious. We should aim to "push" clients into their flow channel, not past it. And sometimes, we may need to be "pulling" overzealous clients into their flow channel, if they've set unreasonable expectations for themselves!

PRACTICE TIP

You know the saying "pulled in different directions?" It always gives me a mental image of being drawn and quartered. Being pushed in many directions isn't fun either. If you are going to push clients, it's worthwhile to push on only one goal at a time. When clients try to work on two goals simultaneously, they have difficulty in allocating resources to both (and end up working only on one, prioritizing one or the other based on whether they believe both are accomplishable). Also, carrying more than one goal increases the perceived overall difficulty which is more likely to lead to goal abandonment (Schmidt & Dolis, 2009).

CHAPTER 43
DO BRING IT TO THE HERE-AND-NOW (DON'T JUST KEEP IT THERE)

The here-and-now is a pretty magical place (Yalom, 2002). It is where clients can change and grow in the moment, where interpersonal feedback can be immediate, where trial and error can become trial and error and trial and error and trial (i.e., a real learning experience). The here-and-now lets us use our (healthy, reality-based) thoughts and feelings about clients to enrich the therapy experience. It's where the evocation and experience of deep emotions (catharsis) can be immediately followed by analysis and integration. It's where the relationship – the foundation of all therapeutic change – is born and grows.

Another way of taking advantage of the here-and-now is using it to develop skills or cultivate new "ways of being" in session that can then be taken outside session. Some of those things might be "typical" therapeutic tasks, like increasing emotional vulnerability (Johnson, 2004) or trying out new relational patterns (Teyber, 2000) *with us*, not just planning how to increase emotional vulnerability with a partner or talking about different relational strategies. And I can't stress too much how important and worthwhile that work is.

We can also improve the utility of our here-and-now time in therapy by bringing the client's "real-life" fears and difficulties into the therapy room, in a highly pragmatic way. I don't mean to suggest that we keep a terrarium full of spiders for doing exposure work. (Not that you can't do that – you would get a lot of very specific referrals.) But is the client struggling to make an important phone call? We could practice it together, and then *pick up the phone in session*. Are they having trouble communicating with their partner? *We could bring the partner in as a guest.* Do they need help with learning how to look for a job? *We could open our laptop and start the search together.* This is even the basis for panic control therapy (Hofmann et al., 2010) – eliciting panic attacks so that clients can practice managing and reducing symptoms with the support and attention of the therapist. We want to enhance (not skip!) the "meat" of the learning process – coaching, processing failures, immediate feedback, supervision – not just leave the practice part for homework.

We need to remember the developmental nature of the therapy process as we do this. Clients typically start out more dependent on us, and that's a good thing – early dependence on the therapist leads to more cooperation and

DOI: 10.4324/9781003125082-48

belief in the therapy process, contributes to therapy efficacy, and is associated with better outcomes (Bornstein & Bowen, 1995; Rotter, 1966). Through the therapy process, clients (hopefully!) grow in independence as they build self-efficacy, change cognitions about self, develop new skills, etc. Doing things in therapy is a wonderful way to make therapeutic progress, as long as we are fostering clients' development, rather than dependence. What is the minimal amount of help that we can give to support a client having a successful, meaningful experience? That's how much we want to give, no more.

PRACTICE TIP

Remember, it will probably be more difficult outside of therapy, when you aren't there for support and help, but it's possible that it is easier! Once a client has come back after a homework assignment or trying out a new skill, be sure that part of the processing is about what was easy/difficult about doing it alone, the different resources/barriers out in the "real world," etc. You can use the session to troubleshoot together before they practice again, if need be.

CHAPTER 44
DO GIVE HOMEWORK AND BROOK NO ARGUMENTS (DON'T MAKE HOMEWORK CRAZY)

If we're lucky, we get to spend 50 minutes per week with a client. That means they spend more than 10,000 minutes a week away from us. So, it will come as no surprise that therapy accompanied by homework generally has better treatment outcomes than therapy without homework (Kazantzis et al., 2000; Kazantzis et al., 2010). So, we need to be giving it! And it's not just for cognitive therapy. Homework improves early treatment gains, even session by session (in CBT for depression; Conklin & Strunk, 2015), improves treatment satisfaction and reduces the number of needed sessions (in parent–child interaction therapy; Danko et al., 2016), reinforces in-session changes (in experiential therapy; Greenberg & Warwar, 2006), and is even useful when clients determine their own homework (in client-centered therapy; Brodley, 2006).

I wish I could give a list of the Top Ten Best Homework Assignments or a decision tree that will lead us to The Perfect Homework for each client, but unfortunately, there is no such thing (although there are a few sources that can give great ideas; e.g., Rosenthal, 2011). Homework needs to be tailored not only to the type of therapy that we are doing, but where clients are in the process, what kinds of emotions they have during homework, and frankly, even what kinds of activities they're willing to do (Harris & Hiskey, 2015). Even if it's not our idea of the perfect homework, homework that gets done is more effective than homework that gets ignored. And you might be tired of hearing this by now, but unsurprisingly, clients are more willing to do homework when the relationship is good. This is especially true when clients perceive that we have good empathy early on during treatment (Hara et al., 2017).

We don't want to activate clients' natural reactance by being too strict or demanding (Branagan et al., 2018), but by and large, we probably need to be a little bit stricter than we naturally want to be. At the very least, we should follow Beck's (1979) advice and check homework every session. It's a simple behavioral principle that underlies the adage, "The first time we don't check homework is the last time they do it." And we want to give homework (or at least set the stage for it) from the very first session – the early impression is a

107

DOI: 10.4324/9781003125082-49

lasting impression (Goffman, 1959) and we can always become more lenient over the course of therapy if that's appropriate.

Now, if we want homework to be done and done well, an additional consideration is that we need to make sure we're not outstripping clients' actual skills or self-efficacy (Bandura, 1977; Bandura et al., 2019). That is, homework needs to be something that clients are both actually capable of doing and believe they're capable of doing. An easy way to make sure that our homework assignments are on target in this way is to do the homework in session first. If that's filling out a thought record, we can fruitfully spend 15 minutes of our time doing this with clients. If it's practicing a brief social interaction, we can walk them out to the front desk and let them have a little practice session with the office staff.

PRACTICE TIP

Make sure you and they know why the homework is important. Assign homework with intention. It's so easy to get into the habit of just assigning and re-assigning the same five homeworks. Instead, make sure you have a clear understanding of the therapeutic value of the assignment. Be able to explain it to yourself, and be overt in telling clients why you are assigning what you are assigning and what benefit you believe it will have for them. If clients believe the homework has value, they're more likely to do it! And, remember that when homework doesn't get done, processing the barriers (internal and/or external) can be just as fruitful as the homework would have been!

CHAPTER 45
DO INSTILL HOPE (DON'T LET THEM BELIEVE IN MIRACLES)

When we ask clients the "miracle question" (i.e., "Imagine that while you're asleep, a miracle happens and the problem you brought to therapy is solved. When you wake up, what will be different? How will you know that the miracle has happened?"), how do they usually answer?

- Unrealistically: "My life would be perfect."
- Vaguely: "Things will just be better." "Everything will be different."
- Emotionally: "I'll be happier." "I'll feel more alive."
- Negatively: "I won't have pain." "Work won't suck."
- Passively: "People will be nicer." "My kids will be more likeable." (emphasis on others)

Not useful. Who knows about miracles? The Solution-Focused Brief Therapy (SFBT) folks do (Dolan & de Shazer, 2007); they're the ones who made up the "miracle question!" And what do they use the miracle question for? To identify how clients would like their lives to be different, that is, *what they hope can change*.

The idea of instilling hope is part of the common-factors literature (see Section One) and a significant part of the group therapy literature (e.g., Yalom & Leszcz, 2006). So, let's talk about what hope is and what it is not. A good working definition for hope might be "a belief that a positive future outcome is possible combined with a desire for that outcome" (Luo et al., 2020).

The future outcome has to be possible and doable. This means that the hopeful vision that we work toward in therapy needs to be something that can be accomplished generally within the systems that the client lives in (or we are looking at major individual and/or societal changes), with the internal and external resources that are available (or attainable), and that we can manage with the efforts of only the people who are in therapy doing the work (i.e., the client and ourselves) or who we can recruit (e.g., family, friends, bosses, other supports). To that end, we want this hopeful future vision to be... decidedly un-miraculous.

- Realistic: "I would be able to meet challenges better and recover from setbacks more quickly and easily."

 DOI: 10.4324/9781003125082-50

- Specific: "I would enjoy my home more, because it wouldn't be as cluttered." "I would spend my evenings with my family, at leisure, instead of working."
- Behavioral: "I would be more active, more engaged in meaningful things, and probably feel happier and more alive because of it."
- Positive: "I would appreciate and fully use the days I have less pain." "I would prioritize the things I enjoy most about work and reduce some of the unnecessary, unpleasant tasks."
- Active: "I would treat others more kindly." "I would create an environment for my kids with less tension and stress." (emphasis on "I")

Here's something *almost* miraculous. Small changes lead to big changes. That's also something the SFBT people know a lot about. We can safely construct solutions that are a series of very small, easy steps. We can aim for moving from a 3.0 on a scale of 0–10 to a 3.25. Each small change sets off other changes that both tend to increase the magnitude of positive difference and allow clients' systems (e.g., families, workplaces) to catch up without huge disruptions.

PRACTICE TIP

A little note about the use of the miracle question. We may need to adapt the original language in order to fit our clients' cultural backgrounds or individual experiences and belief systems better (Kayrouz & Hansen, 2019). For example, if a client who doesn't believe in miracles hears the question literally and therefore doesn't answer, we may not get the information we're looking for at best and may have a rapport rupture at worst. On the other hand, some clients of faith do believe in miracles, and that can cause challenges as well. For these clients, using the word miracle may put them in an external locus of control mindset, rather than the more therapeutically helpful mindset that they can instigate changes in their own lives. One possible language change is to ask clients what would be different if "your best hopes were achieved" or "the life you dream of were real" or "all of your present concerns were gone."

CHAPTER 46
DON'T JUST FOCUS ON BEHAVIOR (UNLESS THEY CAN ACTUALLY CHANGE THINGS)

We already covered a couple of different ways of thinking about when to focus on emotions vs. behaviors, but here is a terribly practical way. Pretty much all clients are coming into therapy with some kind of stress, assuming that we define stress as anything that seems to exceed their current ability to cope effectively. There are two main ways of coping: problem-focused and emotion-focused (Folkman & Lazarus, 1980.) *Problem-focused coping* is any active effort that is put forward to deal with or reduce the actual stressor itself (e.g., changing one's own behavior or changing environmental conditions). *Emotion-focused coping* is any effort aimed at reducing the internal emotional distress we experience because of the stressor without impacting the stressor itself (e.g., venting, seeking social support, reappraising the situation).

It's typical for people (especially in America) to highly value problem-focused coping and to dismiss emotion-focused coping as "useless" or "self-indulgent." Sometimes, that might make sense, because not all of the emotion-focused strategies are helpful (e.g., emotional eating, drug use, denial, avoidance, withdrawal). We might be tempted to do the same – after all, several chapters in this book have been dedicated to the concept of internal locus of control. However, emotion-focused coping can be just as active as problem-focused, just as individually determined, and sometimes more helpful. This is especially true when there is a stressor (or parts of a stressor) that clients actually don't have the power to change or influence. For example, emotion-focused coping is necessary when waiting for test results, when an embarrassing moment is already past, or when nagging a loved one again won't do anything but damage the relationship.

We are sometimes called upon to interact with people in their places of powerlessness (even if it is perceived powerlessness). Clients often come to therapy after they've "tried everything," and "trying more" or "trying harder" aren't good solutions either because they won't work and will further discourage clients or because we need to help reduce negative affect or reframe the situation before they try more problem-focused strategies. Of course, many of the typical Cognitive Therapy (e.g., Clark & Beck, 2011)

DOI: 10.4324/9781003125082-51

techniques are useful for this, as well as the third-wave mindfulness-based therapies such as Acceptance and Commitment Therapy (Luoma et al., 2017) and Mindfulness-Based Stress Reduction (Lehrhaupt & Meibert, 2017). When it comes to bringing negative internal experiences down to more manageable levels, there's probably no better resource than the distress tolerance skills module in Dialectical Behavior Therapy (Linehan, 2014).

The exception to this approach is when clients *do* have some power to change or influence the situation; that's when problem-focused coping is called for. Many clients won't come into therapy in this state, because they are out there already making changes (or trying to). But occasionally, clients will come to therapy in an emotion-focused state even though they have plenty of power to change their situations. In this case, when we notice, we can sometimes use our expert power to shift part of the conversation or assign a homework that will make a quick, significant difference in the client's world. For example, though we may focus most of a session on practicing self-soothing with an overwhelmed client, we could use her calmed state to co-author an email to her boss requesting an extension, or slip in a homework assignment for her to give herself a break by asking her daughter to set the table for dinner. (She may not even notice that she's beginning the process of developing assertiveness to manage her workflow or setting the stage for behavioral training at home!)

PRACTICE TIP

There's one other main type of coping that we didn't discuss: *proactive coping* (Aspinwall & Taylor, 1997). This is a kind of future orientation that leads to behaviors that prevent stress from getting out of control in the first place or set the stage for better coping when needed. For example, a lot of what we talk about being "self-care" is proactive coping – getting enough sleep, eating well, exercising, maintaining regular social supports, etc. (All things we do want to teach our clients when we can!) Other kinds of proactive coping are things like studying throughout the semester rather than waiting to cram for finals, saving money for expectable expenses, having a friend watch out for early signs of another depressive episode, and scheduling regular meetings with a partner to discuss any differences or resentments that have come up lately. (These are also things we'd like our clients to know how to do by the time they leave us!) Just watch out that clients don't convince you that their generalized anxiety is "good proactive coping!"

CHAPTER 47
DON'T TELL CLIENTS WHAT TO DO (BUT DO TEACH THEM HOW TO FIGURE IT OUT)

We've already talked a bit about not giving advice in therapy, but it bears repeating. If we give clients advice, and it turns out badly...that's our fault. They blame us (rightfully so!) and that's not great for the therapeutic relationship. What about if we give advice and it goes well? That's also our fault. They still blame us. Only, under those circumstances, we call it "giving us the credit." But that's *also bad*.

One way of describing it goes like this: "I have learned not to steal my clients' problems from them. I don't want to be the redeeming hero or the *deus ex machina* – not in someone else's story" (Peterson, 2018). This way of thinking really emphasizes the theft of client power when we give advice. We want them to be the heroes in their own stories! At most, we may want to add some healthy alternatives into their pool of choices and help them wade through them. That means teaching a problem-solving model.

Here's the thing – almost none of us was taught the steps in a problem-solving model, but we really should know them, because this is one of those gifts that we can give clients that they can take with them and use long after therapy is over. So, here we go, in summary form (D'Zurilla & Goldfried, 1971; Nezu et al., 2010):

- Step 1: Get your head right
  Set your intention to accept that problematic situations constitute a normal part of life, and that it is possible for us to cope with most of these situations effectively. Recognize problematic situations when they occur. Inhibit the tendency to avoid problem situations or to respond to problems carelessly or haphazardly. (I know, that was a trick. It's really three steps in one!) This is a step in which we are really crucial – helping clients to identify their typical, maladaptive approaches and building their self-efficacy for handling problematic situations.
- Step 2: Do the actual problem-solving
  State the problem, brainstorm possible solutions, pick one, and give it a go. (I know, that was also a trick. It's really four steps in one!) But this is the part that most people are familiar with, when we say "problem

DOI: 10.4324/9781003125082-52

solving." There are some useful tweaks to this sequence, such as making sure to define the problem specifically, having all of the relevant information, and increasing creativity during brainstorming, but by and large, people know how to do this sequence.

- Step 3: See how it went
  This is when we evaluate the solution that was attempted. (This is just one step! Well, it's kind of four steps. Sorry!) How well did the solution work in solving the problem? If it didn't work well, what didn't work? Knowing that, what else can we try? Also, if it went well, for future reference, it's worth asking ourselves how difficult it was and if it is worth repeating.

There is an additional phase that belongs in Step 2 that almost everyone skips — *setting the criteria for an acceptable solution.* For example, any acceptable solution will cost less than $1000 or any acceptable solution must include staying married. Skipping this step (or waiting until the end) not only makes it more difficult to brainstorm solutions, but it makes it much more difficult to choose solutions to attempt and leads to more dissatisfaction with outcomes. Paying attention to it can help with generating useful solutions and also with choosing which solutions to attempt first. It also helps with Step 3, when we evaluate how the process went. Another reason this is helpful is because it can forestall a lot of the frustrating "yes, but..." behavior that clients use during this process. So, we should help clients to do this early in the process, probably immediately after the problem has been identified.

PRACTICE TIP

One other part of problem solving that we can make much easier is the decision-making component. There are two main ways to make decisions (or to choose among alternatives): *maximizing* (which means examining all of the possible options and then deciding which one fits best; Schwartz et al., 2002) and *satisficing* (which means setting the criteria for an acceptable solution and then choosing the first solution presented that meets those criteria, leaving the rest unexamined; Simon, 1955). Most people want to choose a maximizing strategy when it comes to decision making, but it's almost always a bad idea. Maximizing tends to lead to regret, rumination, and continued evaluations of alternative options, which subsequently leads to more choice dissatisfaction and lower well-being (Schwartz, 2004). In contrast, satisficing leads to higher satisfaction, more confidence in one's choice, and less regret (Brough & Chervnev, 2009).

CHAPTER 48
DON'T BELIEVE ANYTHING THEY SAY (EXCEPT GO AHEAD AND BELIEVE IT ALL)

I'm not sure how to break this news to you, but... our memories aren't real. I mean, they're real in the sense that they are something that can be interacted with, but they aren't *accurate*.

Memories are not "pulled out from storage;" they are constructed, or recreated, every time we remember them. We create our memories of the past based on (1) the information that remains in our memories (which itself might not be accurate, because it is influenced when it is encoded by our emotions and perceptions at the time) and (2) supplements to fill in the gaps, such as our general knowledge, the social demands of the retrieval situation, and our emotional state during retrieval. For example, when people are shown a video of a car accident and then asked how fast the cars were going when they "smashed into each other," participants remember the cars going substantially faster than if they are asked how fast the cars were going when they "made contact with each other" – even though they watched the same video (Loftus & Palmer, 1974). If that weren't enough, the people who were asked about the "smashed" cars also remembered broken glass being in the street, even though there wasn't any!

Memories, even personal, emotionally charged memories, can be entirely created (Hyman & Loftus, 1998). Twenty to twenty-five percent of people will create completely false memories of spilling punch at a wedding, getting lost in the mall, and even car accidents or hospitalizations when researchers suggest that their family members reported that these events happened (Hyman et al., 1995; Loftus & Pickrell, 1995).

Let me give just one other example. Consider the events of September 11, 2001, when the twin towers of New York City were hit by terrorist-hijacked planes. If you are old enough to have seen the live video of the plane flying into the first tower that day, you probably have a very clear "flashbulb" memory of seeing that on the news, including where you were and who you were with that day (60–80% of people across the States have this clear memory; Pezdek, 2003).

DOI: 10.4324/9781003125082-53

The thing is, though…there was no video of the first plane hitting the first tower available that day. Video of that didn't turn up until the following day.

The 9/11 research shows that people's memory for the events as they learned them (e.g., on the news) and as they experienced them (i.e., autobiographical memories, such as how they felt or where they were) were shockingly inaccurate by just seven weeks afterwards (Pezdek, 2003). When people recorded their experiences during the week after 9/11 and then were asked questions eleven months later, they were only 85% accurate (on facts that were repeated often on the news) and about 60% consistent on the autobiographical memory (such as where they were or who they talked to first about it), though people were *very* confident that they remembered correctly (Hirst et al., 2009).

This kind of understanding and healthy skepticism regarding memory is really useful in our own lives and might even be useful to teach clients. But that's not how we want to interact with clients from the beginning. We actually don't want to be skeptical about the veracity of their stories. We want to achieve (in Carl Rogers' words) a "gullible caring, in which clients are accepted as they say they are, not with a lurking suspicion in the therapist's mind that they may, in fact, be otherwise. This attitude is not stupidity on the therapist's part; it is the kind of attitude that is most likely to lead to trust" (Rogers & Sanford, 1989 as cited in Thorne, 2003).

Again, knowing this is important, especially because we don't want to be responsible for changing clients' memories! But our work is with the client as they are now. And who they are now depends more on what they believe they have experienced than what they have actually experienced. Or rather, what they remember now is a reflection of who they are now (Adler, 1931/2014).

PRACTICE TIP

Remember this research about September 11 when you're working with couples. In fact, read the article, and read all of Elizabeth Loftus' research, and then teach it to your couples. Once they're on board with the idea that their memories aren't perfect, that their memories are constant recreations based on environmental priming and their own emotions, they can be more open to accepting their partner's view of past events. Not as accurate recreations of the past, but as alternative, functional reconstructions. Then, they're truly on the way to co-creating their future.

CHAPTER 49
DON'T PRAISE THEM
(BUT DO LIKE THEM)

Wait, isn't praise a good thing? If we're making sure to only use positive reinforcement? I mean, especially if we're careful and definitely just praise clients' *behaviors* and not their character? What if we're only reinforcing the behavior that's consistent with their own stated therapy goals?

Well, here's the thing. One of the characteristics of the helping relationship as Rogers (1961) described it is that we want to *free clients from external evaluation.* We spend our entire lives under the scrutiny and judgment of others – our parents, teachers, bosses. And while those influences may be very useful and important (in fact, Freud (1930) suggests that we may not even have civilization without them!), they don't seem to be helpful when it comes to personal growth of the kind that true therapy is. As Rogers puts it, "Curiously enough a positive evaluation is as threatening in the long run as a negative one, since to inform someone that he is good implies that you also have the right to tell him he is bad."

The end goal of therapy, even if we aren't pure Person-Centered therapists, is that clients are self-responsible and able to make their way healthfully through life without our input. Rogers believed that we typically don't need to *train* them, but rather just provide the right kind of environment and clients will be able to shed their old, maladaptive learnings and develop their own inner wisdom. Part of that growth-promoting environment is that we are not – even in our own feelings – evaluating them.

I'm not suggesting that this is easy, or that we'll even be able to do it all the time. Maybe a specific part of our therapy is to evaluate clients' performance (on their self-selected goals) and give them feedback they aren't able to judge yet for themselves (though we probably want to be aiming in the direction of their ability to do this, based on the natural consequences they see in their lives!). Our client might have had such maladaptive learning experiences that many of their self-suggestions are dangerous to themselves or harmful to others, and we might feel ethically obligated to give our opinion. We may be doing cognitive therapy, in which part of our job is to assess clients' thinking, though hopefully we're at least doing this along a spectrum of effective/ineffective rather than good/bad or right/wrong.

But usually clients ask for or "pull for" our approval (probably because they don't yet know how to have a non-judgmental relationship) and we

DOI: 10.4324/9781003125082-54

don't know how to maintain the good rapport without giving it. But, let me suggest this: Choosing not to evaluate them or their behavior is different than expressing *liking* for them. We definitely want to do that.

A warm, positive, accepting, non-possessive, unconditional *prizing* of the client means that we express (congruently!) feelings of liking. Make no mistake – a warm and positive acceptance is *liking*. (If it were a neutral acceptance, it would just be accepting. If it were a cold, negative acceptance, it would be just tolerating.) We don't need to like them because they are like us, because they are good clients, because they're being compliant, because we approve of them, because they are likeable, or *because* of anything at all. Not that we will always experience this (even Rogers didn't!), but when we do, it's good to share it overtly with clients.

PRACTICE TIP

Ethics moment: You can genuinely like and share your liking with clients, overtly and verbally. And you can be friendly without being friends. The therapy relationship is set apart from other relationships – as Yalom (2002), who is the strongest supporter of the authenticity of the therapeutic relationship, says, "Psychotherapy is not a substitute for life, but a dress rehearsal for life...the relationship is not an end – it is a means to an end."

CHAPTER 50
DON'T ASSUME THEIR GOALS ARE REAL (UNLESS THEY ARE)

Consider this – if clients are, by definition, living maladaptively when they begin therapy… how could they initially construct anything but maladaptive goals?

The "problem" that the client brings in the first session is unlikely to be the same problem they have in the second, third, or tenth session (Rogers, 1961). This is especially true if they are changing as a result of the therapeutic work, especially building awareness. That means that the goals from the first session are unlikely to stay the same throughout therapy either.

Recall the definition of hope in Chapter 45: "A belief that a positive future outcome is possible combined with a desire for that outcome" (Luo et al., 2020). Part of the definition that we neglected at that time was that clients need to have a *desire* for the outcome. Chances are that, as clients grow, their *desires* as well as their problems will change. This is what I mean when I say that we should not assume that clients' goals are "real."

Now, do some clients come into therapy with real goals? Maybe. I like to think of the whole therapy process as working on several different levels. The shallowest or easiest level might be something more like coaching. This is when clients are basically high functioning, have healthy intra- and inter-personal relationships, and mostly need a little information and maybe accountability to make a few small changes or build a few skills. In these cases, clients' initial goals may be "real."

However, we often discover that clients, even those who initially identify their distress on what seems like a surface level, need to make deeper changes. A client who comes in with generalized anxiety may actually have intrapersonal work to do in terms of incongruence. One who comes in with depression may actually have significant issues of power in relationships. Difficulty sleeping may be a symptom of trauma, indecision about a relationship may be borderline personality, procrastination may be trouble with emotion regulation, and "feeling stressed" could be *anything*.

Goals may change because of what clients learn in therapy, too. For example, therapy may involve things like changing one's internal view of self, in which case previous goals may no longer apply. A client might realize a relationship is abusive and change their goal from "being a better partner and parent" to earning their own income in order to provide a safety net for

119   DOI: 10.4324/9781003125082-55

leaving. They might resolve trauma that changes an initial goal of sleeping better and reducing anxiety to developing meaning and engaging in pursuits of purpose. They may gain ego strength or self-efficacy and change their goal from something easy to a major challenge now that they believe they can accomplish it. They might discover that their presenting symptom was actually their attempt at a solution to a different problem and choose to address the underlying issue in a new way instead.

Additionally, all significant changes will necessarily impact clients' environment and social systems (reciprocal determinism; Bandura, 1978), but they don't always know that when they come in. We have to be ready (and so do they!) to facilitate the re-establishment of a healthier equilibrium in families, workplaces, and social circles. Those potential and actual changes might lead to goal realignment, or the addition of goals that include the interpersonal realm in a way they didn't initially.

At minimum, we need to consider clients' goals as moving targets!

PRACTICE TIP

With clients' goals always changing, how do you know when to terminate? It's common to suggest that we begin talking about termination from session one (and truthfully, I love the existential energy that gives to therapy). But termination needs to be an ongoing discussion that surfaces often, especially in response to goal transformations. And I think we can help clients let go of the idea that they will accomplish such-and-such goal and that's how they will know that therapy is over. Rather, we should be measuring readiness for termination by something more like "being equipped" – with knowledge, strength, and resources for continuing the ongoing journey without the additional support of therapy. (Bonus tip: I almost never say "termination" anymore, after a client mentioned what a horrible term it was. He suggested therapy "conclusion" and I've been using that ever since!)

REFERENCES

Adler, A. (1931/2014). *What life could mean to you (3rd ed)*. Oneworld Publications.

Aspinwall, L. G., & Taylor, S. E. (1997). A stitch in time: Self-regulation and proactive coping. *Psychological Bulletin, 121*(3), 417–436. https://doi.org/10.1037/0033-2909.121.3.417

Bandura, A. (1978). The self system in reciprocal determinism. *American Psychologist, 33*(4), 344–358. https://doi.org/10.1037/0003-066X.33.4.344

Bandura, A. (2019). Applying theory for human betterment. *Perspectives on Psychological Science, 14*(1), 12–15. https://doi.org/10.1177/1745691618815165

Bandura, A., Adams, N. E., & Beyer, J. (1977). Cognitive processes mediating behavioral change. *Journal of Personality and Social Psychology, 35*(3), 125–139. https://doi.org/10.1037/0022-3514.35.3.125

Berridge, K. C., & Robinson, T. E. (2016). Liking, wanting, and the incentive-sensitization theory of addiction. *The American Psychologist, 71*(8), 670–679. https://doi.org/10.1037/amp0000059

Bornstein, R. F., & Bowen, R. F. (1995). Dependency in psychotherapy: Toward an integrated treatment approach. *Psychotherapy: Theory, Research, Practice, Training, 32*(4), 520–534. https://doi.org/10.1037/0033-3204.32.4.520

Branagan, W. T., & Swanbrow Becker, M. A. (2018). Therapist directiveness and client reactance in the administration of homework in therapy with college students. *Journal of College Student Psychotherapy, 32*(3), 251–266. https://doi.org/10.1080/87568225.2017.1400299

Brodley, B. T. (2006). Client-initiated homework in client-centered therapy. *Journal of Psychotherapy Integration, 16*(2), 140–161. doi:10.1037/1053–0479.16.2.140

Brough, A., & Chernev, A. (2009). Find and keep or keep looking and weep: Satisficing and maximizing strategies in consumer choice [Conference session]. *Society for Consumer Psychology 2009 Conference Advances in Consumer Psychology*, Feb 12–14, 2009. https://doi.org/10.1037/e621092012-090

Bushman, B. J. (2002). Does venting anger feed or extinguish the flame? Catharsis, rumination, distraction, anger, and aggressive responding. *Personality and Social Psychology Bulletin, 28*, 724–731

Chan, E., & Sengupta, J. (2010). Insincere flattery actually works: A dual attitudes perspective. *Journal of Marketing Research, 47*(1), 122–133. https://doi.org/10.1509/jmkr.47.1.122

Clark, D. A. & Beck, A. T. (2011). *The anxiety and worry workbook: The cognitive behavioral solution*. Guilford Press.

Conklin, L. R., & Strunk, D. R. (2015). A session-to-session examination of homework engagement in cognitive therapy for depression: Do patients experience immediate benefits? *Behaviour Research and Therapy, 72*, 56–62. https://doi.org/10.1016/j.brat.2015.06.011

Csikszentmihalyi, M. (2008). *Flow: The psychology of optimal experience*. Harper Perennial Modern Classics.

Danko, C. M., Brown, T., Van Schoick, L., & Budd, K. S. (2016). Predictors and correlates of homework completion and treatment outcomes in parent–child interaction therapy. *Child & Youth Care Forum, 45*(3), 467–485. https://doi.org/10.1007/s10566-015-9339-5

de Shazer, S. (1985). *Keys to solution in brief therapy*. W. W. Norton.

Devlin, A. S., Donovan, S., Nicolov, A., Nold, O., Packard, A., & Zandan, G. (2009). "Impressive?" credentials, family photographs, and the perception of therapist qualities. *Journal of Environmental Psychology, 29*(4), 503–512. https://doi.org/10.1016/j.jenvp.2009.08.008

Dolan, Y., & de Shazer, S. (2007). *More than miracles: The state of the art of solution focused brief therapy.* Routledge Mental Health Classics Editions.

D'Zurilla, T. J., & Goldfried, M. R. (1971). Problem solving and behavior modification. *Journal of Abnormal Psychology, 78*(1), 107–126. https://doi.org/10.1037/h0031360

Erickson, M. H. (2009). Further clinical techniques of hypnosis: Utilization techniques. *American Journal of Clinical Hypnosis, 51*(4), 341–362.

Folkman, S., & Lazarus, R. S. (1980). An analysis of coping in a middle-aged community sample. *Journal of Health and Social Behavior, 21,* 219–239.

French, J. R. P., Jr., & Raven, B. (1959). *The bases of social power.* In D. Cartwright (Ed.), *Studies in social power* (pp. 150–167). University of Michigan.

Freud, S. (1930). *Civilization and its discontents.* (Translated by Joan Riviere). Hogarth Press.

Greenberg, L. S., & Warwar, S. H. (2006). Homework in an emotion-focused approach to experiential therapy. *Journal of Psychotherapy Integration, 16*(2), 178–200. https://doi.org/10.1037/1053-0479.16.2.178

Grogan-Kaylor, A., Ma, J., Lee, S. J., Castillo, B., Ward, K. P., & Klein, S. (2018). Using Bayesian analysis to examine associations between spanking and child externalizing behavior across race and ethnic groups. *Child Abuse & Neglect, 86,* 257–266. https://doi.org/10.1016/j.chiabu.2018.10.009

Hara, K. M., Aviram, A., Constantino, M. J., Westra, H. A., & Antony, M. M. (2017). Therapist empathy, homework compliance, and outcome in cognitive behavioral therapy for generalized anxiety disorder: Partitioning within- and between-therapist effects. *Cognitive Behaviour Therapy, 46*(5), 375–390. https://doi.org/10.1080/16506073.2016.1253605

Harris, D. L., & Hiskey, S. (2015). Homework in therapy: A case of it ain't what you do, it's the way that you do it? *The Cognitive Behaviour Therapist, 8,* Article e20. https://doi.org/10.1017/S1754470X15000549

Hirst, W., Phelps, E. A., Meksin, R., Vaidya, C. J., Johnson, M. K., Mitchell, K. J., Buckner, R. L., Budson, A. E., Gabrieli, J. D. E., Lustig, C., Mather, M., Ochsner, K. N., Schacter, D., Simons, J. S., Lyle, K. B., Cuc, A. F., & Olsson, A. (2015). A ten-year follow-up of a study of memory for the attack of September 11, 2001: Flashbulb memories and memories for flashbulb events. *Journal of Experimental Psychology: General, 144*(3), 604–623. https://doi.org/10.1037/xge0000055

Hofmann, S. G., Rief, W., & Spiegel, D. A. (2010). Psychotherapy for panic disorder. In D. J. Stein, E. Hollander, & B. O. Rothbaum (Eds.), *Textbook of anxiety disorders* (pp. 417–433). American Psychiatric Publishing, Inc.

Hyman, I. E., Jr., Husband, T. H., & Billings, J. F. (1995). False memories of childhood experiences. *Applied Cognitive Psychology, 9,* 181–197.

Jackson, L. A., Hunter, J. E., & Hodge, C. N. (1995). Physical attractiveness and intellectual competence: A meta-analytic review. *Social Psychology Quarterly, 58*(2), 108–122. https://doi.org/10.2307/2787149

Johnson, S. (2004). *The practice of emotionally focused couple therapy (2nd ed.).* Brunner-Routledge.

Judge, T. A., & Cable, D. M. (2004). The effect of physical height on workplace success and income: Preliminary test of a theoretical model. *Journal of Applied Psychology, 89*(3), 428–441. https://doi.org/10.1037/0021-9010.89.3.428

Kazantzis, N., Deane, F. P., & Ronan, K. R. (2000). Homework assignment in cognitive and behavioral therapy: A meta-analysis. *Clinical Psychology: Science and Practice, 7*(2), 189–202.

Kazantzis, N., Whittington, C., & Dattilio, F. (2010). Meta-analysis of homework effects in cognitive and behavioral therapy: A replication and extension. *Clinical Psychology: Science and Practice, 17*(2), 144–156. https://doi.org/10.1111/j.1468-2850.2010.01204.x

Key, M. S., Edlund, J. E., Sagarin, B. J., & Bizer, G. Y. (2009). Individual differences in susceptibility to mindlessness. *Personality and Individual Differences, 46*(3), 261–264. https://doi.org/10.1016/j.paid.2008.10.001

Langer, E. J., Blank, A., & Chanowitz, B. (1978). The mindlessness of ostensibly thoughtful action: The role of "placebic" information in interpersonal interaction. *Journal of Personality and Social Psychology, 36*(6), 635–642. https://doi.org/10.1037/0022-3514.36.6.635

Lehrhaupt, L., & Meibert, P. (2017). *Mindfulness-based stress reduction: The MBSR program for enhancing health and vitality.* New World Library.

Linehan, M. (2014). *DBT Skills Training Manual.* Guilford Press.

Loftus, E. F., & Palmer, J. C. (1974). Reconstruction of automobile destruction: An example of the interaction between language and memory. *Journal of Verbal Learning & Verbal Behavior, 13*(5), 585–589. https://doi.org/10.1016/S0022-5371(74)80011-3

Loftus, E. F., & Pickrell, J. E. (1995). The formation of false memories. *Psychiatric Annals, 25*(12), 720–725. https://doi.org/10.3928/0048-5713-19951201-07

Luo, S. X., van Horen, F., Millet, K., & Zeelenberg, M. (2020). What we talk about when we talk about hope: A prototype analysis. *Emotion.* Advance online publication. https://doi.org/10.1037/emo0000821

Luoma, J. B., Hayes, S. C., & Walser, R. D. (2017). *Learning ACT: An acceptance and commitment therapy skills training manual for therapists* (2nd ed.) Context Press.

Nezu, A. M., Nezu, C. M., & D'Zurilla, T. J. (2010). Problem-solving therapy. In N. Kazantzis, M. A. Reinecke, & A. Freeman (Eds.), *Cognitive and behavioral theories in clinical practice* (pp. 76–114). Guilford Press.

Nissen-Lie, H. A., Rønnestad, M. H., Høglend, P. A., Havik, O. E., Solbakken, O. A., Stiles, T. C., & Monsen, J. T. (2017). Love yourself as a person, doubt yourself as a therapist? *Clinical Psychology & Psychotherapy, 24*(1), 48–60. https://doi.org/10.1002/cpp.1977

Peterson, J. B. (2018). *12 rules for life: An antidote to chaos.* Random House Canada.

Pezdek, K. (2003). Event Memory and Autobiographical Memory for the Events of September 11, 2001. *Applied Cognitive Psychology, 17*(9), 1033–1045. https://doi.org/10.1002/acp.984

Rogers, C. (1961). *On becoming a person.* Houghton Mifflin.

Rosenthal, H. G. (Ed.). (2011). *Favorite counseling and therapy homework assignments* (2nd ed.). Routledge/Taylor & Francis Group.

Rotter, J. B. (1966). Generalized expectancies for internal versus external control of reinforcement, *Psychological Monographs: General and Applied.* 80: 1–28. doi:10.1037/h0092976.

Schmidt, A. M., & Dolis, C. M. (2009). Something's got to give: The effects of dual-goal difficulty, goal progress, and expectancies on resource allocation. *Journal of Applied Psychology, 94*(3), 678–691. https://doi.org/10.1037/a0014945

Schwartz, B. (2004). *The paradox of choice: Why less is more.* Ecco.

Schwartz, B., Ward, A., Monterosso, J., Lyubomirsky, S., White, K., &Lehman, D. R. (2002). Maximizing versus satisficing: Happiness is a matter of choice. *Journal of Personality and Social Psychology, 83,* 1178–1197.http://dx.doi.org/10.1037/0022-3514.83.5.1178

Simon, H. A. (1955). A behavioral model of rational choice. *Quarterly Journal of Economics, 69,* 99–118.

Teyber, E. (2000). *Interpersonal process in psychotherapy: A relational approach* (4th ed.). Brooks/Cole.

Thorne, B. (2003). *Carl Rogers (Key figures in counselling and psychotherapy series; second edition).* Sage Publications.

Vygotsky, L.S. (1978). *Mind in society.* Harvard University Press.

Wong, Y. J. (2015). The psychology of encouragement: Theory, research, and applications. *The Counseling Psychologist, 43*(2), 178–216. https://doi.org/10.1177/0011000014545091

Yalom, I. D. (2002). *The gift of therapy: An open letter to a new generation of therapists and their patients.* HarperCollins Publishers.

Yalom, I. D., & Leszcz, M. (Collaborator). (2005). *The theory and practice of group psychotherapy* (5th ed.). Basic Books.

Zebrowitz, L. A., & Montepare, J. M. (2015). Faces and first impressions. In M. Mikulincer, P. R. Shaver, E. Borgida, & J. A. Bargh (Eds.), *APA handbooks in psychology. APA handbook of personality and social psychology, Vol. 1. Attitudes and social cognition* (pp. 251–276). American Psychological Association. https://doi.org/10.1037/14341-008

Deepening Knowledge (Without a Lot of Spare Time)

Let's face it — we just didn't have time during our training to *really* learn everything the way we wanted to. Classwork, practicum, textbooks, and assignments (often combined with "real life!") meant late nights and skimming everything we could get away with. We told ourselves that we would read it later. We promised ourselves we would read some of those "real books." We agreed that, once we were out of school, we would never read "just the abstract" again. Friends, our time has come. Now we know that *we will never actually have more time*. If we're going to honor those promises to ourselves, we need a plan.

(Are you still in school? I'm so sorry I had to be the one to crush your dreams of long, quiet evenings, surrounded by fireflies, reading *Interpretation of Dreams* with your Sauvignon Blanc.)

Of course, there's no need to do all of these. Any one or a couple will be helpful and rewarding.

CHAPTER 51
READ THE BOOKS

Not all the books. We do have lives, and we have to prioritize. I'd like to suggest that we may get the most "bang for our buck" if we focus on reading some of the classics, rather than whatever's the newest therapy or self-help book on the market. (It's not that these may not be incredibly useful. It's just that these days, books tend to be narrower in scope, and the classics cover more ground. Plus, these are the authors who inspired us!)

Here are two classic texts that are incredibly useful regardless of theoretical orientation. First, Carl Rogers' *On Becoming a Person* (1961) should be required reading in every therapy training program. It is the foundational text for virtually all of the counseling we do, and it addresses the core conditions of therapy in both a theory-driven and incredibly practical way. The second book may come as a surprise: Alfred Adler's *What Life Could Mean to You* (1931/2014). Despite being typically (and not incorrectly) identified as a neo-Freudian, Adler's theory of psychotherapy is remarkably integrative. He manages to incorporate psychodynamic principles (e.g., early childhood learning and development, family of origin dynamics), humanistic principles (the relationship dynamic of therapy and the need for phenomenological understanding), cognitive principles (e.g., private logic), behavioral principles (e.g., reciprocal influence of person and environment), existential principles (e.g., choice, responsibility, meaning), social-constructivist principles (e.g., subjective reality), and more, all tied up in a growth- and future-oriented type of therapy that is surprisingly easy to understand.

We can choose other books almost exclusively by their authors. Do you consider yourself a humanistic-existential therapist? Read Viktor Frankl, Rollo May, Abraham Maslow, Erich Fromm, or Irvin Yalom. Psychodynamic? Try Karen Horney, Carl Jung, Otto Kernberg, and Erik Erikson. Just go for it – try Freud! Consider yourself a behaviorist? John Watson, B. F. Skinner, Joseph Wolpe, and Albert Bandura's books are calling. More cognitive? Aaron Beck and Albert Ellis could share one of our bookshelves, and Donald Meichenbaum is a great supplement. Let's read outside our preferred theoretical orientation, too. Let's read Cloe Madanes, Fritz Perls, Phil Zimbardo, and William Glasser! Philosophy books can be a great adjunct to our therapy foundations, as well. Major influencers of psychology and psychotherapy include René Descartes, John Locke, Martin Buber, Søren

DOI: 10.4324/9781003125082-57

Kierkegaard, and Friedrich Nietzsche. Don't be afraid! We *can* read these, and it's worth the effort!

Another great source is various holy writings. Reading these from different cultures and faith systems at minimum broadens our cultural understanding and gives us more anchors for understanding clients' perspectives. Additionally, the wisdom writings often express foundational psychological principles… after all, psychology as a discipline is an infant compared to the major faith traditions.

Not to be too old-fashioned, but there is a huge benefit in reading these books in a paper format. Meta-analyses on the subject of paper books compared to screens/e-readers show that readers learn and retain more from paper books (e.g., Clinton, 2019; to be clear, the effect is only present when those books are expository. We can certainly keep reading mystery novels on our phones!) Another benefit is that when we re-read the classics every few years, we get to see all of our scribbled notes in the margins, both alerting us to the most important passages and allowing us to experience how we have grown and changed since our last reading.

PRACTICE TIP

Most of us have time to read, but don't *feel like* we have time to read. So, you may need to try one of these two strategies. The first is to set time aside, an hour or two per week. You can call it professional development if that helps you or your family to create time (because it is). The morning is a great time, if you can make that work for your life (not mine, but that's what I hear). Or, you can block out a client hour (especially if you know that you're over-booked and need help to rebalance!). The second idea is to commit to carrying them with you, either as e-books or paperbacks, so that you can use the three- to ten-minute breaks in your day that you usually use for social media for in-depth reading, instead! Also, if you have them with you, you can read during unexpected client no-shows.

CHAPTER 52
STAY IN THE LITERATURE

No one is really asking us to do literature reviews anymore (thank goodness!). But, once we're out of school and we don't *have* to read the research, why should we? Well, because the knowledge half-life (that is, the amount of time it takes for a working professional's competence to practice to fall by 50% because there is new information coming out all the time) of the psychotherapy professions is estimated to be about 7–14 years and getting shorter all the time (Neimeyer et al., 2014). And let's be real, our required amounts and types of continuing education are not making up all of that difference. In general, a few easy ways to stay current on the general trends in our disciplines are to sign up for a *credible* RSS feed or to listen to *credible* podcasts (more on source credibility in the next chapter). Often, our professional associations will offer these, and that's a very reasonable place to start. Let me encourage you to sign up for the feeds, podcasts, magazines, etc. of the "nearby" disciplines as well – when it comes to knowledge about *psychotherapy*, there's less difference between a psychologist and a clinical social worker than we usually imagine.

But we also want to be able to target our new learning not just in the direction of our "niches," but specifically toward what our individual clients need, so that we can improve our therapy week by week, not just year over year. That means that we need access to the current research in a topic-searchable format. Many professional associations also offer an annual package that gives us access to most of the journals in our fields for a reasonable fee. *It is worth it!* Also, signing up for a service like Research Gate is free and can help us get access to full text articles that we might otherwise only find the abstract for.

Plain old Google just won't cut it for us; we have to do better for our clients. So, we need that access to valid, reliable information and we need to use it as at least a first source (if not our only source!), because of the sleeper effect. The *sleeper effect* is a sneaky little social psychology concept that describes how – even though we are more likely to change our opinions or learn from a credible source – over time, we seem to forget where information comes from while remembering the information (e.g., Weiss, 1953; Heinbach et al., 2018). That means that when we get information from a low-credibility source, over time, we might not remember that we aren't supposed to believe it! The terrifying end result of our Google searches might

DOI: 10.4324/9781003125082-58

be that (because we can't not click a clickbait headline) we unintentionally end up giving our clients information or using "treatments" from Reddit or Buzzfeed or Vogue!

PRACTICE TIP

The easiest way to both save time and improve the sources you're gathering information from is just to quit exposing yourself to anything that's not scholarly. At least, quit exposing yourself to anything that's not scholarly that's in the realm of psychology/sociology/counseling/mental health. Oh, also medicine, nutrition, spirituality, and all of the other attendant pieces of information that inform our practices. Unfortunately, that means a ruthless culling of your magazines, your podcasts, and your Netflix list. You can probably keep your comedy specials, but you might have to lose the crime dramas.

CHAPTER 53
KEEP IT CREDIBLE

It would be wrong for me to exhort us all to stay in the research literature and only use credible sources if I didn't also give a quick overview of how to evaluate sources and get the information we need from those research articles. I promise, this will not be a five-minute review of all of Research Methodology squished together with Stats I & II. There are a few quick questions that we can ask ourselves about *any source*, whether it is a research article or some other source, that will get us most of the way toward making sure we're reading something credible, that matters to the client we're thinking about.

First, who is this information about? Any study will have been completed with a specific sample. It's easy enough to skim down to the methodology section and see at least the age, gender, and ethnicity breakdowns of the sample in question. We want to make sure that our client falls into the general categories that are addressed by the study; otherwise, we risk giving them information or delivering treatments that don't actually apply to them. Often, sources that are written for a general audience (e.g., news aggregators, newspapers, magazines, most online sources), don't bother to report the demographic features of a study's sample. Happily, they do often link to the original study. (If they don't, run away from that source!) While you're in the "participants" section, go ahead and check the "n" (the number of people in the study), and make sure that number isn't too small for comfort.

Second, is this information a radical departure from what we already know, or does it basically fit with the rest of the literature on the subject? One clue that an article doesn't have a lot of "fit" with the current body of literature is that the introductory section of the paper will be very short. While that is sometimes just author laziness (and do we want to be taking a lazy author's information to heart?), and often articles from several decades ago have short intros (easy to know by just checking the publication date), that can mean that this author has gone out on a limb and is proposing something that doesn't have much connection to the research that already exists. Also, a quick read of the introduction should give us some anchors into research or theories we're already familiar with.

The third question we should always ask (or maybe it should be the first question!) is "Who stands to make money from this information?" Even with academic sources, it's worthwhile to check. You should be able to scroll to the

DOI: 10.4324/9781003125082-59

end of any article and see the authors' declarations of any potential financial conflict of interest. We should always be very careful in how much credence we give the results of something that could make the author rich (or garner advertisements), regardless of how well put together the study seems. If it's worth following up on, we should be able to find more research done by someone who doesn't have a significant financial interest.

Now, those questions aren't going to do all of the work. We won't be able to find out if the authors of a study artificially created after-the-fact categories so that they could run a statistic that would show significant differences after having run preliminary, non-significant tests unless we can dive into the methodology, instruments, and statistics. And maybe that's too much to ask of ourselves. So, here are two more quick tips. One, keep an eye out for terms like "strong relationship," "large effect size," and "clinically significant difference." Those are specific terms that are probably not being used without the data to back them up. Two, make sure the same or similar information is available in more than one place, from more than one author.

PRACTICE TIP

Teach this to your clients. Use the process to look up something meaningful to them in session to practice it. After that, assign it as homework for them to bring in a source and evaluate it together. (Of course, keep it focused on something related to their therapeutic process!) It can be a little intimidating, but it might be the best long-term gift you can give them, in terms of helping them to move forward independently.

CHAPTER 54
UPDATE YOUR HANDOUTS

Let's just be real. The only reason we might not have some out-of-date client handouts is if we don't have any client handouts. Maybe that's because we have "online resources that we send clients to." (All well and good, as long as we have no technophobes in therapy! And even then, when did we last verify those links? But I digress.)

The point here is that updating psychoeducational handouts can be a series of tiny, useful (dare I say enjoyable?) research projects. They don't need to all be done at once, which is nice. We know that the research we are doing is highly client-oriented and pragmatic. We end with an actual finished product that will kick off a tiny storm of happy fireworks in our neural reward systems (Nakai et al., 2017).

I know, we are tempted to just download something good enough. (Not wanting to kill trees is not an excuse. We can always email handouts to clients or post them on our websites.) Don't give in! Here are the benefits to updating (creating?!) our own handouts:

- We can make them specific to our clients. Even if we see a "general client population," we each tend to see certain kinds of clients. Whether it's word of mouth, our professional reputation, or something in the realm of quantum physics, we do seem to get "runs" of similar clients at times. Tailoring our handouts means that we have specific communication skills instructions on hand for couples, warm and normalizing information about grieving, or gentle and scientific information for parents of transgender teens.
- We can make them specific to our practice. Sure, a pure CBT therapist might be able to find an adequate Thought Record. But if we have an existential streak, where can we expect to find the perfect handout on death anxiety? What about the perfect narrative-style, early childhood experiences worksheet?
- We can make them personal. Clients come to therapy to see *us*. We work hard to form authentic relationships with them, and they risk a lot to build those relationships with us. Giving clients a handout that we have made, that has our personal stamp on it, becomes a therapeutic gift that honors the relationship. Pointing them to a great resource is good, too, but less personal.

 DOI: 10.4324/9781003125082-60

- We can make them "perfect." By perfect here, I mean perfect for us. The National Sleep Foundation obviously has wonderful information on sleep hygiene (NSF, 2020), but my sleep hygiene handout has more than twice the information and emphasizes regular wake times (even though clients hate that) and limiting time in bed awake (because I like to teach classical conditioning). I also don't include information on things like melatonin, diphenhydramine, banana tea, or prescription sleep medication, because – while I'm happy to talk clients through their own decision-making process on those interventions – that's really outside my boundaries of competence. It would be very unusual to find a ready-made handout that already perfectly matched our interests, orientation, clientele, etc.
- We get to own the knowledge. This is perhaps the most important part. It provides an opportunity for us to get into the literature ourselves on things that matter. Then, when we create handouts, we can speak confidently about the information, have answers ready to client questions, and easily troubleshoot any concerns.

PRACTICE TIP

If you are really short on time, and your handouts need to be updated, share the work. If you have access to graduate students or interns, have them do it and you just supervise and provide feedback, before a final edit. That's a win-win! (Interns – ask to do this for indirect hours.)

If you don't, the next best thing is to involve a colleague or two (or maybe your whole office). Get together for a lunch and bring your handouts, digitally or in hard copy. You probably have many similar ones. Pass them around and nominate who has the best current version. Then split up the job of editing the best copies of each one and share them back again to just make final personalizations. Repeat once every couple of years. By the way, that lunch is a "business expense!"

CHAPTER 55
GIVE YOUR KNOWLEDGE AWAY

Why did we get into this field in the first place? (We didn't do it for the money.) Most of us answer this question with something at least partly resembling "helping others" or "giving back." We only need to look as far as our ethics codes to see those values reflected in the field at large – values like beneficence and integrity. Therapy isn't the only way that we can help others; educating each other and the public can be a way to "make the world a better place," too.

We have many professional avenues for giving our knowledge away. Admittedly, things like teaching, presenting, and writing take time. And I know this section is supposed to be about not having much time! But this chapter is about maximizing the benefit of the time we do spend researching and learning (which we're doing anyway just because we're excellent clinicians). Not only can we "pass on the gift," but teaching (and even preparing to teach) helps us learn (Kobayashi, 2019). There are two ways we can capitalize on this: taking the information we've learned recently and turning that into opportunities to teach/present/write or giving ourselves opportunities to teach/present/write in meaningful areas and then doing the research.

First, we can use what we already know. If we've been keeping track of the books we've been reading, or the articles we've been searching, we can turn that knowledge into a gift for our office or our community. When we've bothered to research some new communication strategies for couples and we're implementing them in therapy, why not send a quick email around to the community centers, churches, etc. in our area and ask if they'd be interested in a presentation? If we've just read a great book on using positive reinforcement for behavior change, we could let our contacts at nearby schools know that we'd be happy to share with their teachers. It doesn't even have to be a presentation, per se. What if, as an office, clinicians took turns writing up what they've learned recently in an email newsletter that went out to clients or to each other? And certainly, we don't need to feel limited to these "old school" methods – a YouTube channel or a podcast wouldn't go amiss these days!

Second, we can volunteer for things we wouldn't normally volunteer for. Many of us are more likely to follow through on things (even things we want to do for ourselves) if we're beholden to someone else. So, what kinds

 DOI: 10.4324/9781003125082-61

of things might we be able to commit ourselves to? This doesn't have to be as "big time" as presenting at a professional conference. If the practice has interns, we could ask the group intern supervisor if they'd like a break once a month and use that time to present what we've been learning. We all have an alma mater; we could call up the training director and ask if there are any students who would like to have an informal mentor (whether we're already professionally established or just a few steps ahead). We can send out an email to see if our colleagues would attend a lunch presentation and what topics they might enjoy.

PRACTICE TIP

Doing these things often has additional benefits, beyond the satisfaction of increasing your own knowledge and working meaningfully within your value system. First, task variety and skill variety in your work can reduce your risk of burnout (Zaniboni et al., 2013). (If your boss doesn't want you to do these kinds of things on company time, let them know variety also reduces turnover intentions!) Second, some of these activities will end up getting you more clients. For example, community presentations can be a great source for new referrals.

CHAPTER 56
BONUS LEARNING

Quite a bit of attention is given to understanding the deep cultural dimensions (e.g., time orientation, uncertainty avoidance; Hofstede, 2011) and cultural backgrounds (e.g., gender, age, ethnic background; Sue et al., 2009) of clients, which it absolutely should be. Here, however, I'd like us to think about the individual's particular worldview, and how their internal landscape is populated with many specific references we may not know, like memories of old video games or a book that sparked a career fantasy.

When we engage a client regarding their background, we try to balance encouraging the client to share their specific worldview with doing our own research (so that we don't make them the sole teachers of their cultures and take advantage of their time; Fontes, 2009). We can take the same approach regarding the intricacies of their internal worlds, as well. When we learn that a client relates with a character from a TV show, we can watch an episode. Are they on the path to professional soccer? We can get a basic idea about what that looks like in about ten minutes. Are they struggling with fertility? Do just a little bit of homework. We don't have to watch the whole series, attend pro-am games, or start taking our own basal body temperatures. But we can get our feet wet without too much time or effort. And, the beauty is, we don't even have to get these things totally right. As long as we don't come into the next session like we're experts (which we would never do after such a cursory exposure), we will have opened a very welcoming door for them to educate us, without putting the whole burden on them.

This is wonderful for a few reasons. One, it can help to build the relationship in an authentic way. That is, we can engage with the client on a new, shared experience (rather than trying to connect based on our there-and-then experiences). We can quickly build a shared vocabulary with the client and we may find that "inside jokes" and "conversational shorthand" begin to form. Two, many of clients' outside interests can be used therapeutically, in the form of metaphors, finding strengths, and exploring perspectives. For this reason, one of my favorite client interests is Dungeons and Dragons; it has very cool therapeutic possibilities (e.g., Wright et al., 2020).

This is a really easy and fun kind of learning. We get to use Google and Netflix and YouTube and we don't have to buckle down with a highlighter and a dictionary. This is not "taking our clients home with us." What I'm describing is not stressing about work, planning interventions, or worrying

DOI: 10.4324/9781003125082-62

about clients. It is simply harnessing that intrinsic curiosity we tend to have in a way that happens to benefit clients, and that probably only takes the time we would normally spend browsing and choosing a show to watch or reading more news than is really good for us.

PRACTICE TIP

This isn't something you need to do for every client, every week. But if you don't have time to occasionally learn something new outside of session for a client, you might be overloaded. That might mean having too many clients, so that you just actually don't have time. Or, it might mean having too high of a clinical stress load, so that when you're not in session, you're too busy doing self-care just to make it to the next day.

CHAPTER 57
KEEP A JOURNAL

Here's a different kind of very valuable knowledge building: self-knowledge. Self-reflection is one of the core features of *clinical expertise*, which itself is a core part of evidence-based practice and involves reflecting on our own "experience, knowledge, hypotheses, inferences, emotional reactions, and behaviors" and then using that to improve our delivery of services and grow as therapists (APA, 2007). Journaling can be a way for us to accomplish this kind of additional learning, especially if we use it to reflect on our clients and work (e.g., Cook et al., 2018), and it's helpful across the board, from the earliest practicum classes to the most seasoned clinicians, because it grows with us.

Another useful type of journaling is expressive writing. *Expressive writing* (i.e., writing about our deepest thoughts and feelings, usually for 15–20 minutes per day; Pennebaker & Beall, 1986) has a number of self-reflective properties. It helps us to construct meaningful narratives, decreases emotional reactivity, and promotes self-distancing (Park et al., 2016). That is, expressive writing helps us to sort through our experiences, process the emotions associated with them, begin to understand some of the cause-and-effect patterns, and to think about situations in a way that has more perspective. That's reason enough for us to spend a little time journaling about difficult client experiences, at the very least!

Expressive writing is also incredibly well documented as a therapeutic strategy and we know we must take care of ourselves physically and emotionally if we're going to do good therapeutic work. There are demonstrated benefits of this kind of journaling for physical health functioning (e.g., improved immune functioning) and mental/emotional health functioning (e.g., trauma resolution, reduction in depressive symptoms; Pennebaker, 2003). And we don't even have to write if we don't want to; similar benefits are found from talking aloud. While it would be wonderful to have a quiet half hour alone every night to self-reflect, if we need to hold a little case conference out loud in the car during our commute, so be it. (Also, plants are wonderful targets for our self-disclosure – they are completely non-judgmental, and they grow better when we talk to them!)

Another option might be to start a dream journal. We can let go of the idea that dreamwork is just an old psychoanalytic technique. There are important elements to dreams that are agreed on across theories and even in

139 DOI: 10.4324/9781003125082-63

modern neurological research: Dreams deal with matters that are important to us and involve high-level intrapersonal communication (e.g., symbol use, pattern recognition, holism; Vedfelt, 2020). Every main theoretical orientation has a method for doing dreamwork, including psychodynamic (e.g., Jung, 1974), existential–experiential (Gendlin, 1986; Perls, 1969), cognitive (Freeman & White, 2004), and mixed models (e.g., Hill, 2019). All of them agree that writing down dreams is the beginning of deriving meaning from them.

Can I make a suggestion if you're considering dream journaling? Don't get focused on lucid dreaming. For one thing, it doesn't seem to promote personal growth (Konkoly & Burke, 2019). But mostly, we spend our whole waking lives listening to our conscious minds and only get these few precious hours to hear from our subconscious minds. Why would we want to spoil that?

PRACTICE TIP

If you're still not convinced that journaling is worth the time, ask yourself when the last time was that you assigned journaling as a homework for a client. This is a wonderful opportunity to "practice what you preach," and you get to do it in exactly your own way, on your own timeline, and still reap the benefits.

CHAPTER 58
BE DELIBERATE

When is the last time you watched a video of your own therapy session? Honestly, most of us don't do it much or at all after we're out of supervision. Some of us haven't engaged in something like that for a long time. Some programs didn't emphasize it very much, so we never got comfortable. Some of us might even have had mostly online training, and been able to "escape" being directly observed by a supervisor in the moment, or been able to artfully choose which therapy submissions were reviewed.

But the truth is, simple practice doesn't make perfect (Miller et al., 2020). We know this – it's why we have clients practice social situations in session and give them feedback, make adjustments to their homework, and correct their distorted thinking. Specifically for therapists, not only do we not get better with the passage of time and "experience," all things being equal, we may get worse (Goldberg et al., 2016)! There's also evidence that trainees under supervision have better client outcomes than licensed professionals (Lambert et al., 2003; Minami et al., 2009), and while the jury may be out on why, it's probably a better bet that it has something to do with intentionally working on skills in supervision than it does with professional naiveté.

Deliberate practice (Lehmann & Ericsson, 1997; Miller et al., 2020) is a relatively new model of skills development with four key parts: individualized learning objectives, use of a coach, feedback, and successive refinement through repetition. Choosing an individualized learning objective means identifying an area in which our work needs improvement *that we are invested in improving* and that is at the right level of challenge for us. Though we may not like it very much, an external coach is more effective than being our own coach (and less for the encouragement than specific instruction and corrective feedback, frankly). That feedback works best when it is timely, specific, goal-oriented, and personalized. It allows for successive refinement because each iteration of practice can use the new feedback for improvement.

Though deliberate practice regarding therapy models or techniques may not benefit us as much as making sure that the other common factors are in place (Miller et al., 2020), improving (and perhaps even just maintaining) our skills has an important function in any performance-based career. In our case, that may mean doing deliberate practice to improve our work at the common factors level (e.g., attentive listening) or on specific techniques (e.g.,

DOI: 10.4324/9781003125082-64

Socratic dialogue). Yes, doing this kind of thing takes *extra* time, and it may seem as if I'm violating the principle of this section of the book (again!). Really, though, we're *wasting* most of our therapy time if we aren't engaging with our process in this way.

Admittedly, this is scary for many of us. Here are a few ways to increase our bravery, and maybe our willingness to go the distance on this.

- It's ok to be uncomfortable. We need to remember that feeling nervous and uncomfortable is natural (Biswas-Diener, 2012). No one likes corrective feedback. But this isn't really about us – it's about our clients. And it's not about doing things wrong, it's just about doing things better. We can judge ourselves *positively* as excellent, caring, committed practitioners because we're doing this.
- Do it yourself. Many of us are harder on ourselves than our supervisors ever were. We may be able to access much of the benefit of deliberate practice alone, especially if it's been a long time since we've watched ourselves. (But if you feel wildly brave, you could do this with a partner, or in a group setting, and really maximize the "coach" portion of the procedure!)
- Take it slow. I'm not suggesting that we need to do all of this, or all of this at once. Harnessing even one of these, like intentional goal setting, could help us improve our therapy.

PRACTICE TIP

The first step to doing something like this is to add it to your informed consent document. It doesn't commit you to actually *doing it*, it just helps you take advantage of your moment of bravery (or curiosity!) when it arises. Here's an example of the kind of language you might add:

> "Because I believe in continual professional development, at times, I may video- or audio-record our sessions so that I may review them afterward. This is only used as a tool to help me keep learning and growing as a professional and to provide you with the best possible treatment. I will keep these recordings in a protected place, and I will delete/destroy them within seven days."

CHAPTER 59
SHARE THE LOAD

If you work in a group practice, you may have a readily available group to share the "burden" of learning with. If you don't, it may take a little more work to create one, but you'll be glad you did. Pretty much everyone in this field wants to learn more and wishes they had more time, so it's relatively easy to find other people who would be interested in the kinds of ventures I'm going to suggest here. If going to the gym with a friend increases adherence to an exercise program (and it does; Dalle Grave et al., 2010), I think it's safe to assume it can help us with our learning goals as well.

- Continuing education parties: When you want to do an online or video-based continuing education, invite your work friends to do it with you. Absolutely call this a party, even if you do it at the office during a lunch hour. One of the best parts of sharing continuing education videos is that you can usually share most of the cost. Of course, feel free to be the hero and pick up the tab (it's typically the same cost as you'd be paying alone, anyway). Wine discouraged (at least if you're at work!).
- Research email group: This isn't a flashy idea, but it can be wildly effective and it's really easy. Just set up an email list with likeminded knowledge-seekers and make an arrangement that whenever one of you goes looking for a therapy-related article, you'll pass it on to the rest. (Bonus if you highlight the items from Chapter 53!) Not only will you all benefit from each other's time spent researching, you'll probably be more likely to go hunting up a good study if you know you won't be the only one who benefits. Wine optional.
- Summary book clubs: This is the place to read all of those new topic-specific books that are written for the general population and that you may want to recommend to clients. (You know, the ones I discouraged you from reading in Chapter 51.) Plan to meet every one to three months and have *everyone choose a different book*. The bigger this group is, the better! Do a great job reading your book. Then, spend a couple of hours together and have everyone share a summary of their book, including clients it seems appropriate/not appropriate for. If you have an eight-person group, and you meet every two months, that's six books you've read and 42 books you can get a good handle on each year! Wine recommended.

DOI: 10.4324/9781003125082-65

PRACTICE TIP

Even though you may be getting great recommendations from that book club, please don't recommend books to clients that you haven't read yourself! Just let the group guide you to which books you should follow up on. The primary reason for this is because clients are vulnerable, and there may be things in a book you haven't read that could hurt them – for example, stories that bring up their traumas when they aren't prepared, teaching that's contrary to the therapeutic work that undermines their progress, and frankly, just bad advice or stuff that's not true! As far as the client is concerned, you take responsibility for the information in that book, because you recommended it. So, that can really damage your credibility. Also, it's just not their job. Would you want to pay your physician to have them tell you, "I've heard of a book about your condition, but I haven't read it. You should, though. Oh, and let me know what you think of it, too?"

CHAPTER 60
CHOOSE YOUR COMPANIONS WISELY

I believe that the best gift we can give to ourselves (and each other) as therapists is to develop a consultation partnership. By this I mean an ongoing, regularly scheduled meeting with a colleague we respect and enjoy, to discuss cases, ethical dilemmas, new learnings, and – if we're lucky – maybe even some personal concerns.

Continually available clinical supervision leads to greater personal growth and protection against burnout (Linley & Joseph, 2007). And what is consultation but a less formal, more enjoyable kind of co-supervision experience without a difficult power differential? While it doesn't replace formal training and supervision when we want to learn a new skill or type of therapy, it can be a good place to gently expand our boundaries of competence. If we have a really trusting relationship, the benefits are even better – we never have to be afraid of processing difficult countertransference, or worry about mentioning an ethical dilemma, and it might even save us some of the cost of our own therapy.

Here are some ideas about how to make the most of this relationship:

- Who to choose? While there is more research about consultation groups, I'd like to suggest the value of a consultation *partner*. It's easier to find someone who we truly get along with, to create a trusting relationship, to work out schedules for meeting, and to get enough time to talk. (That's quite important for maximizing the time. In a larger, group setting, these meetings often feel like a waste of time because of a couple monopolizers or the devolution of the conversation.) In a perfect world, we might have two of these relationships – one with a person who is similar to us in terms of therapeutic style/theoretical orientation and one with someone who is quite different. In this way, everyone gets to maximize the opportunity for growth in both depth and breadth.

- When to do it? It may sound strange, but we should schedule these meetings for about twice as often as we think we should. That's mostly just for practical purposes. There will be times that someone needs to miss, and it makes it easier than rescheduling. Also, we won't get the growth benefit if we don't meet often enough (just the same way we know that clients don't typically do effective work when they only come in once a month). The right frequency might be different for each of us, and

 DOI: 10.4324/9781003125082-66

depend on things like how much support we get in the office (great office support may mean less often is ok), how many clients we have (more clients should probably mean higher frequency, by the way, not a reason to meet less), or client turnover (if we only keep clients for few weeks, we need to meet more often or we won't get any consultation in about them before they're gone).

- How to go about it? Largely, this is a personal question, and we can structure this however we like, as long as we do basic things like protect client confidentiality. A couple of things can help when it comes to doing great case consultations. First, every couple of months, we should schedule a special meeting to talk about the clients we usually don't talk about. Whether that's a countertransference reaction (so that we find those clients "boring" or "forget" about them) or we just have such a good handle on them that they feel "easy," a second perspective can be really helpful (Hayes et al., 2018). Second, playing "devil's advocate" or defense/prosecution with each case helps us stretch our conceptualizations and avoid groupthink (Janis, 1972).

PRACTICE TIP

If you're able to, you might want to choose your consultation partners from outside your office (Thomas, 2010). While it might be more convenient (and hopefully, lots of day-to-day consultation continues to happen in the office), a number of things make it more appealing to make this an outside relationship. You get the "special factor" (kind of like the sacred space of therapy), and you'll be less likely to try to cram it into a lunch hour or into two minutes between clients. You get to avoid the natural competitiveness of the office, and you don't have to worry about gossip or reputation, which makes it a great deal safer. Also, if at some point you decide to move on, there are fewer social/professional repercussions.

REFERENCES

Adler, A. (1931/2014). *What life could mean to you (3rd ed)*. Oneworld Publications.

American Psychological Association, Presidential Task Force on Evidence-Based Practice. (2006). Evidence-based practice in psychology. *American Psychologist, 61*(4), 271–285. https://doi.org/10.1037/0003-066X.61.4.271

Biswas-Diener, R. (2012). *The courage quotient: How science can make you braver*. Jossey-Bass

Clinton, V. (2019). Reading from paper compared to screens: A systematic review and meta-analysis. *Journal of Research in Reading, 42*(2), 288325.

Cook, J. M., Simiola, V., McCarthy, E., Ellis, A., & Stirman, S. W. (2018). Use of reflective journaling to understand decision making regarding two evidence-based psychotherapies for PTSD: Practice implications. *Practice Innovations, 3*(3), 153–167. https://doi.org/10.1037/pri0000070

Dalle Grave, R., Calugi, S., Centis, E., El Ghoch, M., & Marchesini, G. (2011). Cognitive-behavioral strategies to increase the adherence to exercise in the management of obesity. *Journal of obesity.* https://doi.org/10.1155/2011/348293

Fontes, L. A. (2009). *Interviewing clients across cultures: A practitioner's guide*. Guilford Press.

Freeman, A., & White, B. (2004). Dreams and the dream image: Using dreams in cognitive therapy. In R. I. Rosner, W. J. Lyddon, & A. Freeman (Eds.), *Cognitive therapy and dreams* (pp. 69–87). Springer Publishing Co.

Gendlin, E. T. (1986). *Let your body interpret your dreams*. Chiron Publications.

Goldberg, S. B., Rousmaniere, T., Miller, S. D., Whipple, J., Nielsen, S. L., Hoyt, W. T., & Wampold, B. E. (2016). Do psychotherapists improve with time and experience? A longitudinal analysis of outcomes in a clinical setting. *Journal of Counseling Psychology, 63*(1), 1–11. https://doi.org/10.1037/cou0000131

Hayes, J. A., Gelso, C. J., Goldberg, S., & Kivlighan, D. M. (2018). Countertransference management and effective psychotherapy: Meta-analytic findings. *Psychotherapy, 55*(4), 496–507. https://doi.org/10.1037/pst0000189

Heinbach, D., Ziegele, M., & Quiring, O. (2018). Sleeper effect from below: Long-term effects of source credibility and user comments on the persuasiveness of news articles. *New Media & Society, 20*(12), 4765–4786. https://doi.org/10.1177/1461444818784472

Hill, C. E. (2019). The cognitive-experiential dream model (CEDM). In R. J. Hoss & R. P. Gongloff (Eds.), *Dreams: Understanding Biology, Psychology, and Culture* (pp. 571–575). Greenwood Press/ABC-CLIO.

Hofstede, G. (2011). Dimensionalizing cultures: The Hofstede model in context. *Online Readings in Psychology and Culture, 2*(1). https://doi.org/10.9707/2307-0919.1014

Janis, I. L. (1972). *Victims of groupthink: A psychological study of foreign-policy decisions and fiascoes.* Houghton Mifflin.

Jung, C. G. (1974). *Dreams* (trans. R.F.C. Hull). Princeton University Press

Kobayashi, K. (2019). Learning by preparing-to-teach and teaching: A meta-analysis. *Japanese Psychological Research, 61*(3), 192–203. https://doi.org/10.1111/jpr.12221

Konkoly, K., & Burke, C. T. (2019). Can learning to lucid dream promote personal growth? *Dreaming, 29*(2), 113–126. https://doi.org/10.1037/drm000010

Lehmann, A. C., & Ericsson, K. A. (1997). Research on expert performance and deliberate practice: Implications for the education of amateur musicians and music students. *Psychomusicology: A Journal of Research in Music Cognition, 16*(1–2), 40–58. https://doi.org/10.1037/h0094068

Linley, P. A., & Joseph, S. (2007). Therapy work and therapists' positive and negative well-being. *Journal of Social and Clinical Psychology, 26*(3), 385–403.

Miller, S. D., Hubble, M. A., & Chow, D. (2020). What is (and is not) deliberate practice? In S. D. Miller, M. A. Hubble, & D. Chow, Better results: *Using deliberate practice to improve therapeutic effectiveness* (pp. 31–39). American Psychological Association. https://doi.org/10.1037/0000191-004

Minami, T., Davies, D. R., Tierney, S. C., Bettmann, J. E., McAward, S. M., Averill, L. A., ... Wampold, B. E. (2009). Preliminary evidence on the effectiveness of psychological treatments delivered at a university counseling center. *Journal of Counseling Psychology, 56*, 309–320. http://dx.doi.org/10.1037/a0015398

National Sleep Foundation. (2020). *Sleep hygiene.* Retrieved from https://www.sleepfoundation.org/articles/sleep-hygiene

Nakai, T., Nakatani, H., Hosoda, C., Nonaka, Y., & Okanoya, K. (2017). Sense of accomplishment is modulated by a proper level of instruction and represented in the brain reward system. *PloS one, 12*(1), e0168661. https://doi.org/10.1371/journal.pone.0168661

Neimeyer, G. J., Taylor, J. M., Rozensky, R. H., & Cox, D. R. (2014). The diminishing durability of knowledge in professional psychology: A second look at specializations. *Professional Psychology: Research and Practice, 45*(2), 92–98. https://doi.org/10.1037/a0036176

Park, J., Ayduk, Ö., & Kross, E. (2016). Stepping back to move forward: Expressive writing promotes self-distancing. *Emotion, 16*(3), 349–364. https://doi.org/10.1037/emo0000121

Pennebaker, J. W. (2003). Writing about emotional experiences as a therapeutic process. In P. Salovey & A. J. Rothman (Eds.), Key readings in social psychology. *Social psychology of health* (pp. 362–368). Psychology Press.

Pennebaker, J. W., & Beall, S. K. (1986). Confronting a traumatic event: Toward an understanding of inhibition and disease. *Journal of Abnormal Psychology, 95*(3), 274–81. doi:10.1037/0021–843x.95.3.27

Perls, F. S. (1969). *Gestalt therapy verbatim.* Real People Press.

Ranganathan, P., Pramesh, C. S., & Buyse, M. (2015). Common pitfalls in statistical analysis: Clinical versus statistical significance. *Perspectives in clinical research, 6*(3), 169–170. https://doi.org/10.4103/2229-3485.159943

Rogers, C.R. (1961). *On becoming a person.* Houghton Mifflin.

Sue, S., Zane, N., Nagayama Hall, G. C., & Berger, L. (2009). The case for cultural competency in psychotherapeutic interventions. *Annual Review of Psychology, 60*, 525–548. doi: 10.1146/annurev.psych.60.110707.163651

Thomas, J. T. (2010). Consultation and supervision groups. In J. T. Thomas, *The ethics of supervision and consultation: Practical guidance for mental health professionals* (pp. 163–181). American Psychological Association. https://doi.org/10.1037/12078-007

Vedfelt, O. (2020). Integration versus conflict between schools of dream theory and dreamwork: Integrating the psychological core qualities of dreams with the contemporary knowledge of the dreaming brain. *The Journal of Analytical Psychology, 65*(1), 88–115. https://doi.org/10.1111/1468-5922.12574

Vincent, J. (2016). Students' use of paper and pen versus digital media in university environments for writing and reading – a cross-cultural exploration. *Journal of Print Media and Media Technology Research, 5*(2), 97–106.

Weiss, W. (1953). A "sleeper" effect in opinion change. *The Journal of Abnormal and Social Psychology, 48*(2), 173–180. https://doi.org/10.1037/h0063200

Wright, J. C., Weissglass, D. E., & Casey, V. (2020). Imaginative role-playing as a medium for moral development: Dungeons & Dragons provides moral training. *Journal of Humanistic Psychology, 60*(1), 99–129. https://doi.org/10.1177/0022167816686263

Zaniboni, S., Truxillo, D. M., & Fraccaroli, F. (2013). Differential effects of task variety and skill variety on burnout and turnover intentions for older and younger workers. *European Journal of Work and Organizational Psychology, 22*(3), 306–317. https://doi.org/10.1080/1359432X.2013.782288

Ethics for Practice (Not Just the School Stuff)

This is a tough profession in some ways. It's professional and intimate; structured and messy. We have ethical issues that no other profession has, and – for reasons passing understanding – training programs don't always cover all of the difficult things. Or manage a nuanced view when they do cover difficult things. This section isn't going to cover much about ethics codes and laws, partly because there is too much slight (but important!) variation across states and disciplines, but also because I know you already know that stuff. Instead, we'll look at some of the very commonly experienced, but less commonly discussed ethical issues in practice.

CHAPTER 61
MAKE MISTAKES AND ADMIT THEM

We are going to be less than perfect, and understanding that is the foundation of any discussion of ethics, so let's just go ahead and begin with the *therapeutic apology*. If we haven't said "I'm sorry" to a client this month and meant it, we might need to check in with ourselves. In real relationships, we blow it sometimes. So, if we're having authentic, therapeutic relationships with clients, apologizing will be a part of the deal. Not only is it an important part of a real relationship, it models something very important for clients, too – apologizing is indicative of low shame, appropriate guilt, and high empathy (all good things!; Howell et al., 2012). Here are some thoughts about how to apologize to clients.

- Recognize when to apologize
  - When we have violated part of the explicit or implicit contract
    - Running late, mistaken charges, delays in providing requested documentation, unclear communication, etc.
  - When we haven't honored clients well
    - Made an assumption, not listened well, gotten distracted, interrupted, followed our own agenda, etc.
  - When we made a mistake we shouldn't have made
    - Forgot to check their homework, started into a stock metaphor we often use but then realize it's not well tailored to this particular client, overstepped a boundary, pushed too hard that day
    - Note: When we make a mistake that was reasonable at the time, and not due to a lack of knowledge/ethics/conscientiousness on our part, we can just explain it without apologizing. This is *excellent* modeling!
- Only apologize for things we have control over (i.e., our own *behavior*)
  - Avoid the "habitual apology." That's when we say "I'm sorry" when no offense actually occurred.
    - "I'm sorry (for taking up space in the hallway because I have a body and walk at the same time as you which is obviously not my fault)"
    - "I'm sorry (because you were speaking very softly and the air conditioner is loud so I couldn't hear you which is obviously not my fault)"

DOI: 10.4324/9781003125082-68

- Resist the urge to apologize just because they don't like something (e.g., for the email/contact policy, for ending session on time, experiencing difficult feelings, referring them appropriately)
  - Apologize for what we *did*, not for what *happened.*
    - NO: "I'm sorry we had a misunderstanding just then."
    - YES: "I'm sorry I wasn't listening well just then and assumed incorrectly."
  - Two exceptions to this rule:
    - Go ahead and say, "I'm so sorry to hear that …" when something unfortunate has happened to a client. Even though sorry isn't exactly the right word, that's so culturally established that if we *don't* say it, the moment will be really weird, and that moment is also usually a moment when we need to not be weird, and really be attentive and present, and not explaining weird cultural, linguistic idiosyncrasies.
    - Go ahead and apologize if the administrative staff, office management/maintenance people, etc. have done something unpleasant or insensitive. The client often sort of sees them as an extension of us.
- Apologize WELL.
  - No beating around the bush; we need to be specific and own it.
    - "I'm sorry for getting distracted just then." "I'm sorry for not listening well." "I'm sorry for running late today."
  - No passive aggression. We should avoid giving our "reasons," unless we're sure they're really reasons (not excuses, which are things we say to reduce our responsibility) *and* the reason is actually important to the process. In that case, be specific.
    - NO: "I'm sorry for getting distracted just then. I have a lot going on personally right now." (excuse)
    - YES: "I'm sorry for getting distracted just then. Will you repeat that?"
    - YES: "I'm sorry for getting distracted just then. What happened was that what you said really struck a chord with me around grief, and I'm wondering now if or how grief is playing a role for you?"
  - Add what we're planning to *do* about it.
    - "You have my full attention now." "Can we go back and you can describe it to me again so that I can understand better?" "I'm going to make sure I adjust your fee for the missed time today."
    - Oh, and then do that.

PRACTICE TIP

When we have rightly made an apology, we need to follow up. In your next session, even if it's uncomfortable, *bring it back up*. Not to apologize again, but to check in that the apology was heard and that any action that was needed because of the offending behavior has been taken care of. Honestly, they're quite likely to say something like "Oh, no worries" or "It doesn't matter." So, follow up on that with something like "Thanks for your patience" or "You do matter to me, so I just wanted to let you know."

CHAPTER 62
WHEN THEY DON'T CARE
AS MUCH AS WE DO

Clients can be weird sometimes. They seem to think it's ok to continue talking about their personal stuff out in the waiting room, even though other people are definitely listening – with interest. They see us at the grocery store and approach us, even though they're with their families and we're with ours. They invite us to join their book clubs. (Though, let's be real, we probably walked into this last one with some kind of unnecessary self-disclosure.) Clients don't always have the same feelings as we do about things like boundaries and confidentiality, even though we discussed it in the beginning of therapy. We often want (or legally need!) to protect them more than they want to be protected.

There are two main ways that we can react when clients don't join with us in managing important issues like these (or really any issues that we disagree on). This is especially true when they "know better," which they usually do. First, it's easy to get frustrated with them. Follow that to its unmitigated conclusion and we're going to end up with rapport breakage. Second, it's easy to shrug and say to ourselves, "Well, therapy is about them; if they don't care, I don't need to." Obviously, neither of these is a great idea.

So, what can we do differently? *Confront*.
Wait, what? Didn't you just say we didn't want to break rapport?
Yes, yes, I did.

Therapeutic confrontation is not what it sounds like. It's not even what you may have been taught. It's definitely not anything that reminds you of Dr. Phil, which is something like a hostile way of calling people out on their bad decisions or stupidity. And it's not "carefrontation" (e.g., Post & Neimark, 2007), which is like a nicer way of calling people out on their bad decisions or stupidity. *Therapeutic confrontation* is about recognizing our own confusion about two (or more) things in seeming conflict and bringing them forward to be addressed by our client.

First things first – it has to be legitimate confusion. If we haven't adopted a position of true confusion and curiosity, it's going to come out as patronizing or manipulative. The other benefit to making sure we're truly confused and curious is that it helps us notice the assumptions we may have been making and put them aside, so that we can interact with what is truly

DOI: 10.4324/9781003125082-69

present for the client. If we assume they don't care about their confidentiality or our boundaries, even if we approach it very gently, the best we're going to get is a mild teaching moment.

Instead, we might say something like "I'm finding myself confused about something. On the one hand, you have these really important things to say in therapy that I know you want time to process, and on the other hand, it seems like they always come out at the very end, or even in the waiting room, and then you don't get to have the time and privacy you deserve. Can you help me puzzle this out?" Possibly the client's answer is "I don't care about other people hearing my very personal business and I have poor time management skills." That answer is probably what we would be addressing if we gave a little psychoeducation about confidentiality or a little passive-aggressive punishment in the form of "reminders about the time."

But that's probably not their answer. Do they have difficulty warming up in session? Are we spending too long addressing their homework and so they run out of time? Are they actually afraid to process and so they leave it for the end so they can escape? Are they jealous for our time and attention? Do they want to be seen or heard by others? Do they feel like therapy is really expensive and they're trying to eke out every moment's worth? We don't know, and we can't interact with what's really going on unless we bring up the conflict with curiosity.

PRACTICE TIP

This type of confrontation is good for all kinds of therapeutic situations. Consider the client who says they really want to quit drinking but – despite all appearances of doing good work in therapy – has not reduced their drinking. A therapeutic confrontation might be "I'm sort of struggling to understand. I know on the one hand you definitely want to reduce your drinking and you've been making progress around that in session. At the same time, it seems like out of session, that same kind of progress isn't happening. What do you think might be going on?" Then, we can get at real barriers, resistance, and difficulties, rather than relying on exhortation and teaching.

CHAPTER 63
SEXUAL ATTRACTION
(FROM CLIENTS)

Clients having sexual attraction for their therapists is normal, common, and – depending on how psychoanalytically inclined you are – maybe even good (Kernberg, 1995; Reich, 1933). Also, it's happening whether we believe it is or not, whether we notice it is or not. As with most things, it's better to be aware of it than not be aware of it, because then we can handle it better. (And as we'll see in Chapter 68 – we need to be able to handle it well!)

Why does this happen? One reason is because we are, generally speaking, both healthy and nice. This means people are quite likely to be interpersonally attracted to us. *Interpersonal attraction* is a very broad construct, which may include sexual attraction but also includes any way that we are likely to turn toward someone, such as respect, liking, or perceived similarity. It's the basis for all types of social influence, including that expert power that we've talked about so much (French & Raven, 1959). Interpersonal attraction can set the stage for sexual attraction.

Another reason is because what we do is really intimate, and many people aren't good at separating emotional intimacy from physical intimacy. So, clients may begin to feel romantically attracted to us because it is safe to share their deep thoughts and feelings or because we talk openly about topics like sex and relationships that they aren't used to talking about.

Whether it is because clients are generally becoming healthier (because it is healthy to be attracted to healthy people!) or because the therapy process really helps clients to work through the fixations of their sexual energies, it's worth treating the attraction as something that might not be pathological in nature.

So, how do we handle this? Aside from setting our boundaries early and keeping them (which we definitely already know!), here are a couple of thoughts:

- Err on the side of not leading anyone on. We can argue out in the world that people should not mistake us for having sexual interest just because we are wearing short pencil skirts or putting hands on shoulders. In the therapy room, we can take responsibility for dressing and behaving in ways that are beyond reproach and leave no room for misinterpretation.

DOI: 10.4324/9781003125082-70

- Explain what's happening when it comes up. Often, all clients need is for it to be normalized. Then, they don't need to be worried about it because we will hold our clear boundaries and they also don't need to feel rejected. It often wanes after they've said it out loud and we've responded well.
- Process it. That can feel awkward or uncomfortable, but we can't be afraid to process it. Would we avoid processing it when a client is angry or disappointed with us? No! This needs to happen whether the client has brought it up (e.g., "umm ... I had a weird dream about us ... ") or if they are expressing sexual interest nonverbally (e.g., moving closer to us, bringing up provocative topics, finding reasons to "accidentally" touch us).

But yes, sometimes we do all of this and it's still a problem. And if it's getting in the way of the client's work, we may have to refer.

It's good to have a little speech already prepared, just like we do for going through the basics of informed consent, so the conversation about sexual attraction can happen more easily. If they bring it up overtly, this is quite straightforward. Something like "I hear that you're noticing some attraction towards me, and that it's noticeable enough that you brought it up. Thank you for doing that. It's very common for clients to have some attraction for their therapists because what we do is very intimate. It's just a different kind of intimacy than people are used to. You might find that it goes away now that you've told me, or that it diminishes more slowly over the course of therapy. Since there's no possibility that we're actually going to become romantically involved, let's both just keep an eye on it and make sure it's not getting in the way."

PRACTICE TIP

If they don't bring it up overtly, you can use basically the same info, but start it with something like "I've noticed that you keep bringing up very provocative topics, and that is sometimes a sign that clients are feeling some attraction ..." or "I've noticed that you've brushed your shoulder up against mine when you've left session these last two times. I don't know if that's because you're feeling some attraction, but if so ..." Then just give your little speech *anyway* (this is why it's crucial for it to be a short, well-practiced speech!). Then it's ok to drop the subject for now if they want to or if they deny it.

CHAPTER 64
SEXUAL ATTRACTION (TO CLIENTS)

Let's just go ahead and say it – this happens, too. If we pretend it never happens, we're much more at risk for not handling it appropriately (Pope & Vasquez, 2011). And the answer is not always "just refer them out," even if that seems like the safest option. We need to consider whether and how our feelings might be managed, and the damage it might do to our clients for us to "send them away."

There seem to be three main times that therapists experience sexual attraction or romantic feelings towards clients. The first is when the client first walks in the door and they are H-O-T. Statistically speaking, it just has to happen sometimes that we get a new client who is objectively attractive or who meets our personal definition of "dreamy." Often, there isn't that much to worry about in these instances; by the end of the intake session, the initial attraction has often waned. This happens because our assessment of the client's physical attractiveness diminishes as we recognize that we are not very attracted to their personalities or because we have spent a little time in the therapist role and imagined the work that will ensue, which can also dampen an initial attraction.

The second time that this happens is with clients who didn't seem that attractive to start with, but they seem to be getting more and more interesting, enjoyable, and attractive over the course of therapy. What may be going on in these circumstances is that our clients are getting *healthier*. This can actually be a clue that they are growing well and maybe even getting ready to terminate therapy. So, if we notice this and can allow it to give us information and help them transition out, that's not only not a problem, it might be really great. (If the idea of them terminating sounds awful and we really really really want them to stay, it may be more the next type!) Note that this can happen in non-sexual ways, too; for example, feeling as if we wish we could be friends with clients outside of session or after therapy is concluded.

The third time we might be attracted to clients is (dun-dun-*dun*) countertransference. Whether we conceptualize countertransference in the deeply psychoanalytic way (e.g., clients elicit unconscious reactions from us because they are displaying the undertones of a disordered personality or – if we're not well analyzed ourselves, they represent an object from our past that we have unresolved conflicts with) or in the more contemporary way (e.g., our thoughts and emotions toward the client may be more about ourselves and not really about what's happening in therapy), we will need to work on this kind of attraction. That might best be done in a supervision relationship, consultation relationship, or in our own therapy.

This is the kind of attraction that is most likely to need to result in referral (but it's still sort of unfair, because it's not the client's fault). So, if it is possible to work on our thoughts and feelings outside of the session (not "just handle our emotions alone" – that's a dangerous thinking trap!), maintaining the therapeutic relationship is an option that should be considered, rather than outright, immediate referral. While we may realize that we need deep or intensive therapy to really handle some countertransference issues (not just erotic ones, by the way), one very pragmatic way of handling this kind of attraction (at least initially) is Acceptance and Commitment Therapy (Blonna, 2014). The emphasis on mindfully recognizing thoughts as thoughts (not as truth, and not as something requiring action) along with the focus on acting in accordance with values can go a long way toward making the situation more comfortable for us and more fair and helpful for our clients.

PRACTICE TIP

We simply have to have a safe place for consultation (see Chapter 60). A great consultation relationship means that you won't be nervous about admitting attraction to a client, which is the first step to handling it ethically. Your consultation partner can help you figure out if you have an unmet childhood need for being wanted and liked or if this client just happens to wear the same cologne as your ex. They can also help recognize some of the factors that might contribute to taking attraction into an inappropriate space (like underlying impulsivity or substance use) or see the early warning signs (like changes in the way you talk about or avoid talking about a specific client).

CHAPTER 65
PERFORMANCE RANGE VS. PRACTICE RANGE

In performance professions (e.g., vocals, dance, surgery) there is always a difference between our practice range and our performance range. No performer goes out on stage and tries to sing for an audience a song that hits both the highest note and lowest note they're capable of squeezing out on their best day, well hydrated and vocally rested. No dancer who can barely pull off a triple pirouette intentionally choreographs one into a performance piece. And no surgeon goes into surgery alone when they've just learned a new procedure. So, why do we do that, all the time?

Training and practice are where we stretch ourselves – extending our range, improving our vibrato, getting stronger and more flexible, learning and finessing new skills, etc. Ostensibly, we do this all until these new skills have become part of our *performance range* – what we can do comfortably, competently, and reliably – before we take those skills out on stage.

There's a little bit of a language issue here, because we talk about the "practice" of therapy (not the "performance" of therapy) even though it's much closer to the latter. We are performing our therapy skills when we are in session with clients … that's not a practice space. And if we blow it, it's not just an embarrassing performance – it can have very serious consequences, more like those in a "surgical theater" than an opera house. And here's something terrifying: Many of us – after we're out of our training programs and internships – never truly have a practice space again.

That's all an introduction to the idea that our boundaries of competence are probably better described as what's in our performance range than what's in our practice range. *Competence* may be defined as "the habitual and judicious use of communication, knowledge, technical skills, clinical reasoning, emotions, values, and reflection in daily practice for the benefit of the individual and community being served" (Epstein & Hundert, 2002). Working within our boundaries of competence maximizes our chances of helping clients make positive changes; going beyond our areas of competence increases the chance for harm. For example, we may fail to provide the most appropriate treatment or not recognize potentially risky or dangerous situations (Nagy, 2011).

What falls inside our *boundaries of competence* is usually based on education, training, and supervision (e.g., APA, 2017), which implies that we have

DOI: 10.4324/9781003125082-72

practiced enough and gotten enough feedback through supervision that we have moved those new skills out of our practice range. It's possible that I'm going to ruffle some feathers, but it's hard for me to imagine that we are ready to *perform* new skills after a six-hour continuing education program – even if it's live and experiential. (Let's not get started on recorded videos with true/false quizzes that you can print out before you even start watching.)

There's evidence to suggest that the fact that we do a training, get a certificate, or even participate in supervised practice doesn't necessarily mean that we know enough to be doing a good job. How can we know? The *most important way* is the evaluation of our supervisors; another is by checking to see if clients are improving.

Routine outcome monitoring (sometimes called feedback-informed treatment or measurement-based care) is a way of assessing clients' outcomes session to session so that we get data about their progress through treatment. This helps us to time interventions appropriately and switch gears if we need to. It's objective and may be a more effective way to determine our competence than our own personal judgment (Pinner et al., 2018). With the caveat that sometimes clients who are doing great work and making excellent progress might *feel* worse for a while (and therefore not answer an outcome survey in the way we would hope), getting objective, measurable feedback from clients can help us to make sure we're on the right track.

I get that this is potentially really scary. What if we're not as good at this as we hope we are? What if the data shows it?! Here's the truth: If we're not as good as we want to be, we *need to know it* so *that we can get better.*

PRACTICE TIP

Vocal, dance, and surgical training happen slowly, and so does therapy training. Please *do* find your edges and grow! Choose wisely – get involved in a serious training program for something you really care about developing – one that lasts six months or more and includes live supervision as well as continued consultation as you take the skills to your clients. Allow yourself to enjoy the process. You don't need to be an opera singer today (or maybe ever)! No matter where you are in your career, there's plenty of benefit clients can derive from your performance range, and you can develop your practice range without rushing.

CHAPTER 66
IT'S OK TO BE CREATIVE
IF WE'RE GROUNDED

You know how people sometimes look at abstract art and say, "My four-year-old could have painted this?" Well, it turns out that people *can* tell the difference between professional abstract art and art made by kids (and animals!), even when they are lied to about who painted it (Hawley-Dolan & Winner, 2011). There really is something important about training and skills fidelity, even when the content is highly creative. We could also think about this related to the professions from the previous chapter – we definitely expect a trained musician to be able to write better music than an untrained one and a trained dancer to be a better choreographer than a novice. We would definitely trust an experienced surgeon to perform exploratory surgery and just "fix whatever they found wrong in there" much more than a first-year med student with a scalpel.

Creativity is good for many reasons. Maybe the best reason is because it's part of being a fully functioning, self-actualized person (Maslow, 1962; Rogers, 1961) and it's central to the ability to love, work, and play (Carson & Becker, 2003). Contrary to the common belief that people are most creative when they are most free to imagine, creativity flourishes more under constraints (e.g., Acar et al., 2019). I'd like to submit that the best time to utilize our therapeutic creativity is when clients present constraints on the typical process of therapy.

The process of being creative in therapy (Carson & Becker, 2003) has a good deal in common with the typical problem-solving process. It starts with preparation – acquiring the skills and background information and resources needed, as well as clearly defining the problem to be handled creatively. It requires intense concentration – both a time of clear focus away from other demands or distractions and a willingness to engage in the frustration of trial and error. We must also allow ourselves to engage in ideation – like brainstorming, this is the generation of ideas that are not judged or dismissed at the outset. Specific to the creative process are the phases of *incubation* (slightly withdrawing from the problem in a relaxed way, allowing it to be integrated and clarified at an unconscious level) and *illumination* (the "aha" moment, the emergence and acceptance of an image or idea that suggests a solution or direction). To finish the process, we need to test out the new ideas – implement and evaluate, then adjust or return to the drawing board as needed.

DOI: 10.4324/9781003125082-73

So, the fundamental principle here is that we need to know the fundamental principles. We should choose or identify the theoretical orientation we're working from (assuring that we know it well and are already skillful in its use). Then, we should start by using all of the basic concepts and skills with *fidelity*. After that, we can address the constraints of therapy — client's particular needs, preferences, skills, situations — by accessing our creativity!

PRACTICE TIP

If you find yourself needing to be creative with almost all of your clients, it might be because you're trying to fit everyone into your theoretical orientation. Beware of treating every problem like a nail, just because what you have is a hammer (Maslow, 1966). Your client may need an electrician or a gardener rather than a carpenter, or maybe even just someone who is handy with a screwdriver. We need to be aware when clients may need something that's genuinely not in our wheelhouse (rather than trying to "create" a way to fit their needs to our skills), and that's where an excellent referral list needs to come into play.

CHAPTER 67
SLIDING SCALES & PRO BONO WORK

You knew this was coming, right? This book doesn't pull any punches, so we can't ignore this ethical issue, even though it is one that *everyone seems to want to ignore.* We'd rather talk about sex or politics than money. And we have to pay our rent, we do. You won't hear me say that I don't think we should be paid a fair wage. We might have a little discussion about what a fair wage is, though.

Here's the deal. The American Psychological Association (APA, 2017), American Counseling Association (ACA, 2014), American Association of Marriage and Family Therapists (AAMFT, 2015), and the National Association for Social Workers (NASW, 2017) all include in their respective codes of ethics something very like this: "We are encouraged to contribute a portion of our professional time/activities to services for which there is little or no financial return." Each one ties this to professional values, such as justice (the idea that our services should be accessible to everyone) and service (the idea that what we do is more than focus on our self-interest). Seriously, we can't avoid this.

So, how can we approach this idea without feeling awful or bankrupting ourselves? Here are some thoughts:

- When clients suggest that they might need to leave therapy, or reduce their frequency, before just agreeing, we can ask if finances are the reason (even if they didn't bring it up) and make arrangements to reduce their fee so that they can continue the work they (and we!) have committed to.
- Periodically, maybe we can review our caseloads. Or, if we have staff who handle most of our financial and billing responsibilities, we can ask them to alert us if they notice that we have only full-fee clients. (Yes, we may have to explain ourselves!)
- Sometimes, we think that if we supervise practicum students or interns, and they offer reduced fees, that the moral value of that transfers to us and we are "doing our duty" and don't need to see anyone at a reduced fee ourselves. Maybe, if we're not charging for their supervision hour, that's sort of true?
- Maybe this is sort of cheating, but giving community presentations for free (like we discussed in Chapter 55) can be a way to both donate professional time to the community and also do a little marketing.

DOI: 10.4324/9781003125082-74

- Oh, and consider whether taking insurance gets us out of this requirement. It can feel like it does, because we're seeing clients for low out-of-pocket cost. But none of our ethics codes make any such distinction!

In indigenous communities, healers are given gifts "in gratitude for services given [which] help the elder or healer to meet his or her subsistence needs … a gift of money, though it is still *literally* money, can still be used to express gratitude for help received; it need not be a payment or a fee for services" (Katz, 2017). That's not the way we usually think of things, but it might be a helpful perspective for keeping our fee situation in, well, perspective.

PRACTICE TIP

This is a bit unusual for this book, but I'd like to share with you something that I learned specifically from a clinical experience of mine, with no reference to show for it. Once I had a supervisor who, in his private practice, held a philosophy that "an hour of my time is worth an hour of your time." He turned no one away, and everyone provided a copy of their most recent pay stub as part of their initial paperwork. Whatever that person made per hour is where they set the fee. Because of this virtuous arrangement, he regularly had clients who, when their pay increased, requested that they increase their fee. And it made it easy and shame-free for clients to pay lower than typical fees, or to request that their fee be reduced during times of hardship. Not that we all need to or even can do this, but it's a really great model.

CHAPTER 68
NOT GETTING SUED

First, don't be terrified. For example, only about 2% of psychologists have licensing board complaints filed against them each year, and there are even fewer disciplinary actions taken (Novotney, 2016; Van Horne, 2004). However, 40–50% of psychologists can expect to have a complaint filed against them at some point in their careers (Knapp et al., 2013). Actual legal action in the form of malpractice suits is much lower, around 2% (Novotney, 2016). But all that doesn't mean that we don't worry about it, or that we shouldn't.

So, let's start with what gets us into legal trouble. It can be very difficult to get aggregate data about malpractice claims (in part because there are many different providers) and a little easier to get data on disciplinary actions. For example, we can often find at least some data through our state licensing boards – many of them publicly post sanctions and disciplinary actions. The Association of States and Provincial Psychology Boards (ASPPB, 2020) keeps a running list of complaints, and we can get a good idea from this about what kinds of complaints are most often made: unprofessional conduct (15.6%), sexual misconduct (14.9%), negligence (11.0%), non-sexual dual relationship (9.7%), and conviction of crime (8.5%). The other categories common enough not to be called "Other" include failure to maintain adequate or accurate records, failure to comply with continuing education or competency requirements, incompetence, improper or inadequate supervision or delegation, substandard or inadequate care. Malpractice claims identified the counseling relationship as the problem 58.7% of the time, professional responsibility 20.6% of the time, and issues of confidentiality/privacy 17.5% of the time (Healthcare Providers Service Organization, 2014). Similar to the ASPPB findings, most claims were about inappropriate relationships (39.7%), boundaries of competence (15.8%), and improper sharing of confidential information (12.7%). It will be interesting to see if The Great Telehealth Migration of 2020 changes these numbers in the near future!

Of course, at least some of the factors in why therapists get sued are client factors, and things we can't do much about. For example, patients who have family or friends who support them in suing, who have informal legal resources to contact ("lawyer friends"), or who have sued someone before and have knowledge of the process are more likely to sue their physicians than

DOI: 10.4324/9781003125082-75

dissatisfied patients who don't (May & Stengel, 1990). Clients who are angry, mistrustful, focused on compensation, involved with substance abuse, or who had severe punishment in childhood are more likely to consider suing (Fishbain et al., 2007).

That means we need to prepare to get sued anyway, even if we're always super ethical and legally flawless. And that means having our malpractice insurance all sorted out and it means *documenting* all of those legal and ethical things we do but that we're not really addressing here – protecting records and confidentiality, managing or avoiding dual relationships, setting clear expectations with clients, etc. (Novotney, 2016).

There also isn't much data about what therapist factors help us not get sued. However, physicians are less likely to get sued when they educate patients about what to expect, laugh and use humor, involve patients in the work (e.g., ask for their opinions, check their understanding), and when they spend more time with them – the largest difference in physicians who don't get sued vs. those who do is an extra three minutes spent with patients, on average (18.3 vs. 15.0 minutes; Levinson et al., 1997). When patients believe their doctors are competent and that their doctors are concerned about the personal effects of their care, they are less likely to sue (May & Stengel, 1990). There are lessons we can learn from that data, as well. When we prioritize the relationship, and clients view us as competent, trustworthy, and human, they are probably less likely to want to take us to court, even if we did something they think was wrong.

PRACTICE TIP

I know this is going to sound corny, but please do read over your ethics guidelines and relevant laws twice a year. It will surprise you what kinds of things you find that you didn't notice or remember. For example, many practitioners in Texas don't know that they can see minors without the consent of their guardians for substance abuse (Texas Family Code, 2013) and many professional counselors don't know that the ACA Code of Ethics prohibits them from looking up their clients on social media (ACA, 2014)!

CHAPTER 69
IT'S NOT UNETHICAL IF ...

Most of us are conscientious, moral people with good intentions to do the best work, maximally help our clients, and fully conform to our laws and ethics codes. Still, we are human. So, we can fall victim to mistaken beliefs and justifications, especially when we're stressed, conflicted, or under pressure. There are somewhat exhaustive lists of such phenomena (e.g., Pope & Vasquez, 2011), but here is a quick summary of a few of the most insidious ones!

- It's not unethical if it's not illegal (or if the ethics code doesn't mention it specifically, or our supervisor never said explicitly not to).
  - We've all tried to put together a bookshelf and ended up with extra screws, right? It's perplexing and frustrating, and our first instinct is to shrug and assume it's fine because it seems sturdy enough. We don't usually take the whole thing apart and start over unless something breaks. We are more comfortable when we have clear directions, and when there aren't clear directions, it can be easy to shrug off the more delicate parts of an ethical dilemma.
- It's not unethical if we feel like we're doing the right thing (or we didn't mean for anyone to get hurt).
  - There's a strange emphasis in mental health ethics on a clinician's "guts." Some Ethical Decision-Making Models even include "checking your gut reaction" as a step! (This is a little terrifying. How, for example, are young clinicians supposed to have clinical wisdom or "guts" to trust?) Maybe most of us have a good internal *moral* compass and checking our gut reaction will help us know if that's been violated, but guts are of limited use in the much more complex world of mental health ethics and laws.
- It's not unethical if we did our best, or the best we could at the time and under the circumstances (e.g., stress, time pressure).
  - Sometime between bringing up Boomers and raising Millennials, schools and parent training programs started emphasizing the praise of effort over outcome (even though both are important! Wubbolding, 2007) and this may be why this one sneaks up on us. But when it comes to whether something is ethical, it's not about our intentions or effort. We can do our best, we can struggle against difficult circumstances, and sometimes we still don't do the right thing.

DOI: 10.4324/9781003125082-76

- It's not unethical if doing the really ethical thing is unreasonably difficult or impossible.
  - I know, I can even hear myself balking at the idea that the right thing might be impossible, but it's still the right thing. It feels unfair to be held to such a standard! But the care of human lives and minds and hearts is a high calling; we need to be willing to take the narrow road, even if it challenges us to our limits!
- It's not unethical if nothing bad happens or no one complains.
  - This is an example of consequentialism – a philosophy that the moral worth of an action is determined by what happens, not by whether it follows a set of ethical guidelines or laws. This is often written as "the ends justify the means" and attributed largely to Machiavelli – yeah, *that* Machiavelli! And even when we don't mean in it in a sinister way, if we do something wrong and nothing bad happens, we're only more likely to do it again.
- It's not unethical if someone else (a book we read, an insurance reviewer, another therapist, our client) suggested it or agrees that it's ok.
  - Don't get me wrong – there is some value in what I call "conformity ethics." Aside from issues like groupthink, it may be worthwhile to consider the opinion of the group, and it certainly helps when it comes to having a plausible defense for our actions, should we need one. The real danger is in getting an idea about what we would like to do and then finding sources who give us permission.

Even the best of us can get trapped in some of these thought patterns. And we all have different personalities, histories, and values that make us each vulnerable in different ways.

PRACTICE TIP
_____

Therapist, know thyself. If you've been to yoga, you've probably heard some yoga instructor say, "Just notice what you feel like you want to do when the pose gets difficult … Do you send yourself criticism? Do you want to give up? Do you want to compare yourself to others? Instead, just notice what you want to do … and stay with the pose … and breathe." Some of us find refuge in the "safety" of conformity, in passing the blame, in giving ourselves excuses. Take a nice, hard look – where do you want to run when things are tough?

CHAPTER 70
WHEN IS NOTHING BETTER THAN SOMETHING?

Which ethical dilemmas are most common? As we saw in Chapter 68, the most common violations that end in discipline or legal suits are inappropriate relationships. But that's not really the same as how we experience our practices – it may be that many of our ethical predicaments are resolved in ways that don't show up in those kinds of reporting. This is borne out in some of the limited research that's been done on the topic; psychologists, when polled, order them with confidentiality, blurred or dual relationships, payment issues, and teaching/training concerns topping the list (Pope & Vetter, 1992).

But I would like to submit that most of the ethical dilemmas that we come up against (in clinical practice, at least) are some variation on one theme: I don't believe I can provide the perfect standard of care – is providing something less than that better than not providing it?

What are some reasons we might not be able to provide the best standard of care?

- Our laws and/or ethics codes and/or ethical principles might be in conflict about what best practice is.
  - We're pretty confident about these. Generally speaking, laws take precedence over ethics codes, and specific codes take precedence over principles. We do get into muddy waters sometimes when we have to balance different principles, but we can usually get through that with a bit of consultation or a good ethical decision-making model. And once we've done that, we tend to feel quite a bit better about it and also have something defensible to say about our choice.
- We might not have the competencies to provide the best practice.
  - If this is the case, we can get into supervision/consultation to develop the necessary competencies or we can refer. This might also happen because we have some kind of conflict of interest – we know the client from outside of therapy or we can't keep our countertransference at bay. OK, simple. Refer. (Although referring isn't always that *easy*, especially when therapy is the way we pay our rent, that doesn't mean the decision isn't *simple*!)
- We might not want to do the work or make the sacrifices to provide the best practice.

DOI: 10.4324/9781003125082-77

○ Uh-oh. Now we're in the really difficult territory. This happens when we know what we should do, but we don't want to do it. We don't want to refer our favorite client even though the erotic countertransference that's making them our "favorite" is probably the reason we should. (Anyway, isn't the fact that we have such a personal connection a good reason to keep them?) We don't want to bother doing continuing education when we're totally sure that Exposure and Response Prevention Therapy is self-explanatory. (Anyway, *only* 15% of change comes from the theory, so what does it matter if it's not perfect?) We don't want to see our downtrodden client for $15 even though they've invested a lot in this work and relationship. (Anyway, wouldn't a prac student also be fine?) We don't want to provide teletherapy to a high-risk client, even though they live over an hour away from another therapist. (Anyway, aren't some clients just not appropriate for distance work?)

○ It's kind of a tough message, but we need to hear it – "We can usually find a way to do almost anything we really want to do and to do it with at least a temporarily soothed conscience" (Pope & Vasquez, 2011).

Thinking about any ethical dilemma from this standpoint can give us a quick bit of clarity: Do I know what the best standard of practice is? If I can't or don't want to do it, who can? If no one else can, what's the best I can do?

PRACTICE TIP

Ethical decision-making models (EDMMs; e.g. Forester-Miller & Davis, 2016; Pope & Vasquez, 2011) aren't just for school. And they're not just for documentation in case we get called to the Board. They're for *us*.

How much time do you spend fretting about an ethical dilemma? Even doing a really thorough job, it's not going to take more than a couple of hours to go through a model. The structure helps to avoid bias and writing it out helps with perspective. You'll feel so much clearer and better about your decision if you do it. There's not a time in our practices, not after 50 years, that we're not better off going through a model than skipping it.

And if you catch yourself thinking, "I really ought to do an EDMM," and then finding excuses not to do it ... that's a sign that you *really* ought to do it.

REFERENCES

Acar, O. A., Tarakci, M., & van Knippenberg, D. (2019). Creativity and innovation under constraints: A cross-disciplinary integrative review. *Journal of Management, 45*(1), 96–121. https://doi.org/10.1177/0149206318805832

American Association of Marriage and Family Therapists. (2015). *Code of ethics.* Retrieved from https://www.aamft.org/Legal_Ethics/Code_of_Ethics.aspx

American Counseling Association. (2014). *2014 ACA code of ethics.* https://www.counseling.org/docs/default-source/default-document-library/2014-code-of-ethics-finaladdress.pdf

American Psychological Association. (2017). *Ethical principles of psychologists and code of conduct* (2002, amended effective June 1, 2010, and January 1, 2017). https://www.apa.org/ethics/code/

Association of States and Provincial Psychology Boards (2020). *ASPPB Disciplinary Data System: Historical Discipline Report – Reported Disciplinary Actions for Psychologists*: 1974–2019. https://www.asppb.net/page/DiscStats

Blonna, R. (2014). An acceptance commitment therapy approach to sexual attraction. In M. Luca (Ed.), *Sexual attraction in therapy: Clinical perspectives on moving beyond the taboo: A guide for training and practice* (pp. 80–96). Wiley-Blackwell. https://doi.org/10.1002/9781118674239.ch6

Epstein, R. M., & Hundert, E. M. (2002). Defining and assessing professional competence. *JAMA: Journal of the American Medical Association, 287*(2), 226–235. https://doi.org/10.1001/jama.287.2.226

Fishbain, D. A., Bruns, D., Disorbio, J. M., & Lewis, J. E. (2007). What patient attributes are associated with thoughts of suing a physician? *Archives of Physical Medicine and Rehabilitation, 88,* 589–596. doi:10.1016/j.apmr.2007.02.007

Forester-Miller, H., & Davis, T. E. (2016). *Practitioner's guide to ethical decision making* (Rev. ed.). Retrieved from http://www.counseling.org/docs/default-source/ethics/practioner's-guide-toethical-decision-making.pdf

French, J. R. P., Jr., & Raven, B. (1959). *The bases of social power.* In D. Cartwright (Ed.), Studies in social power (pp. 150–167). University of Michigan.

Gendlin, E. T. (1978). *Focusing.* Bantam.

Hawley-Dolan, A., & Winner, E. (2011). Seeing the mind behind the art: People can distinguish abstract expressionist paintings from highly similar paintings by children, chimps, monkeys, and elephants. *Psychological Science, 22*(4), 435–441. https://doi.org/10.1177/0956797611400915

Healthcare Providers Service Organization. (2014). *Understanding counselor liability risk.* http://www.hpso.com/Documents/pdfs/CNA_CLS_COUNS_022814p_CF_PROD_ASIZE_online_SEC.pdf

Howell, A. J., Turowski, J. B., & Buro, K. (2012). Guilt, empathy, and apology. *Personality and Individual Differences, 53*(7), 917–922. https://doi.org/10.1016/j.paid.2012.06.021

Katz, R. (2017). *Indigenous healing psychology: Honoring the wisdom of the first peoples.* Healing Arts Press.

Kernberg, O. (1995). *Love relations: Normality and Pathology.* Yale University Press.

Levinson, W., Roter, D. L., Mullooly, J. P., Dull, V. T., & Frankel, R. M. (1997). Physician-patient communication: The relationship with malpractice claims among primary care physicians and surgeons. *JAMA: Journal of the American Medical Association,* 277(7), 553–559. https://doi.org/10.1001/jama.277.7.553

Maslow, A. H. (1962). Creativity in self-actualizing people. In A. Maslow, *Toward a psychology of being* (pp. 127–137). D Van Nostrand. https://doi.org/10.1037/10793-010

Maslow, A. H. (1966). *The psychology of science: A reconnaissance.* Unknown Publisher.

May, M. L., & Stengel, D. B. (1990). Who sues their doctors? How patients handle medical grievances. *Law & Society Review, 24*(1), 105–120. doi: 10.2307/3053788

Nagy, T. F. (2011). Competence. In T. F. Nagy, *Essential ethics for psychologists: A primer for understanding and mastering core issues* (pp. 67–88). American Psychological Association. https://doi.org/10.1037/12345-004

National Association for Social Workers. (2017). *Code of ethics.* Retrieved from https://www.socialworkers.org/about/ethics/code-of-ethics

Novotney, A. (2016). 5 Ways to Avoid Malpractice. *Monitor on Psychology, 47*(3), 56. https://doi.org/10.1037/e509622018-001

Pope, K. S., & Vasquez, M. J. T. (2011). *Ethics in psychotherapy and counseling: A practical guide* (4th ed.). John Wiley & Sons Inc. https://doi.org/10.1002/9781118001875

Pope, K. S., & Vetter, V. A. (1992). Ethical dilemmas encountered by members of the American Psychological Association: A national survey. *American Psychologist, 47*(3), 397–411. https://doi.org/10.1037/0003-066X.47.3.397

Post, S. G., & Neimark, J. (2007). *Why good things happen to good people: The exciting new research that proves the link between doing good and living a longer, healthier, happier life.* Broadway Books.

Reich, W. (1933). *Character-analysis.* Orgone Institute Press.

Texas Family Code (2013). Title 2. Child in relation to the Family. Subtitle A. Limitations of Minority. Chapter 32. Consent to treatment of child by non-parent of child. Subchapter A. Consent to medical, dental, psychological, and surgical treatment. Sec. 32.003 Consent to treatment by child.

Van Horne, B. A. (2004). Psychology licensing board disciplinary actions: The realities. *Professional Psychology: Research and Practice, 35*(2), 170–178. https://doi.org/10.1037/0735-7028.35.2.170

Wubbolding, R. E. (2007). Glasser Quality School. *Group Dynamics: Theory, Research, and Practice, 11*(4), 253–261. https://doi.org/10.1037/1089-2699.11.4.253

It's a Lifelong Journey (Real Professional Development)

What's professional development even really about? Sure, it's about staying current and growing our boundaries of competence (APA, 2013). It's about much more than that, too – developing ourselves in knowledge but also as clinicians and professionals more broadly. And I won't avoid the practical parts here, but couldn't professional development be *more* than just a continuing education requirement? Couldn't it be this incredibly rich journey of exploration, change, and growth? I know that sounds a little idealistic, but don't we all need my type of idealism in our lives sometimes?

When it comes to professional development, once we're out of training, we have to become our own mentors. We are the only ones who we will continue to be responsible to, so we have to learn how to support ourselves, grow ourselves, and hold ourselves accountable. Hopefully, this little chapter can help build up and give some ideas to our Internal Mentors to keep us in tip-top shape for every session. This section will address general professional development concepts, some specific topical areas that we all need to be competent in, and some ways of thinking about our different roles as psychotherapists.

CHAPTER 71
DON'T CHEAT YOURSELF

We say this to our kids and our clients in slightly different ways. To our kids we say, "I'd rather you earn that B- than cheat your way to an A+" or "I'm paying for your college, so take a class that matters even if it's hard, not a blow-off class!" To our clients we say, "If it's a worthwhile goal, it's worth the effort" or "There aren't shortcuts to meaningful change." So, what do we say to ourselves?

If we're going to have to be our own mentors, we should be choosing our learning experiences with care. How can we judge whether a learning experience is going to be worth our time and effort (the effort we *are* going to put in, because we're exercising our best selves!)? Some guidelines exist to help us; for example, quality professional development should be presented by legitimate experts, should build on the training we already have rather than repeat it, use evidence-based learning strategies, reflect current research on diversity, include active engagement with us as learners, and have a clear connection to improving our practice (e.g., APA, 2013).

A few other considerations that might help us to evaluate: Do we have to *work* to pass the test? (We want to earn our continuing education, not buy it.) Would the best supervisor we ever had approve? (It's ok to internalize their voices as part of our own.) Will we get to practice and have supervision? (We'd rather actually be expanding our boundaries of competence than pretending to.)

We may want to prioritize getting trained deeply in a type of therapy we really want to do, rather than getting a few hours' lecture on ten different therapies in the next two years. If we want to dip our toes in, we can still verify first that there is substantial, additional training to be earned in follow-up in case we're interested. This can also help us avoid traps of programs that sound very interesting but aren't well grounded, which often don't have multiple levels of training.

We need to be wary of all the available "mental health certifications," especially the ones that are offered online, charge exorbitant fees, and could be passed by an eighth grader with no mental health background (yep, that's real! Rosen et al., 2020). Instead, we should consider types of training that are regulated by a state board (e.g., does your state license play therapists or art therapists or sex offender treatment providers?), a national board certification (e.g., American Board of Professional Psychology specialty in

                                                  DOI: 10.4324/9781003125082-79

Forensic or Geropsychology, Master Addictions Counselor from National Board for Certified Counselors), or at least those that are associated with reputable state, national, or international associations.

Let's not get obsessed with extra "letters" behind our names. Most letters beyond our licensures are more about us paying money than they are about adding value to our practice (with rare exceptions). And putting relatively insubstantial letters alongside our real credentials might even be unethical, in the sense of misleading the public about our credentials (American Counseling Association, 2014; APA, 2017). Clients don't know the difference between a reputable, meaningful licensure that we earned and a four-hour, inconsequential certification that we paid for, and it's not their responsibility.

PRACTICE TIP

Please, don't spend years and/or tens of thousands of dollars to get a doctorate if all it means to you is "fancy letters." By which I mean, the title doesn't make you worth more – certainly not as a clinician and likely not even in terms of wealth (after you factor in the additional debt, the small potential difference in insurance payout, and the increased licensing, liability, and association fees). Do your research and if it will open career doors for you that you want to explore, like research or graduate-level teaching, by all means – pursue it. And then pursue an *excellent* program – if you're going to pour yourself out for it (time, energy, money, relocation, etc.), don't settle!

CHAPTER 72
DON'T TRY TO GO IT ALONE

Development doesn't happen in a vacuum. We will be affected by the people in our systems whether we like it or not, so we probably want to give careful attention to the environment we're growing in. There's no shortage of research showing that the people who surround us impact us in profound ways, including health behaviors (Christakis & Fowler, 2008), academic performance (e.g., Cooc & Kim, 2017), cognitions, decision making, pursuit of goals and success (Westaby, 2012), and emotional functioning (e.g., Fowler & Christakis, 2008).

So, if we have the capacity to influence the "gardens we grow in," we should definitely take an active role in cultivating them.

There are a few types of people we should probably all have ongoing relationships with:

- Veterans in the field: Whether this means keeping close relationships with a couple of supervisors or actively seeking out new mentors, people who have been in the field for a long time have a certain comfort and familiarity even with difficult questions. These people are the soil we grew in, and transplanting can make it very difficult to put new roots down. Even if we do make a big change, veteran clinicians can be the mature trees in a garden that provide sheltering shade and break damaging winds.

- Current students or interns: Keeping relationships with people who are "young" in the field is helpful to us because they often have an enthusiasm and vivaciousness for the work that is infectious, and they also can keep us in touch with new research and trends. These colleagues are the water that keeps the garden fresh.

- Clinicians who are "culturally different" from us: I absolutely mean this in the way it is typically used (e.g., people with different ethnic / national backgrounds, but I'll address that more in Chapter 95). I also mean this in the way that we are trained in different therapy styles from different training "families of origin" (i.e., different programs focused on different models). This helps prevent isolation and the risks associated with groupthink and the like. If we grow with only other plants like us, we're not growing in a garden anymore ... we're growing on a farm.

DOI: 10.4324/9781003125082-80

- Non-therapists: Honestly, it can be sort of easy between training programs and then internships and then work environments to find ourselves surrounded almost entirely by mental health people. And then we run the legitimate risk of forgetting how to be a regular person and interact in normal situations! These are the flowers that make the garden more beautiful, and the companion crops that keep us healthy (like how planting strawberries with asparagus maximizes nutrient exchange).
- Consultation partner: I know, I simply will not let this go! This person, well chosen, can be the sun that keeps us growing in the best directions.

PRACTICE TIP

Let me say one more piece about how development doesn't happen in a vacuum. You know how we always warn clients that as they change in therapy, their systems will be affected? So, they need to know that their families, and especially their partners, are going to be affected. That's true for us, too. I know you can't do anything to change your family of origin, and friends are easier, because we can drift in and out of friendships as we change. You're going to want to give some serious thought to a conversation about this with your partner, though — whether you're still looking for that person or you've been together a few decades. You'll need them to know they need to be open to and expecting you to change over time, and you'll need to figure out how to balance the changes you make personally and professionally with their own developmental changes in complementary ways.

CHAPTER 73
DON'T STAY IF IT'S NOT RIGHT

Assuming that we're getting about as much sleep as we're supposed to (ha!) and working as much as we're supposed to (ha!), we spend one third of our lives in bed and one third of our lives at work. (So, bonus tip – make sure you have an excellent bed.) We don't sleep well in a bed that's full of lumps, or bed bugs, or snoring partners. If we're wise, we solve the problems we can, and when they're beyond fixing, we sleep somewhere else. When it comes to work, this is a part of professional development we don't talk about very much – getting out of bad situations. These are some of the signs which might lead us to consider leaving the job we're in:

- We don't feel safe: Whether this is because of the actual work environment, the organization's practices, or the behavior of colleagues, this is not something we usually have a lot of power to fix. Certainly, if laws are being broken or there is physical danger, we should run and not look back. (And report if we feel we can!)
- We're walking on an ethical tightrope: Especially when we're new to an environment, and learning the "ways things are done" there, we can feel a little off-balance regarding they gray area between unethical and not-what-we're-used-to. But if we are feeling the need to work EDMMs every couple of weeks or we don't feel free to consult on ethical concerns with our colleagues, this is a warning sign.
- We don't like the people there: If we don't get along with any of our colleagues, there are probably other ways that the job is a poor fit, too. But even if it is a good fit, stressful work relationships aren't worth the strain they put on us in the long term. We can't expect to get along with everyone, but we should get along with a few people, including administrative staff and our direct boss/supervisor.
- We're edging toward burnout: Once burnout hits – exhaustion, cynicism, and reduced professional efficacy (Leiter & Maslach, 2005) – it's too late. No amount of self-care or moderate work changes will bring us back once we've crossed over. So, it's important that we pay attention to our personal signs of stress (which come before burnout), so we don't get caught unawares.

The mental health field is huge and varied, and – despite our fears – there are jobs out there that will be a good fit for us. The key is to start looking early,

DOI: 10.4324/9781003125082-81

when we first notice these signs, rather than waiting until we're miserable, burnt out, or desperate.

No job will be perfect, and we will have to choose our priorities (e.g., Is the pay more important than the interpersonal climate? Is having an interesting caseload worth working difficult hours?). But it's worth knowing the things that contribute to a long, healthy, satisfying career sans burnout for most people: a sustainable workload, meaningful personal control, a good community, a sense of fairness, consistency with values, and appreciated rewards (Maslach & Leiter, 2008). If we have some of each of these, we're probably in a pretty good place. If one or more of these is absent, our professional development may need to take a sharp turn!

PRACTICE TIP

This might sound a little weird, but I'd be remiss to talk about professional development without saying part of it might be career change. You may have gotten into this career path because someone "expected" it of you, or because you like kids but didn't want to be a teacher, or because you like helping but didn't want to be a nurse, or because you majored in Psychology and this was the only thing you could think to "do with your degree." You may have even gotten into this field for all the "right reasons," but it still might not be the right fit. If this field is *truly not for you*, you probably already know it, deep down. And if you've gleaned something from this book, I hope it's the courage to examine that feeling and allow it to guide you.

CHAPTER 74
WE'VE GOT TO KNOW
IT WELL: DIAGNOSTICS

Does it seem strange to say that the reason we need to know diagnostics well is *integrity*? For one thing, our commitment to accuracy, honesty, and truthfulness (e.g., APA, 2017; ACA, 2014 has 'veracity' for 'truthfulness') doesn't extend only to clients – it extends to insurance providers, too.

We don't have to like diagnosing to do it well. We don't even really have to believe in it to do it well! But we often have to do it, and in that case, we need to do it well. That's part of integrity, too. Here are some ideas about how to go about that:

- Read the book. I really don't like it when people call the DSM-5 (American Psychiatric Association, 2013) the "Bible" of mental health diagnosing, but they do have one thing in common – most people who base a large portion of their lives on it haven't read it all the way through even one time. If you haven't read it through, you don't have to admit it to anyone. You can just read it, alone, and rectify the situation. We can't diagnose with integrity if we don't know what we're diagnosing. (And you're in for a treat – the diagnostic criteria are the least interesting part!)

- Be specific. Reading the DSM will help with the natural instinct to give the same few diagnoses over and over and it will help us avoid the inclination to over-diagnose with "Adjustment Disorder" or "Unspecified XYZ Disorder." This helps with treatment, too. A client who has "anxious distress" with their depression needs different treatment than one with "melancholic features." And even if we harken back to Section One and say we would do the same kind of treatment either way, there's a difference in the efficacy of certain medications for each condition. So, being specific helps us and it helps with the primary function of diagnosis – professional communication. Let's use the specifiers and modifiers to paint the clearest, most accurate pictures we can.

- Update often. Clients' diagnoses will usually change over the course of therapy if we're doing a good job. For example, after 16 weeks of CBT, a client may not meet criteria for "Social Phobia, Situational" anymore. When our client with Bipolar II Disorder moves from a depressive episode to "Bipolar II Disorder, current episode hypomanic, with mixed features," we update it. This is important for insurance, but it's even more important for the integrity of our records, and possibly for the clinician who takes over for us in an emergency.

 DOI: 10.4324/9781003125082-82

Some of us might like diagnosing a little too much. We should be aware of the tendency toward "reification" of diagnoses – this means that we sometimes treat an idea as if it is a real thing. But a map is not the actual territory and a ticking clock is not the actual passage of time, no matter how accurate either is. Likewise, a diagnosis is just a way of talking about a person's experience; it's not their actual experience.

Diagnoses are, first and foremost, attempts at professional communication between researchers and clinicians. Just like other kinds of language, they are constantly changing as we learn more and use the terms in different ways. Also, diagnoses are moving targets. A "gross stress reaction" in the original DSM isn't the same as Post Traumatic Stress Disorder in DSM-5, and it won't be the same in DSM-10. That's not because it wasn't accurate back then; it's because we can become more accurate and more specific over time. (There are more known, named types of cancer, autoimmune disorders, skin conditions, etc. this year than last year, too.)

It's important for us to know this, and also to teach our clients: A mental health diagnosis is a descriptive term. It's not something you are, and it's not something you have.[1] It's a way of describing how things are for you and an imperfect way at that.

PRACTICE TIP

When clients ask about their diagnoses, it can be difficult to know what to do. I typically do the opposite of whatever they ask for. If a client is scared about diagnostics and really doesn't want a label, I often see an opening there for psychoeducation (these are just a set of signs and symptoms, nothing more), normalization (letting them know they aren't alone), and instilling hope (having a diagnosis means we can research and improve treatment). When they come in really pushing for a diagnostic label, especially a specific label, I'm immediately a bit skeptical and wonder about things like secondary gain and how much they've been Googling. In those cases, I'm more likely to focus on areas of distress and dysfunction, reducing emphasis on diagnosis.

NOTE

1   The medical/disease model suggests that mental health diagnoses are something people *have*. This can be useful in reducing shame, but also risks over-emphasizing uncontrollable factors. We don't want to do the opposite either – mental health conditions are also not something people choose. We need to identify the actual sources of internal and external locus of control, maximize what clients can change and help them manage what they can't.

CHAPTER 75
WE'VE GOT TO KNOW IT WELL: PSYCHOPHARMACOLOGY

Why? Why should we need to know psychopharmacology when we aren't allowed to have anything to do with clients' medications? Allow me to use this metaphor (even though it's controversial, maybe, to equate physicians with bartenders!)

Bartenders, who are responsible for knowing all about drinks and also giving drinks to customers should definitely know the signs of alcohol poisoning and be able to gauge when someone's had too much. They do get training in that; most bartenders have the authority to "cut someone off" and they can certainly call an ambulance if there's a need. But they also have to stay behind the bar. So, they only get to see someone if they come up to the bar, and they're often really busy, and only see each person for a moment. (Are you with me? This is the psychiatrist, or physician, who is being responsible to the degree that they are able, given that they tend to see clients for 15 minutes every three months for med checks.)

So, what's our role? We're not the best friend and designated driver who follows the "client" to the bathroom and who should *definitely* be aware of what's going on with them. Hopefully, our clients do have people in their social support groups who they have trusted enough to tell about their medications, who are also responsible enough to do the research on what they should be looking for, and who are paying attention most of the time. But they don't all have that.

We are something like a really excellent server. We don't have as many customers as the bartender does, so we can give each of them much more time and attention. We're the ones who know better how many drinks they've had, how many have been carbonated, how quickly they were drunk, if they were taken with food or water in between. We get to see everyone at the table, and their appearance and behavior. (That is, we get to observe clients about 600 minutes for every psychiatrists' 15 minutes, and we're more likely to have good rapport so they may be more likely to tell us things like "I didn't feel good, so I just quit taking that one.")

So, what should we know about medications? Probably:

- The basic types of psychotropic medications and what they're used for (including common off-label uses)

DOI: 10.4324/9781003125082-83

- Generally, the common side effects of all of those, along with how well they work and any problems there might be associated with their use (e.g., potential for dependence, interference with therapy work)
- Maybe also the common medications that tend to have psyc-related side effects (e.g., hormonal birth control, beta blockers, thyroid medications)

What?! How can we learn all that without going back to school?

- We can start by reading one very good book or attending one very good training (following all of the guidelines from Chapter 71 and making sure it's as newly updated information as possible). There are typically several options for books or trainings that are specifically geared toward therapists (rather than medical doctors; e.g., Preston et al., 2017)
- Then, we can get comfortable with reading the "Full Prescribing Information" documents that go along with medications. Don't worry – you do often have to click the button on the website that says "Health Professionals Only" but there's not a password. Also, it's easier than you think. You'll quickly learn which parts you can skip and where to find the Adverse Effects and Clinical Trials portions.
- We can then build our "mental libraries" of medications slowly, by committing to giving ourselves the homework of looking up any medication that a new client is taking as soon as we learn they are taking it. That keeps us up to date on the medications that are most important (because those are the ones our clients are taking!) without being the overwhelming task of trying to learn about all of them at once.
- And we can listen carefully to clients and observe them closely. Remembering that they are taking medications gives us something else to consider when they report more difficulty sleeping, appear to have gained weight, seem like zombies, etc.

PRACTICE TIP

This is an ethical issue in two directions. Of course, remember that no matter how much we know, it's outside our boundaries of competence to give clients advice about their medications (e.g., AAMFT, 2015; ACA, 2014; APA, 2017; NASW, 2017). On the other hand, if we allow clients to suffer because we ignore or are ignorant about their medication issues, that's not ok. If we recognize when we should, we can engage them with questions, help them educate themselves, and encourage them to be honest and assertive with their prescription providers without stepping over any lines.

CHAPTER 76
WE'VE GOT TO KNOW IT WELL:
THE UNAVOIDABLES

As a clinical teacher and supervisor, I can't tell you how many times I heard students say something like, "I'm just not going to work with people with personality disorders." And no matter how hard I tried, I was rarely able to contain my laughter. There are just a few things that we will come across in practice, in virtually every setting, whether we want to or not. Even in the settings where we might have a fair amount of choice in who we see (e.g., a group practice that shares intake duty and then staffs out cases by expertise, availability, or preference), there are some things we have to know how to recognize and handle at least somewhat because they will come up without warning after therapy is well established.

- Personality Disorders: To be fair, we don't see the Cluster A personality disorders much in therapy, unless they come in for another reason, like depression. Cluster B and C personality disorders show up quite a bit, though. And, especially with Cluster B, they come off as relatively high functioning (even charming! Back et al., 2010) so we don't usually know for a few weeks at least. Fear not, though! Despite the common myth, personality disorders are treatable (e.g., with psychodynamic therapy, Keefe et al., 2020; with DBT, Linehan 2014; with CBT, Sperry & Sperry, 2016).
- Trauma: Sometimes clients don't bring up trauma right away because it's too uncomfortable, or because they don't realize that it's impacting them, or occasionally because they don't even know their trauma was trauma. This means that clients often don't go to a therapist who specializes in trauma work (e.g., Cognitive Processing Therapy, Resick et al., 2008; Prolonged Exposure Therapy, Foa et al., 2007). Without going the distance to develop our own specialty in trauma treatment, we can still increase our knowledge base and perhaps target some of our training toward enhancements to our primary therapy to make it more inclusive of trauma (e.g., with Trauma-Focused CBT; Ehlers, 2013).
- Substances: Often, despite our reassuring introductions about confidentiality, clients don't feel safe (for legal or other reasons) to bring up substance use issues at the beginning of therapy. They may not believe that the substance use is related to their "real problems" (of course,

DOI: 10.4324/9781003125082-84

that's almost never true). Depending on client needs, a Motivational Interviewing (MI; Miller & Rollnick, 2013) approach may serve. MI is a broadly useful therapy that improves our practice in many areas, and is worthwhile getting trained in, regardless of our intention to work with substance use problems. Of course, with serious or long-term substance use, we may need to refer if it's not our specialty.

- Sexual Issues: Embarrassment or discomfort is usually the reason that clients don't bring up sexual issues at first. Again, a question on our intake to smooth the way, along with our ability to talk about sex in a relaxed way will help clients open up. Sometimes when clients do bring up sexual issues, they are looking for a quick-fix technique and we may believe that they need a referral to a certified sex therapist, though often it's a relational or intrapersonal issue (e.g., relationship conflict, performance anxiety) that we can treat in our typical modality (including use of common factors; Donahey & Miller, 2001) as long as we don't run away from it.

- Prejudice/discrimination: Clients often don't know that this is "the kind of thing you can talk about" in therapy. A question that asks about past or current experiences of prejudice and/or discrimination on the intake form can help to open the door for these conversations, but it still often takes time. We need to demonstrate our cultural competence before it can feel safe, and it also helps if we bring it up. Of course, once the topic is open, we need to be able to be helpful (for example, by following appropriate guidelines; e.g., APA, 2019).

PRACTICE TIP

These are definitely not all of the things that may come up in therapy and depending on your geographic location, typical clientele, and the type of setting you work in, different issues may be prevalent that you need to watch out for. For example, in some parts of the country, human trafficking is an issue that you'll see whether you notice it or not. Working primarily with women means interpersonal violence and eating disorder symptoms will be more prevalent. In schools, it can be important to watch out for homelessness and bullying that sometimes don't present overtly. Having continuing consultation with colleagues who have worked in your area for a while can be invaluable in helping to "know what you don't know" you should be looking for.

CHAPTER 77
BE A SCIENTIST

What makes a scientist? For our purposes, I'm going to say *curiosity plus methodology*.

Curiosity can be defined as "desire for information in the absence of any extrinsic benefit" (Lowenstein, 2000). Sure, scientists sometimes have ulterior motives, like advancing their careers or getting the next grant, but they didn't start out that way. Before they knew the dog-eat-dog world of publishing, promotion, and tenure, they became scientists because they just *wanted to know more*. Some of us came into this field because of infinite curiosity about the human condition or people's stories, and it helps us want to know clients in a pure, unbiased way. Hopefully, each of us can take this attitude – of interest, attention, and exploration – into each session.

It's funny how people generally think that scientists have all the answers, but it is scientists themselves who are most likely to say things like "under some circumstances" and "with a 95% confidence interval" and "we don't have enough data to make that conclusion." Scientists have more intellectual humility than almost anyone else, and it's one of the things that makes science keep working. Intellectual humility serves our curiosity by helping us not get too wrapped up in silly things like "being right," which is helpful not only for keeping the client center-stage but also for maintaining a balance of trying something new long enough to really give it a chance and also being willing to abandon that something when it clearly isn't helpful.

Regarding methodology, I think it's safe to dispense with the details and consider the overall features of the scientific method. We can think of each client as an n = 1 study. First, we begin with observations and early data (from the intake). Then, we hypothesize (about diagnosis and treatment acceptability/effectiveness). Then, we gather more data and (here's the crucial point!) *update our hypotheses*. Rinse and repeat. This is how we get rich, useful bodies of literature on various subjects in the sciences. And a human life, complete with growth and progress in therapy, is definitely as complex and deserving of an approach that we revise as needed.

It can be wonderful for clients to structure therapy as a scientific study and to give them the lead role as "principal investigator." What do they want to change? What are their hypotheses? What variables would they like to manipulate first? How will they measure the changes that occur? Then we get to be the consulting partner in the investigation, helping to design

DOI: 10.4324/9781003125082-85

the "study" and implement the "experimental conditions" and analyze the "results," but leaving them in control of their experience. And the mentality of a scientist (it reminds me of a mindfulness meditation, "holding it lightly") is such that it's ok to experiment and fail and see what happens and just be interested without being overly *invested* in the outcome.

PRACTICE TIP

Stay curious and teach curiosity overtly to clients. Hands down, curiosity is the most useful emotional approach to, well, just about everything. Definitely relationships (curiosity about the other's experiences and phenomenological world) and self-study (curiosity about their own thoughts, feelings, reactions, responses, history, etc.). Also great for things like "different ways of being" or "stuff I've never tried before." And you know, many clients never learned how to approach the world this way. Yet another gift we can give them that transcends the boundaries of the therapy experience.

CHAPTER 78
BE AN EXPERT

In the recent past, a popular idea has developed that all one needs to become an expert is 10,000 hours of practice (Gladwell, 2011). Even if that were true (and it's not – just wait!), that wouldn't be just five years' worth of clinical practice – to get 10,000 hours of face-to-face client time would take much longer. But, of course, just practice isn't enough. Both the *quantity* and *quality* of practice in any complex skill, including psychotherapy, is required for the development of expertise (Miller & Ericsson, 2013). This process includes assessing your current baseline, soliciting ongoing feedback, and engaging in deliberate practice (as mentioned in Chapter 58).

Even if we did that, then we'd be "experts" in therapy, broadly defined (as opposed to being an expert in CBT or working with men or play therapy). So, if we consider that we might need 10,000+ hours of this kind of practice in *each domain* we want to improve or become experts in, we can see clearly that this field is never-ending, and we will always have growth edges.

Because this is such an undertaking, we may need to start by cultivating the attitude it takes to be an expert:

- Growth Mindset: In order to grow in any area (e.g., improving academics, decreasing aggression, enhancing willpower), it is important that we believe that these qualities can be developed through nurture and persistent effort (Dweck, 2016). This is in contrast to believing that these core qualities are "inborn" or "fixed." In fact, when we believe we're already good at something (e.g., "naturally therapeutic"), that can even be a barrier to improving.
- Love–Hate Relationship with Failure: There are many factors in how we respond to failure, some of which don't seem to be very changeable (e.g., personality traits). We can respond to failure in varied, maladaptive ways (e.g., avoidance, self-criticism) and these tend to reduce our goal-pursuit. We need to discover our particular vulnerabilities regarding failure and what we can do to reframe failure as something to be embraced as a necessary part of the process of becoming an expert (e.g. it's not the end of the world and might be valuable).
- Drive: I'm sure we're all doing this job (or reading this book) because we're passionate about the field and highly motivated to work with excellence. But we can be honest here – we're not equally passionate

DOI: 10.4324/9781003125082-86

about all areas of the field, all populations, all types of therapy. It's worthwhile to aim our development of expertise in directions that we have the most intrinsic motivation to pursue. Not that stretching ourselves into other areas is bad, but expertise requires such a time commitment and high level of perseverance that most of us won't be able to manage it unless we've chosen wisely. This is especially true if we're not naturally high in trait conscientiousness, which seems to be an important component of or at least highly related to the concept of "grit" (Crede et al., 2017; Duckworth et al., 2007).

Unsurprisingly, these are all wonderful attitudes for clients to have, too! We can model them as well as teach them overtly.

PRACTICE TIP

As a caveat, don't just develop a niche and abandon everything else, even in service to deliberate practice. It's dangerous to become too narrow, in the same sense that it's dangerous for a family to live alone out in the wilderness with no contact with the rest of the world for decades – closed systems tend to accumulate unresolved errors, decrease in organization, and succumb to early ends (Walonick, 1993). That means that seeing only the same kinds of clients, going to only the same kinds of trainings, trading supervision/consultation with only the same couple of people can lead to poorer outcomes, even as we develop expertise.

CHAPTER 79
BE AN EXPLORER

When we meet a client, we aren't just meeting a person. We're meeting a person and all of their *territory*. By "territory," I mean all of their thoughts, feelings, and neurophysiological responses that are based in the totality of their history and experiences. All of the features and dimensions of this internal landscape are fundamentally *different* from our own territory and fundamentally *unknowable* without that person's willing guidance. As Rogers (1961) says, "It is the client who knows what hurts, what directions to go, what problems are crucial, what experiences have been deeply buried."

There are three ways to approach a new territory:

- As a conqueror
  - A conqueror knows they know what's right and best. They force or coerce to get their own way. They take over – abolishing what was, in favor of what they want. They destroy and replace. They wage war – loudly and quietly. We can tell a conqueror by their actions and their language. They are forceful, uncompromising. They listen poorly (distorting) or not at all. They say things like, "Yes, but …" and "You should …" Everyone is a conqueror sometimes, whether we wish to think it about ourselves or not. This is more subtle than we think and it's sinister. It feels right when we're doing it. It feels … righteous.
- As a colonizer
  - A colonizer is pleased with their own way. They believe they can bring good things to the new situation. Manners, refinement, worthy (if different) traditions. Changes … but only good changes (or so they protest)! We can tell a colonizer by their actions and their language, too. They seem accommodating at first, and then we're surprised when we've acquiesced. They listen, but artfully dismiss. They say things like, "I think …" and "How about instead …" Everyone is a colonizer sometimes, whether we wish to think it about ourselves or not. (Oh! Therapists are so guilty of this, so often!) It's much, much more subtle than conquering. It's (ostensibly) gentler. It feels *more right.*
- As an explorer
  - An explorer wants only to be exposed and educated. They do not have pre-formed opinions. They are completely open and prepared to handle surprises gently and with curiosity and grace. They simply

DOI: 10.4324/9781003125082-87

want to know more, hear more, understand more fully and accurately. They have no desire to change what is. We can also tell an explorer by their actions and words. They make space for what is new. They ask honest questions to clarify what is new or unclear. They go slowly, without encroaching. They listen. As therapists, we hope to be explorers almost all the time. It's important in all relationships, but in therapy exploring is crucial. It takes a *lot* of work and self-management ... and it's not our natural instinct, no matter what we'd like to believe about ourselves. But we can cultivate it!

Explorers don't enter territory unannounced or without invitation. They tread lightly, not wanting to trample any indigenous plant or wildlife. They tread slowly, knowing their guide has more knowledge of the terrain and its challenges. They come equipped for a journey – with nourishment and protection and a traveling journal and camera (not with flags of ownership and certainly not with machetes). When the guide enters a dark or unexplored area that even they know little about, the explorer follows closely and slightly behind, and holds up the lantern.

Though I would say that being an explorer is definitely the preferred modality for therapists, I know that may be showing my humanistic/existential core. Depending on our theoretical orientation, we may sometimes need to act as "colonizers." When we do, though, it's very much worth noticing what we're doing. That will help us remember to explore when possible and help us avoid edging into being conquerors.

Once we develop the mindset of being explorers, we can approach not just clients this way, but also new experiences (hint: like professional development or continuing education!). We're much better learners when we're in explorer-mode than when we feel the need to demonstrate our knowledge or competence.

PRACTICE TIP

Some couples really respond to this metaphor, as well. It seems to give them a little distance to identify their own trespassing and assuming behaviors. Also, the specialized vocabulary tends to make it easier for me to "call them out" (and for them to call each other out, for example, when they're in "conquering mode"). It handles embellishments well, too, such as conquerors coming in with "swords and shields" (i.e., criticisms and defensiveness). Feel free to steal it and try it out in therapy!

CHAPTER 80
BE AN ADVENTURER

Life is a *quest*. If you are thinking now about *Lord of the Rings*, Gilgamesh, *The Alchemist*, *Star Wars*, or even Dungeons and Dragons, you are absolutely thinking in the right direction. What are the fundamental ingredients in a quest? We need a hero (that's us!). The hero needs a journey. The journey needs adventure – obstacles, mysteries, and enemies – and the hero needs to engage them courageously and grow into their true self in the process!

So, let's be actual adventurers! Or at least professional adventurers. What does that look like?

- Travel well prepared. We wouldn't go backpacking without the appropriate gear, and we don't want to start off on a professional adventure without being well equipped. That means having our basic self-care well in hand (e.g., nutrition, exercise, good sleep patterns), resources for resilience when things get tough (e.g., social supports, available consultation), and maybe even a wise, enjoyable traveling companion. And it's ok to wait until we're ready – we don't want to start an adventure when we're not well or when we're in recovery from a significant injury. (But beware of these preparatory steps becoming excuses to avoid the adventure; it can be easy to keep putting it off until the "right time," which probably never arrives.)

- Go with a target in mind. In the language of Acceptance and Commitment Therapy, we want to move in "valued directions" (Luoma et al., 2017). Chances are, we won't be able to adventure up the mountain, down the valley, across the savannah, through the ocean, and into outer space. We definitely won't be able to do all of those at once! Once our values are clarified, it helps us to set meaningful directions. That doesn't mean we'll find what we want or grow the way we're expecting, but we're certainly more likely to end up somewhere we want to go if we don't wander aimlessly (Peterson, 2008). We also don't have to go into completely uncharted territory in order to be going into new territory for *us*.
  - If we *do* go into completely uncharted territory, we need to be especially well prepared and cautious. And we should go *wisely*, with all of our experience behind us. Creating "new" types of therapy, mixing treatments in ways that haven't been done before, even

DOI: 10.4324/9781003125082-88

learning the hottest new (read: unsupported by research) therapy trends can be dangerous territory. Go armed with a firm ethical footing and tread carefully.

- Embrace the "side quests." Be open to what may happen along the way. The more we are lightly scanning the environment as we progress, the more likely we are to notice opportunities for potential new growth. This is known as "planned happenstance" and it involves tentative yet meaningful forays into new territory as the chance arises (Krumboltz, 2007). It's good to venture out one step at a time, rather than commit wholesale to a path (even one we're passionate about!) and it's better to take almost any appropriate action rather than waiting passively for opportunities to find us. This is an adventure, after all, and that implies that we are *doing* the adventuring, not allowing the adventure to just happen.

PRACTICE TIP

Be an adventurer in your "real" life, too. That doesn't have to mean trips to exotic lands. It means approaching the edges of the life you have now as the adventure they are. Is there something honest you need to tell your partner? Is there a job you know you need to quit? A part of self you haven't explored? Existential anxiety is "the signpost of unlived possibilities, but until pursued as such, the anxiety is the mark of untimely deadness, of a too narrow existence" (Gendlin, 1973). Where in your life is the existential arrow pointing? You'll know it by the excited-sort-of-terrified trembling inside when you imagine going there.

REFERENCES

American Counseling Association. (2014). *2014 ACA code of ethics.* https://www.counseling. org/docs/default-source/default-document-library/2014-code-of-ethics-finaladdress.pdf

American Psychiatric Association. (2013). Diagnostic and statistical manual of mental disorders (5th ed.). Arlington, VA: Author.

American Psychological Association. (2013). *Quality professional development and continuing education resolution.* https://www.apa.org/about/policy/improving-quality

American Psychological Association. (2017). *Ethical principles of psychologists and code of conduct* (2002, amended effective June 1, 2010, and January 1, 2017). https://www.apa.org/ ethics/code/

American Psychological Association. (2019*). APA Guidelines on race and ethnicity in psychology.* American Psychological Association. https://www.apa.org/about/policy/guidelines-race-ethnicity.pdf

Back, M. D., Schmukle, S. C., & Egloff, B. (2010). Why are narcissists so charming at first sight? Decoding the narcissism–popularity link at zero acquaintance. *Journal of Personality and Social Psychology, 98*(1), 132–145. https://doi.org/10.1037/a0016338

Berlyne, D. (1960). *Conflict, arousal, and curiosity.* New York: McGraw Hill.

Christakis, N. A., & Fowler, J. H. (2008). The collective dynamics of smoking in a large social network. *New England Journal of Medicine, 358*(21), 2249–2258.

Cooc, N., & Kim, J. S. (2017). Peer influence on children's reading skills: A social network analysis of elementary school classrooms. *Journal of Educational Psychology, 109*(5), 727–740. https://doi.org/10.1037/edu0000166

Credé, M., Tynan, M. C., & Harms, P. D. (2017). Much ado about grit: A meta-analytic synthesis of the grit literature. *Journal of Personality and Social Psychology, 113*(3), 492–511. https://doi.org/10.1037/pspp0000102

Donahey, K. M., & Miller, S. D. (2001). "What works" in sex therapy: A common factors perspective. In P. J. Kleinplatz (Ed.), *New directions in sex therapy: Innovations and alternatives* (pp. 210–233). Brunner-Routledge.

Duckworth, A. L., Peterson, C., Matthews, M. D., & Kelly, D. R. (2007). Grit: Perseverance and passion for long-term goals. *Journal of Personality and Social Psychology, 92*(6), 1087–1101. https://doi.org/10.1037/0022-3514.92.6.1087

Dweck, C. S. (2012). Mindsets and human nature: Promoting change in the Middle East, the schoolyard, the racial divide, and willpower. *American Psychologist, 67*(8), 614–622. https://doi.org/10.1037/a0029783

Ehlers, A. (2013). Trauma-focused cognitive behavior therapy for posttraumatic stress disorder and acute stress disorder. In G. Simos & S. G. Hofmann (Eds.), *CBT for anxiety disorders: A practitioner book* (pp. 161–189). Wiley Blackwell. https://doi. org/10.1002/9781118330043.ch7

Foa, E. B., Hembree, E. A., & Rothbaum, B. O. (2007). *Treatments that work. Prolonged exposure therapy for PTSD: Emotional processing of traumatic experiences: Therapist guide.* Oxford University Press. https://doi.org/10.1093/med:psych/9780195308501.001.0001

Fowler, J. H., & Christakis, N. A. (2008). Dynamic spread of happiness in a large social network: Longitudinal analysis over 20 years in the Framingham Heart Study. *British Medical Journal, 337*, 2338.

Gendlin, E. T. (1973). Experiential psychotherapy. In R. Corsini (Ed.), *Current psychotherapies* (pp. 317–352). Itasca, IL: Peacock. From http://previous.focusing.org/gendlin/docs/ gol_2029.html

Gladwell, M. (2011). *Outliers: The story of success*. Bay Back Books.

Keefe, J. R., McMain, S. F., McCarthy, K. S., Zilcha-Mano, S., Dinger, U., Sahin, Z., Graham, K., & Barber, J. P. (2020). A meta-analysis of psychodynamic treatments for borderline and cluster C personality disorders. *Personality Disorders: Theory, Research, and Treatment, 11*(3), 157–169. https://doi.org/10.1037/per0000382

Krumboltz, J. (2007). *Promoting Career Development by Capitalizing on Chance*. APA 115th Annual Convention, San Francisco, California. https://doi.org/10.1037/e674312007-001

Leiter, M. P., & Maslach, C. (2005). A mediation model of job burnout. In A.-S. G. Antoniou & C. L. Cooper (Eds.), *New horizons in management. Research companion to organizational health psychology* (pp. 544–564). Edward Elgar Publishing. https://doi.org/10.4337/9781845423308.00046

Linehan, M. (2014). *DBT Skills Training Manual*. Guilford Press.

Loewenstein. G. (1994). The psychology of curiosity: A review and reinterpretation. *Psychological Bulletin, 116*, 75–98.

Loewenstein, G. (2000). Curiosity. In A. E. Kazdin (Ed.), *Encyclopedia of psychology* (Vol. 2, pp. 414–415). American Psychological Association.

Luoma, J. B., Hayes, S. C., & Walser, R. D. (2017*). Learning ACT: An acceptance and commitment therapy skills training manual for therapists* (2nd ed.) Context Press.

Maslach, C., & Leiter, M. P. (2008). Early predictors of job burnout and engagement. *Journal of Applied Psychology, 93*(3), 498–512. https://doi.org/10.1037/0021-9010.93.3.498

Miller, S., & Ericsson, K. A. (Mar 21 – Mar 24, 2013). In search of excellence: Part 1 & part 2. Taking your practice to the next level. *Psychotherapy Networker Symposium*, March 21–24, 2013. https://doi.org/10.1037/e506242013-029

Miller, W. R., & Rollnick, S. (2013). *Motivational interviewing: Helping people change (3rd edition)*. Guilford Press.

Peterson, J. B. (2018). *12 rules for life: An antidote to chaos*. Random House Canada.

Preston, J. D., O'Neal, J. H., & Talaga, M. C. (2017). *Handbook of Clinical Psychopharmacology for Therapists (8th ed)*. New Harbinger Publications.

Resick, P. A., Monson, C. M., & Chard, K. M. (2008). *Cognitive Processing Therapy Veteran/ Military Version: Therapist's manual*. US Department of Veterans Affairs (VA). https://doi.org/10.1037/e514742018-001

Rogers, C.R. (1961). *On becoming a person*. Houghton Mifflin.

Rosen, G. M., Washburn, J. J., & Lilienfeld, S. O. (2020). Specialty certifications for mental health practitioners: A cautionary case study. *Professional Psychology: Research and Practice*. Advance online publication. https://doi.org/10.1037/pro0000324

Shand, A. F. (1914). Curiosity. In A. F. Shand, *The foundations of character: Being a study of the tendencies of the emotions and sentiments* (pp. 438–454). MacMillan Co. https://doi.org/10.1037/10666-032

Silvia, P. (2006). *Exploring the psychology of interest*. Oxford University Press.

Sperry, L., & Sperry, J. (2016). *Cognitive behavior therapy of DSM-5 personality disorders: Assessment, case conceptualization, and treatment* (3rd ed.). Routledge/Taylor & Francis Group.

Walonick, D. S. (1993). *General systems theory*. Retrieved from http://www.statpac.org/walonick/systems-theory.htm

Westaby, J. D. (2012). Dynamic goal pursuit: Network motivation, emotions, conflict, and power. In J. D. Westaby, *Dynamic network theory: How social networks influence goal pursuit* (pp. 33–95). American Psychological Association. https://doi.org/10.1037/13490-002

We Are Not Immune (Common Cognitive Distortions)

The human brain is marvelous … and *strange*. We've been told it's the most complex supercomputer in existence, yet most of us can't add two four-digit numbers in our heads. What gives? In general, most of the ways our brain behaves that we don't like are caused because the human brain has to make tradeoffs between being fast and being accurate (e.g., Spieser et al., 2018). It's no good being able to use complex modeling to plot the most energy-efficient path away from a tiger … we'd be eaten before we got to our start-up screen. Maybe the coolest thing about the human brain, though, is the capacity for metacognition. (Remember this from Chapter 38?) That means that we can learn about the kinds of tradeoffs our brains make and do some work to account for them.

This list isn't comprehensive, but it might feel a bit daunting anyway because there are simply so many ways that our brains make these tradeoffs. So, I have two tips for you reading this chapter – first, don't get discouraged (remember how important all the other stuff is, especially the relationship … you're doing *fine*!) and second, don't feel compelled to remember all of the names! Hopefully, this will just increase our awareness of some of the cognitive biases, logical fallacies, and mental heuristics that befall us and help us strategize how to create protective environments and processes that can help us to combat some of the potentially negative effects for therapy.

As we read, let's use William James' (1890) *psychologist's fallacy* as our foundation – "The great snare of the psychologist is the confusion of his own standpoint with that of the mental fact about which he is making his report." That is, let's make sure we're not assuming that the way we experience things is the way things really are.

CHAPTER 81
WE SEE THROUGH OUR OWN LENSES

We are fundamentally self-centered. Not in the sense of being selfish, of course, but we are each the center of our own universe. There's no way to fully escape the fact that we perceive and think about and interact with the world through our own nervous system and no one else's, and our nervous system is completely unique, both genetically and also crafted moment by moment by every experience we ever have. So, we are necessarily limited in how we experience the world. Being limited in this way means that we are subject to a few special cognitive errors that keep us front and center (to ourselves), operating by different rules than we apply to everyone else.

You've probably heard of the *fundamental attribution error* (FAE). It's the tendency to underestimate the impact of situational forces and overestimate the role of dispositional factors (i.e., character traits) when making judgments about people's behavior (Ross, 1977). But of course the FAE doesn't apply to *us* — we are more likely to attribute our behavior to situational factors than to personal characteristics, probably because we know much more about ourselves, see ourselves in many more different roles than we see others, and have access to our own inner experiences (that's the *actor-observer bias;* Lay et al., 1974). We even take it one step further, because we have a tendency to ascribe successes to our own abilities and efforts, but failures to external or situational factors (*self-serving bias*; e.g., Campbell & Sedikides, 1999). My, oh my! The take home message here is that accurate empathy is probably much more difficult than we believe it is! A metacognitive balancing strategy that we could use here is to consistently maintain our focus on the necessity of the Rogerian skills, including his "gullible caring" (mentioned in Chapter 48).

Not to hammer the point home too painfully, but we also tend to think that we contribute more than we actually do to group efforts (*egocentric bias*; e.g., Ross, 1979), have more confidence in our beliefs and answers than we rightfully deserve (*overconfidence effect*; e.g., Pallier et al., 2002), and believe we have control over situations we actually have no control over (*illusion of control*; e.g., Langer, 1975). Think how precarious this makes our judgments of what is going on in therapy! We are probably chronically overestimating how much work we're doing compared to clients, delivering our psychoeducation and suggestions with more authority than is warranted, and assuming that we are more responsible for clients' positive changes than we really are. Yikes!

DOI: 10.4324/9781003125082-90

And we need to be especially careful about all of this because of the *bias blind spot*, in which we tend to see ourselves as less biased than other people or better able to identify our own biases (e.g., Pronin & Kugler, 2007)! Maybe this is the reason for the lesson that we learned in Chapter 41 about professional humility — that therapists with a fair amount of self-doubt have better outcomes (Niessen Lie et al., 2017). That humility could be what protects us from some of these errors, so it's ok to feel a bit tender or terrified right now! (Remember, we're also doing *fine*. Plenty of therapists never learn all of this — it's just gravy.)

PRACTICE TIP

One form of this that you'll see with clients (especially couples) is the *false consensus effect* (Choi & Cha, 2019) — the tendency to believe that your own opinion (or judgment, or choice) is what any reasonable person would think or do, while thinking that any opinion/judgment/choice contrary to yours is bad, weird, or ridiculous (Ross et al., 1977). You can be sure this is happening when you or a client uses the word "obviously." (Sometimes accompanied by an eyeroll, for effect!) For example:

- "Obviously, when I kissed her before bed, it meant that I was sorry."

- "Nobody wants to be promoted over their best friend at work, obviously."

Some responses that can help might be things like:

- "I hear you saying that seems obvious to you. I wonder where that learning comes from?"

- "That surprised me just now. I imagined it meant XYZ before you told me what it meant to you."

CHAPTER 82
WE SEE WHAT WE LOOK FOR

Here's another we may be familiar with – *confirmation bias*. The part about confirmation bias that most of us don't know is how many different ways it works … it is the tendency to search for, interpret, focus on, and remember information in a way that confirms our preconceptions (Lilienfeld, 2020; Mynatt et al., 1977). Let's explore that (because we're *explorers*; remember Chapter 79?) and talk about how we create our maps of clients' internal worlds.

First, our tendency to *search for* information in a way that confirms our preconceptions means that we are at risk for bias before we even meet a new client. It's like instead of taking out a blank sheet of paper to begin drawing the map of the client's world, we have already outlined the continent, and that changes how we ask questions. We may be looking for valleys (problems) and forgetting to ask about the mountains (strengths). We may focus on the mouth of the client's river (current distress) and neglect the headwaters (origins), or vice versa. If we don't ask about islands, we may never know they're there. Confirmation bias is especially perilous at this early point in therapy because we may entirely miss important features of the landscape and never get back to them (orchards, mesas, cliffs, undersea trenches, black sand beaches?!). We might get a more interesting view of the landscape if we finish our intake with, "What else is important that I didn't ask you about today?"

Second, we *interpret* information in a way that confirms our preconceptions, which means that we are at risk during the intake session and beyond, as we put data together about clients and continually integrate and update our mental maps about them. They may say stream and we draw a river or a brook, over- or under-emphasizing different facets of their experience. We may interpret mountains as molehills and valleys as canyons, even when we're listening carefully. So, now we have an incomplete map to which we add inaccurate features. While that will always be true, no matter our best efforts, the way to increase accuracy the most is to continually show clients the map we're drawing and ask for corrections. In practice, this means reflecting and clarifying relentlessly.

Third, we *focus on* information in a way that confirms our preconceptions, so we don't pay equal attention to all of the data we get from clients. Though clients may have mentioned the sweeping wheat fields (e.g., social support

DOI: 10.4324/9781003125082-91

in the form of friends or community), we might not attend to them if we're focused on the backyard garden (e.g., social support in the form of family and partner). We may lose track of the islands that clients described in the beginning because we are reasonably focused on an erupting volcano, but islands can be volcanos, too! Sometimes, this isn't a problem, as long as we aren't neglecting something that's going to explode. This is one reason good notes are so important. When our client is engaging with the mountain ranges, we may not want to interrupt that work. But next session, we may want to ask after that dark forest they mentioned a few weeks ago.

Fourth, we *remember* information in a way that confirms our preconceptions. That means that we are at risk when we write our notes and when we see clients next session. (Wait, what? There was a swamp?!) One (terrible) solution to this is to write notes continuously all session, every session. Please don't – the divided attention, rapport damage, and hand cramps are not worth what we gain in completeness. Instead, consider checking in briefly with the client at the end about what was most important for them; it's surprising how often we don't guess this correctly. (Bonus if you ask this right before assigning homework and incorporate it!) And, of course, write notes immediately!

PRACTICE TIP

Our map *will never be perfect* and since we can't escape having an inaccurate map, we should at least have one that is similar to the one the client is using. But part of why clients come to us to help them navigate their inner worlds is because they haven't explored all of their own territory (and when they have, they've done it in a biased way, too). Two ways we can potentially improve clients' experiences are to explore their internal worlds more *broadly* or more *deeply*.

Exploring more broadly might look like having a standardized, carefully and thoroughly constructed intake, that intentionally addresses a wide array of current and past symptoms, potential resources, and all areas of life. (Bonus if you also trade intake forms with a colleague from a different practice occasionally, to see if they're attending to something interesting that you aren't.) Exploring more deeply can be choosing a theoretical orientation and following through with it faithfully and thoroughly, rather than bouncing around.

CHAPTER 83
WE NEED THINGS TO BE EASY, EVEN IF THEY'RE WRONG

Life is too complex to take time learning everything in specific detail. Just imagine what it would be like if, every time we saw a chair that we'd never seen before, we had to examine it and discover its purpose. If the grocery store were out of our normal dish soap, we'd be in a panic until someone came along to teach us that, in fact, all of these pleasant-smelling, jewel-colored liquids near each other can clean dishes (and even some of the powders – what?!). And we would have to be bitten by *all* the snakes before we learned our lesson.

One of our brains' solutions to this problem of complexity is to utilize a this/not-this strategy. When we encounter something new, we examine it and say to ourselves, "Is this like something I've seen before?" If the answer is yes, we *assimilate* this new object or experience into a category we already have; if the answer is no, we *accommodate* by creating a new category (Piaget, 1952). Generally speaking, accommodating takes a little more brain power, and the more complex or ambiguous the new object or experience is, the more difficult it is to sort out. If we grow up with dogs in our home, and then we see a cat, we often think it's some kind of funny dog until we make a category for "cats." But then what happens when we see a fox?

Attribute substitution occurs when we face a difficult or complex judgment and – without thinking about it or noticing that we're doing it – we ask ourselves to make a simpler judgment instead (Kahneman & Frederick, 2002). For example, instead of asking, "What is this creature?" we might ask ourselves, "Is that a dog or a cat?" In diagnostics, we might ask ourselves, "What category does this fit?" rather than "How can I conceptualize this infinitely complex person in this moment of time?" And instead of thinking, "How can this best be treated?" we might ask ourselves, "What distorted cognitions are present?"

Our brains also use certain kinds of biases to help this process go along even more quickly and smoothly (but, of course, less accurately). One is the *anchoring bias*. This is the tendency to rely too heavily on one trait or piece of information when making decisions, usually the first piece of information acquired on a given subject. If the first part of a fox that we see is its long snout peeking out from behind a tree, we're likely to think "dog" and it's going to be harder to change our minds later. Clinically, this means that it's

DOI: 10.4324/9781003125082-92

pretty hard for us to get past the first information that clients give us, and it turns out that's especially true if that information is indicative of more problems or pathology (e.g., Pain & Sharpley, 1989). For example, clinicians are more likely to diagnose PTSD than Borderline PD when childhood sexual abuse is presented at the beginning of a vignette and Borderline PD when it's presented at the end of the vignette (Woodward et al., 2009). Yikes!

We're also probably more likely to label a fox as a dog if we just saw a dog, just saw a movie about a dog, have a neighbor with a dog, saw an advertisement for dog food, or had a dog when we were growing up. This is called the *availability heuristic*, and it means that we overestimate the likelihood of events with greater "availability" in our memory (i.e., that we are exposed to a lot or have been exposed to recently; e.g., Schwarz et al., 1991). In therapy, that means our previous client, our typical clients, our last consultation, the last book we read, and the last training we went to all may contaminate our thinking about *this* client in the here and now.

By the way, in both cases, we'd technically be right about the fox. Foxes are of the family *Canidae* – descendants of wolves, as dogs are. However, they don't live in packs, they hunt by stealth, they play with their food, and they even climb trees (Nobleman, 2007). That is, behaviorally, they're much more like cats. Reality is rarely as simple as we think.

PRACTICE TIP

It's inescapable – we have to simplify in order to function. The best we can do is mitigate these well-intentioned but unhelpful shortcuts our brains use. So, here are a couple of ideas: (1) Read your intake notes backward (informationally backward, not word-for-word backward!) before your second session; that can help with anchoring bias. (2) Asking yourself "What *else* might this be?" instead of "Could this be what I'm thinking?" can help with availability heuristic.

CHAPTER 84
WE GET DISTRACTED EASILY
FROM WHAT'S IMPORTANT

Our diagnostics are terribly at risk from some specific cognitive biases. To help protect the integrity of the diagnostic process, we have to keep these things in mind. Let me begin with three short client descriptions. As you read, imagine your initial diagnostic impression.

- George is a 38-year-old, married, White male, referred by his wife for "depression," but he doesn't think he has it. He reports feeling not much of anything (apathy) and sometimes irritability. He also reports lack of motivation and low interest in work, socializing, and sex. He notes a reduced appetite, difficulty sleeping, little exercise, some alcohol use, no other substance use beyond caffeine (two to three cups of coffee).
- Ana is a 21-year-old, single, Venezuelan-American college student. She presented to the university counseling center for an intake as part of a class project to learn about mental health services. During her intake, she described (truthfully) that her biggest concern was probably having "ups and downs" (but which her roommate called "mood swings"). Details of her "ups" included partying, drug use, and indiscriminate sex, but she said it wasn't a problem because she was still going to class and getting her work done.
- Sasha is a 14-year-old, Black female. Her mother brought her in because last month Sasha was a witness to a brutal school shooting – her school was on lockdown, the assailant broke into her classroom, and though she wasn't hurt, she saw six people shot, and remembers scooting back into the corner to stay away from the spreading blood. Two of them died, including the teacher, while she was watching. Sasha reports trouble concentrating, and worry about school, grades, and her parents. She's not sleeping well and feels tired a lot but also restless, and she has headaches.

The first cognitive bias we'll consider is *base rate neglect*. This is the tendency to ignore general information about the probability of an event and instead focus on the details of a specific instance (Baron, 1994; Kahneman & Tversky, 1973). Regarding George's case – are you leaning toward thinking he does have depression, as his wife suggests? After all, men can appear apathetic or irritable rather than sad when they are depressed. However, we probably

 DOI: 10.4324/9781003125082-93

want to take the diagnostic base rate into account – based on population data about adult men, George is about six times more likely to have Alcohol Use Disorder than Major Depressive Disorder! Oh … now that we think about it, alcohol use can also be associated with apathy, irritability, low motivation, sexual performance problems, and sleep disturbance!

The second bias we'll consider is the *contrast effect,* which is the change or enhancement in how we perceive one stimulus depending on what we've just recently perceived (Bower, 1961; Plous, 1993). So, if you thought that Ana might have Bipolar Disorder, consider that it probably sounds more like mania than just "being in college" in part because her description followed straight after we were thinking about depression.

Finally, let's consider the *availability heuristic.* Yes, we just talked about this (with the dogs). But the availability heuristic is also operating when things are very emotionally charged – that makes something more "available," too (e.g., Schwarz et al., 1991). Sasha's recent trauma probably leads us in the direction of PTSD, but look again. If we take the trauma out, those symptoms are more consistent with Generalized Anxiety Disorder, and she doesn't report any of the PTSD criteria besides having had trauma. It would be easy to assume that her symptoms started after the trauma, but we don't have that information yet. (It's also worth noting that the availability heuristic is also why, after we go to an interesting training, we suddenly realize that (magically!) half of our clients have *that exact* diagnosis or would benefit from *that exact* treatment.)

PRACTICE TIP

Have you ever watched *House*, the medical drama featuring Hugh Laurie as a (somewhat misanthropic) brilliant diagnostician? What makes him incredible isn't just his insane knowledge base (though that certainly helps!). We don't have to memorize the DSM-5, but it helps to have it on our desks, instead of our bookshelves. There's plenty of information about base rates in there! Dr. House pays attention to details that other people dismiss and asks useful questions – not just to confirm his theory, but to ask *what else* it might be. Also, Dr. House has a luxury that we don't have, probably; he tends to see just one patient per episode. Since we can't do that, we can help reduce contrast effect by "wrapping up" each client by writing their progress note and giving ourselves a small intentional break between sessions.

CHAPTER 85
WE SEE THINGS THAT AREN'T THERE

Apophenia is the tendency to perceive meaningful patterns where none exist, and if that sounds like a hallmark of hallucinations and delusions, you're right (Blain et al., 2020). It's also a completely non-pathological phenomenon associated with openness to new experience (the Big Five trait) and when it's put together with high intelligence, is probably the basis for creativity (Oleynick et al., 2017).

Some of us will remember learning about the Gestalt perceptual principles in PSYC101 (not to be confused with Gestalt therapy!) about how our brains really want to make complete, meaningful pictures. For example, our brains naturally group things together that have some obvious similarities. (In a perfect grid of black and white dots, if the black dots are in rows, we see rows. If the black dots are in columns, we see columns.) Let's look at a few of the instances in which we might just make things up in therapy, without realizing we're doing it:

- Applying apophenia and the Gestalt principle of grouping to our perception of events gives way to *magical thinking*, which is the tendency to believe that unrelated events are causally connected, because they seem to form a meaningful pattern (and especially if they happen close together in time). Kids do this a lot – it's why a six-year-old will often think their parents are getting divorced because they broke the lamp. But we are not immune! This misperception of causality can happen in two main ways – we might assume incorrectly that something in a client's world (past or current) is related to their current distress (and then we waste treatment time working on it, to no avail) or we may assume incorrectly that something we're doing in therapy is related to a client's progress (and then we waste treatment time continuing to do that, to no avail).

- Our memories are not sorted into neurons by date, they are clustered together into meaningful categories and thus activated together (i.e., *associative memory*). The classic study of this involves participants remembering lists of words like dream, rest, pillow, bed, blanket, etc., and recalling the word "sleep" though it wasn't on the original list (Roediger & McDermott, 1996). And think of all of the lists of associated symptoms we have in the DSM just waiting to be misremembered! Did that client who obviously worries too much and has insomnia and feels on

DOI: 10.4324/9781003125082-94

edge report any muscle tension? We're sure she did … she must have … right?

- *Priming* is the activation of thoughts or feelings by something in the current or recent situation, without our awareness (e.g., Higgins et al., 1977; Weingarten et al., 2016). It's the real version of what we imagine when we hear the term "subliminal messages." It comes from a plethora of stimuli (e.g., words, letters, sounds, images, sensations) and can impact our thoughts, feelings, and (in some cases) behaviors. Sometimes priming effects won't hurt us in session – who cares if the reason a certain metaphor pops into our heads is because of the last song we heard on the radio, as long as it's working for the client? But we know that priming can be dangerous – if being primed with a gender question leads to poorer math performance for girls (Gibson et al., 2014), what stereotypes might we be at risk for enacting with clients?

PRACTICE TIP

Go look at the clouds for five minutes. Seriously. I've been very challenging with you in these last few chapters, and I want you to be able to have an experience, rather than just hearing it from me. Don't say it's a perfectly sunny day. In that case, go look at a few tree trunks. See what you see. And you *will* see something. (This is called *pareidolia,* by the way.) And as you realize you really are at risk for all of these things, also allow yourself to be awed … truly, your brain is an amazing thing. While we're talking about how to manage its mistakes, remember how your mind is the very thing that allows you to contemplate it.

Oh, and if that wasn't as practical a tip as you'd hoped, here's another bonus tip: Keep your office slightly warm or offer a warm cup of coffee – physical warmth primes clients to feel socially warm (Bargh & Melnikoff, 2019).

CHAPTER 86
WE CAN'T UN-SEE IT ONCE
WE'VE SEEN IT

So, now we know there are about a million ways to get things wrong, and it's often pretty difficult to notice when we've done it. And now we need to talk about how it's extra hard to fix anything, even when we do notice, because we get stuck.

The law of the instrument (which we briefly mentioned in Chapter 66) goes like this: "I suppose it is tempting, if the only tool you have is a hammer, to treat everything as if it were a nail" (Maslow, 1966). When it comes to our clinical skill set and theoretical orientation, if we are significantly limited in the way that we view clients or the skills we have for treating them, we will be stuck both in conceptualization and treatment. For example, based on the same client information, psychodynamic therapists are more likely to diagnose Borderline PD while cognitive behavioral therapists are more likely to diagnose PTSD (Woodward et al., 2009). Luckily, there are a couple of ways to get out of this stuckness, and we've already discussed them: continual training and great consultation partners!

This next one isn't quite so easy. *Conservatism bias* has nothing to do with our political leanings, or even our therapy style; it is the tendency to revise our beliefs *insufficiently* when we are presented with new evidence. That is, it happens when we update our client maps (or diagnoses, or treatment plans) in response to their feedback (or new symptoms, or little progress), but we don't update them enough. So, we escape the trap of getting things wrong, only to end up closer to right but not all the way there.

As if that weren't enough, there's also the *continued influence effect*, which is the tendency to believe previously learned misinformation even after it has been corrected; sometimes we even believe the old misinformation more (Swire et al., 2017)! This can be a problem in so many ways – for example, we read article corrections or retractions, but our brains can't let go of the originally reported findings. (For example, it turns out that standing in Superman pose doesn't raise our testosterone (Ranehill, 2015) and infants don't imitate our facial expressions (Oostenbroek et al., 2016)). Unfortunately, just by mentioning these, I may have contributed to your believing the old finding instead of the new one!

In session, the continued influence effect means that once we've thought about something wrongly, even if we're blessed with clients who notice and

DOI: 10.4324/9781003125082-95

correct us, we're quite likely to fall back into the same pattern of thinking we had before or at least to allow that previous misinformation to affect how we take in new information. It's kind of like we're drawing our client map with a poor eraser — the badly drawn features are still there, and we can't not see them.

PRACTICE TIP

For sure, be as accurate as possible early on by using reflection and clarification like it's the life and breath of therapy (which it is), so that your map is as accurate as possible. When you do learn something in session that means you need to re-draw part of the map, don't let it go in passing. Ask for lots of details, then use your new information immediately and connect it to the client's overall narrative (Swire et al., 2017). This is like re-drawing the map in ink. You might still see the old pencil marks, but you have a clearer, more correct picture.

CHAPTER 87
WE KNOW TOO MUCH

We know a lot more about some things than our clients do. (At least, we'd better!) And while that's basically the foundation of our profession, there are a couple of ways that it can get us into trouble if we're not careful.

First (play some ominous music in your head, please), the *curse of knowledge*! This is a way of saying that better-informed people often find it difficult to think about problems from the perspective of lesser-informed people (Birch & Bloom, 2003). This is probably what's happening when we get that blank, spacey look from clients after we just developed a beautiful metaphor or the tentative-but-unresponsive head nodding as we explain the theoretical foundation of the homework assignment. (Side note: The curse of knowledge is also one of the reasons that a great therapist doesn't necessarily make a great supervisor!) But it simply isn't useful to try to communicate with clients from our place on the psychological-knowledge mountaintop. We've got to let them lead the way, starting from where they are.

Another problem that can arise from knowing a lot about the "best" way to do things – to communicate with a partner, to solve a problem, to get over a fear – is that we may get stuck teaching clients our way, when there's an equally good way that's easier. This is called *Einstellung*, and officially it is the tendency, after solving many problems in one way, to apply that solution to later problems, even when a better or simpler solution exists (Luchins, 1942). Once we've gotten in the habit of skills training, or cognitive restructuring, or behavioral activation, or going with the feelings, or using a fabulous metaphor … that can become our "go-to" method. Even though our way might be a great way that usually works well, it may not be the most accessible way for every client. We may be trying to fit them to our solution, rather than fitting our process to them.

Another misperception that can get us is the *Dunning-Kruger effect*. Some will be familiar with it from the graphs featuring "Mount Stupid" that are popular online, but it is better expressed like this: Poor performance is associated with unrealistically high perceptions of competence (Kruger & Dunning, 1999). Or we could say that part of being incompetent is the inability to know how incompetent we are. Once we are experts, we are more likely to make accurate judgments about our abilities (or to slightly underestimate ourselves).

DOI: 10.4324/9781003125082-96

This will apply to each of us differently, depending on where we are in our careers. New therapists will likely overestimate their own competence (after the brief phase of complete terror and imposter syndrome). But longtime or expert therapists aren't immune – Dunning-Kruger hits us after we read a new book or attend a one-day training; it's easy to assume that we are competent to bring those things into therapy with us even if they are specialized knowledge or skills. I'm convinced that continuing education providers capitalize on this bias of ours, and we should combat this by choosing training programs that are more extensive and that involve supervision of new therapeutic procedures (like we discussed in Chapter 71). In the areas that we truly are experts, it's ok to embrace that little bit of underestimation and keep ourselves humble.

PRACTICE TIP

If you have the opportunity to teach Introduction to Psychology, do it. It's a very powerful experience in learning how to un-do the curse of knowledge because you will have to simplify all the basic concepts that you already know so well, learn to sequence them in ways that support learning more complex concepts, and do that for 20–300 different people all at once. If not, then you may want to try yoga. Seriously! It's a great place to learn "beginner's mind," which is an openness, a freshness, an ability to approach even something you're an expert in without preconceptions.

CHAPTER 88
WE DO TOO MUCH

We've all heard the adage that we "shouldn't be working harder than our clients," right? There are different reasons for that saying, like burnout reduction or lowering the risk for developing clients' dependence on us. But here are a couple of reasons that it works well for clients to do some specific parts of the work themselves.

First, the *self-generation effect*: Information is better remembered if it is generated from our own minds rather than simply read (Jacoby, 1978). If we want clients to remember the important things from session, it will go better if they say them in their own words. Second, the delightfully named *IKEA effect*: This is the tendency for people to place a disproportionately high value on objects that they worked hard to create themselves, such as furniture from IKEA (Norton & Ariely, 2005). Clients will have more pride and ownership of anything that they co-create or work to build in therapy than something that we just give to them. (Here's a caveat: One part of the IKEA effect is that we value things more if we work hard on them, *regardless of their actual value*, so we do need to stay invested and involved while clients are "building" to ensure that what they take with them is indeed a high-quality product.)

In addition, though we want to make the most of each of those tiny 50 minutes, I'd like to suggest that we could change our focus (a little bit) to helping clients make more therapeutic use of the 10,000 minutes they have between sessions. One way we can do that is to take advantage of the *Zeigarnik (incompletion) effect*: An activity that has been interrupted may be more readily recalled than one that feels completed (Zeigarnik, 1938). This means we actually may want to leave the therapy session a bit open or incomplete at the end, rather than painstakingly monitoring the time and forcing ourselves to tie everything up perfectly at the 50-minute mark. (Of course, I don't mean that we should just shove weeping clients out the door in mid-process. Just that we don't need to do a complete round of practice homework or "finish" every couple's conflict.) Clients may be more likely to ponder therapy thoughts or do their homework during the week.

We also don't need to work hard to present the perfect "gem" for clients to take with them. Unless we somehow manage to make it rhyme (Bower & Bolton, 1969), they're only going to remember the "gist" of what we said anyway, not the exact words (the *verbatim effect*; e.g., Loosen, 1981). And

DOI: 10.4324/9781003125082-97

that's actually fine — conceptual precision or exactness during conscious deliberation (such as in therapy with us) makes for better decision making in the moment. But it turns out that decision making actually improves during a distraction period (e.g., the whole week before they come back), and during that time, clients are just using the "gist" of what they remember (Abadie et al., 2017). (Remember in the intro to this section, when I advised you not to bother with trying to remember the specific name of every bias? This is why.)

PRACTICE TIP

It's really easy to take advantage of these processes: Just always have clients summarize the important things from the session before they go. That will give them the opportunity to put it in their own words and give you the opportunity to check their "gists" for fidelity.

CHAPTER 89
WE HANG ON TOO LONG

Have you ever finished your plate after you were full because it was already paid for? Worn a scratchy dress because it cost $100 or kept watching a bad movie because you'd already finished an hour of it? Held your position in an argument because you just can't back down now, after everything you've said? We've all experienced the *sunk cost fallacy* – when we overvalue what we've already invested in, often to the point of continuing on with it despite negative outcomes (Arkes & Blumer, 1985). That makes it hard for us (sometimes for clients, too) to let go of a therapy direction or strategy once we've started it, even if it's not going well. We didn't spend all that time teaching cognitive distortions and practicing thought records just to abandon the effort! The client finally just got the hang of journaling, we can't change the homework now! It's been a year, we must be getting close to figuring out the childhood learning that led to this terrible relationship!

If we're deep in it, we might double down with *escalation of commitment* – this is where we justify increasing our investment (time, money, discomfort, effort, etc.) just because of how much we've already invested, even though the data suggests that the first decision or direction was probably the wrong one. This is really easy to slip into, because we're now very reluctant to switch gears and "maybe the problem is just that we need to work harder ... "

The next level is when we really need to be paying attention, but unfortunately, by this time, we're typically not good at noticing this or judging it anymore. This stage is *self-justification,* when we go so far as to change our beliefs instead of changing our behavior. This is when we begin to ignore (or just stop noticing) the feedback in session that things aren't changing. It's when we start imagining progress that's not really happening. It's when reluctance to change isn't evident, because the possibility of change isn't even on our radar anymore. It's our consultation partner who is probably going to notice that this is going on, and it will be because we start saying, "yes, but ..." to every question or suggestion that they make.

There's a saying that's called the Law of Holes: "If you find yourself in a hole, stop digging." And how do we know if we're in a hole? We know that client distress, discomfort, or preference isn't necessarily a great metric (because often therapy is difficult and uncomfortable, and tough emotions are sometimes actually signs of progress), so we probably don't want to change course on their whims alone. We can determine if we're actually in a

217

DOI: 10.4324/9781003125082-98

hole, though, based on the metric that our working theoretical orientation gives us. Is anxiety increasing or simply changing targets after a well-done systematic desensitization process? Are negative thoughts becoming ruminative instead of more realistic after a few good cognitive restructuring sessions? Are walls going up with decreased vulnerability after emotion-focused therapy? Nightmares and startle responses getting worse after somatic experiencing work? This is another reason that it is worthwhile for us to use a theoretical orientation with intention, rather than being "eclectic" with each client — it gives us a "measuring stick" for how well therapy is going. And it's another reason that it's good to be reasonably competent in at least a few different modalities, so that we can fully get out of the hole and start on a new path, if need be.

PRACTICE TIP

Occasionally, the thing you're holding on to too long is the client. Whether that is because you really aren't a great fit (but you wish you were) and they deserve a referral, or simply because you both enjoy the time even though they honestly don't need it anymore. I get it – "losses loom larger than gains" (Kahneman & Tversky, 1979). *Loss aversion* means that we experience greater unpleasantness when we lose something of value than the pleasantness we experience when we gain something of the same value (and even monkeys have it! Silberberg et al., 2008). So, it makes sense that we would be loath to let clients go in return for an unknown replacement. But let me suggest two things: First, because we aren't accurate about loss and gain, it's pretty safe to assume that our bank accounts will be the same shortly and we're quite likely to still have clients on our caseload who we enjoy. Second, it's unethical (and in some places illegal!) to keep clients in therapy once they aren't benefiting anymore.

CHAPTER 90
WE'RE ONLY HUMAN

We are human, and we have bodies, and those bodies are amazing. When our bodies are in good working condition, we can absolutely listen to their wisdom. Our body sensations can alert us to danger and to directions for existential growth. Now, what I'm about to say is going to shock you, because by now you know me as a big proponent of listening to one's internal wisdom, but sometimes our bodies talk crazy talk! And we need to know how to know the difference.

The *interoceptive bias* is the tendency for sensory input from our bodies to impact our thoughts or feelings about external, *unrelated* circumstances. When we have internal sensations (e.g., physiological arousal, discomfort, "butterflies," tension) but no clear way of explaining that to ourselves, we search for possible explanations by looking at the environment without realizing we are doing that. For example, when given a stimulant and then sitting in a waiting room with either a happy or angry confederate, people interpret the excess arousal in their bodies as indicators of emotion, specifically an emotion similar to whoever was in the room with them (Schachter & Singer, 1962). And this can have serious real-life consequences – for example, parole judges who are hungry give harsher sentences than they do straight after lunch (Danziger et al., 2011)!

Another thing that human people need is sleep. I know, I know; this sometimes feels like a foreign concept to us. But really, adequate sleep helps us do a better job as therapists. Almost everything our brains do, they do worse when we haven't slept enough. Sleep deprivation (which doesn't have to be total – it can just be not sleeping the full amount we need each night) impairs functions that are really important for the therapy room, like working memory, attention, vigilance, logical reasoning, and decision making (Alhola & Polo-Kantola, 2007).

Taken together, all of this means that we want to make sure that our bodies aren't giving us cues that we misinterpret – hunger, muscle tension, headache, arousal (either kind), tiredness, heat or cold, pain, any kind of gastrointestinal distress, etc.[1] And we don't want to give clients half our brain power; they deserve better. So, if we needed another reason that self-care is an ethical mandate, here it is – we must eat well and sleep well to be able to trust the interoceptive cues we're getting during session and act on them appropriately. This doesn't mean the same thing for everyone, of course.

DOI: 10.4324/9781003125082-99

We each need to know if the coffee will help us return to normal after a poor night's sleep or give us the jitters, if the protein bar in the vending machine will quell our "hangry" feelings or give us heartburn, and if nine hours of sleep will give us mental clarity or zombie-brain. And when in doubt, we need to take the Advil, because pain gets in the way of us doing a good job, too (Eccleston & Crombez, 1999).

PRACTICE TIP

Here's one final thing about being human that I'd really like to close with. We're not perfect. And the *nirvana fallacy* (you didn't think I'd miss the chance to throw in just one more cognitive bias, did you?) is the idea that we compare everything to the perfect thing it could be – how's that for dichotomous thinking (He, 2016)? Let's not. It's worth knowing we'll never be perfect and it's worth working our whole careers to keep doing better. Let's also not let the perfect be the enemy of the good.

NOTE

1   Ladies, small note – the cognitive and emotional changes related to the reproductive cycle are real, so let's get educated about that, so we can account for it, rather than letting our clients pay for us not knowing.

REFERENCES

Abadie, M., Waroquier, L., & Terrier, P. (2017). The role of gist and verbatim memory in complex decision making: Explaining the unconscious-thought effect. *Journal of Experimental Psychology: Learning, Memory, and Cognition, 43*(5), 694–705. https://doi.org/10.1037/xlm0000336

Alhola, P., & Polo-Kantola, P. (2007). Sleep deprivation: Impact on cognitive performance. *Neuropsychiatric Disease and Treatment, 3*(5), 553–567.

Arkes, H. R., & Blumer, C. (1985), The psychology of sunk costs. *Organizational Behavior and Human Decision Processes, 35,* 124–140.

Bargh, J. A., & Melnikoff, D. (2019). Does physical warmth prime social warmth? Reply to Chabris et al. (2019). *Social Psychology, 50*(3), 207–210. https://doi.org/10.1027/1864-9335/a000387

Baron, J. (1994). *Thinking and deciding* (2nd ed.). Cambridge University Press. ISBN 978-0-521-43732-5.

Birch, S., & Bloom, P. (Feb 6 – Feb 8, 2003). The curse of knowledge: Biased assessments of the knowledge and beliefs of others [Conference session abstract]. *4th Annual Meeting of the Society for Personality and Social Psychology,* Los Angeles, California. https://doi.org/10.1037/e633872013-792

Blain, S. D., Longenecker, J. M., Grazioplene, R. G., Klimes-Dougan, B., & DeYoung, C. G. (2020). Apophenia as the disposition to false positives: A unifying framework for openness and psychoticism. *Journal of Abnormal Psychology, 129*(3), 279–292. https://doi.org/10.1037/abn0000504

Bower, G. H. (1961). A contrast effect in differential conditioning. *Journal of Experimental Psychology, 62*(2), 196–199. https://doi.org/10.1037/h0048109

Bower, G. H., & Bolton, L. S. (1969). Why are rhymes easy to learn? *Journal of Experimental Psychology, 82*(3), 453–461. https://doi.org/10.1037/h0028365

Campbell, W. K., & Sedikides, C. (1999). Self-threat magnifies the self-serving bias: A meta-analytic integration. *Review of General Psychology, 3*(1), 23–43. https://doi.org/10.1037/1089-2680.3.1.23

Choi, I., & Cha, O. (2019). Cross-cultural examination of the false consensus effect. *Frontiers in Psychology, 10,* Article 2747. https://doi.org/10.3389/fpsyg.2019.02747

Eccleston, C., & Crombez, G. (1999). Pain demands attention: A cognitive–affective model of the interruptive function of pain. *Psychological Bulletin, 125*(3), 356–366. https://doi.org/10.1037/0033-2909.125.3.356

Gibson, C. E., Losee, J., & Vitiello, C. (2014). A replication attempt of stereotype susceptibility (Shih, Pittinsky, & Ambady, 1999): Identity salience and shifts in quantitative performance. *Social Psychology, 45*(3), 194–198. https://doi.org/10.1027/1864-9335/a000184

He, X. (2016). When perfectionism leads to imperfect consumer choices: The role of dichotomous thinking. *Journal of Consumer Psychology, 26*(1), 98–104. https://doi.org/10.1016/j.jcps.2015.04.002

Higgins, E. T., Rholes, W. S., & Jones, C. R. (1977). Category accessibility and impression formation. *Journal of Experimental Social Psychology, 13*(2), 141–154. https://doi.org/10.1016/S0022-1031(77)80007-3

Jacoby, L. L. (1978). On interpreting the effects of repetition: Solving a problem versus remembering a solution. *Journal of Verbal Learning & Verbal Behavior, 17*(6), 649–667. https://doi.org/10.1016/S0022-5371(78)90393-6

James, W. (1890). *Principles of Psychology Volume I.* Dover Publications.

Kahneman, D., & Frederick, S. (2002). Representativeness revisited: Attribute substitution in intuitive judgment. In T. Gilovich, D. Griffin, & D. Kahneman (Eds.), *Heuristics and biases: The psychology of intuitive judgment* (pp. 49–81). Cambridge University Press. https://doi.org/10.1017/CBO9780511808098.004

Kahneman, D., & Tversky, A. (1979). Prospect theory: An analysis of decision under risk. *Econometrica, 47*(2), 263–291. doi:10.2307/1914185

Kahneman, D., & Tversky, A. (1973). On the psychology of prediction. *Psychological Review, 80*, 237–251. http://dx.doi.org/10.1037/h0034747

Langer, E. J. (1975). The illusion of control. *Journal of Personality and Social Psychology, 32*(2), 311–328. https://doi.org/10.1037/0022-3514.32.2.311

Lay, C., Ziegler, M., Hershfield, L., & Miller, D. (1974). The perception of situational consistency in behaviour: Assessing the actor-observer bias. *Canadian Journal of Behavioural Science/Revue canadienne des sciences du comportement, 6*(4), 376–384. https://doi.org/10.1037/h0081883

Lilienfeld, S. O. (2020). Embracing unpopular ideas: Introduction to the special section on heterodox issues in psychology. *Archives of Scientific Psychology, 8*(1), 1–4. https://doi.org/10.1037/arc0000072

Loosen, F. (1981). Memory for the gist of sentences. *Journal of Psycholinguistic Research, 10*(1), 17–25.

Luchins, A. S. (1942). Mechanization in problem solving: The effect of Einstellung. *Psychological Monographs, 54*(6), i–95. https://doi.org/10.1037/h0093502

Marcatto, F., Cosulich, A., & Ferrante, D. (2015). Once bitten, twice shy: Experienced regret and non-adaptive choice switching. *PeerJ, 3*. doi: 10.7717/peerj.1035

Maslow, A. H. (1966). *The psychology of science: A reconnaissance.* Unknown Publisher.

Mynatt, C. R., Doherty, M. E., & Tweney, R. D. (1977). Confirmation bias in a simulated research environment: An experimental study of scientific inference. *The Quarterly Journal of Experimental Psychology, 29*(1), 85–95. https://doi.org/10.1080/00335557743000053

Nissen-Lie, H. A., Rønnestad, M. H., Høglend, P. A., Havik, O. E., Solbakken, O. A., Stiles, T. C., & Monsen, J. T. (2017). Love yourself as a person, doubt yourself as a therapist? *Clinical Psychology & Psychotherapy, 24*(1), 48–60. https://doi.org/10.1002/cpp.1977

Nobleman, M. T. (2007). *Foxes.* Benchmark Books.

Norton, M. I., & Ariely, D. (Nov 11– Nov 14, 2005). *The "IKEA effect": Why labor leads to love {Conference session abstract}.* Society for Judgment and Decision Making 2005 Annual Conference, Toronto Canada. https://doi.org/10.1037/e640112011-015

Oleynick, V. C., DeYoung, C. G., Hyde, E., Kaufman, S. B., Beaty, R. E., & Silvia, P. J. (2017). Openness/intellect: The core of the creative personality. In G. J. Feist, R. Reiter-Palmon, & J. C. Kaufman (Eds.), *Cambridge handbooks in psychology. The Cambridge handbook of creativity and personality research* (pp. 9–27). Cambridge University Press.

Oostenbroek, J., Suddendorf, T., Nielsen, M. … Davis, J., Clark, S., & Slaughter, V. (2016). Comprehensive longitudinal study challenges the existence of neonatal imitation in humans. *Current Biology, 26*(10), 1334–1338. doi:10.1016/j.cub.2016.03.047

Pain, M. D., & Sharpley, C. F. (1989). Varying the order in which positive and negative information is presented: Effects on counselors' judgments of clients' mental health. *Journal of Counseling Psychology, 36*(1), 3–7. https://doi.org/10.1037/0022-0167.36.1.3

Pallier, G., Wilkinson, R., Danthir, V., Kleitman, S., Knezevic, G., Stankov, L., & Roberts, R. D. (2002). The role of individual differences in the accuracy of confidence judgments. *Journal of General Psychology, 129*(3), 257–299. https://doi.org/10.1080/00221300209602099

Piaget, J. (1951). The biological problem of intelligence. In D. Rapaport, *Organization and pathology of thought: Selected sources* (pp. 176–192). Columbia University Press. https://doi.org/10.1037/10584-007

Plous, S. (1993). *The psychology of judgment and decision making*. New York: McGraw-Hill. ISBN 978–0–07–050477–6.

Pronin, E., & Kugler, M. B. (2007). Valuing thoughts, ignoring behavior: The introspection illusion as a source of the bias blind spot. *Journal of Experimental Social Psychology, 43*(4), 565–578. https://doi.org/10.1016/j.jesp.2006.05.011

Ranehill, E., Dreber, A., Johannesson, M., Leiberg, S., Sul, S., & Weber, R. A. (2015). Assessing the Robustness of Power Posing: No Effect on Hormones and Risk Tolerance in a Large Sample of Men and Women. *Psychological Science, 26*(5), 653–656. https://doi.org/10.1177/0956797614553946

Roediger, H. L., & McDermott, K. B. (1995). Creating false memories: Remembering words not presented in lists. *Journal of Experimental Psychology: Learning, Memory, and Cognition, 21*(4), 803–814. https://doi.org/10.1037/0278-7393.21.4.803

Ross, L. (1977). The intuitive psychologist and his shortcomings: Distortions in the attribution process. In L. Berkowitz (Ed.), *Advances in experimental social psychology* (Vol. 10, pp. 173–220). San Diego, CA: Academic Press.

Ross, L., Greene, D., & House, P. (1977). The "false consensus effect": An egocentric bias in social perception and attribution processes. *Journal of Experimental Social Psychology, 13*, 279–301. doi: 10.1016/0022–1031(77)90049-X

Ross, M., & Sicoly, F. (1979). Egocentric biases in availability and attribution. *Journal of Personality and Social Psychology, 37*(3), 322–336. https://doi.org/10.1037/0022-3514.37.3.322

Schachter, S., & Singer, J. (1962). Cognitive, social, and physiological determinants of emotional state. *Psychological Review, 69*(5), 379–399. https://doi.org/10.1037/h0046234

Schwarz, N., Bless, H., Strack, F., Klumpp, G., Rittenauer-Schatka, H., & Simons, A. (1991). Ease of retrieval as information: Another look at the availability heuristic. *Journal of Personality and Social Psychology, 61*(2), 195–202. https://doi.org/10.1037/0022-3514.61.2.195

Silberberg, A., Roma, P. G., Huntsberry, M. E., Warren-Boulton, F. R., Sakagami, T., Ruggiero, A. M., & Suomi, S. J. (2008). On loss aversion in capuchin monkeys. *Journal of the Experimental Analysis of Behavior, 89*(2), 145–155. https://doi.org/10.1901/jeab.2008.89-145

Spieser, L., Kohl, C, Foster, B., Bestmann, S., & Yarrow, K. (2018). Neurodynamic evidence supports a forced-excursion model of decision-making under speed/accuracy instructions. *eNeuro, 5*(3), ENEURO.0159–18.2018. doi: https://doi.org/10.1523/ENEURO.0159-18.2018

Swire, B., Ecker, U. K. H., & Lewandowsky, S. (2017). The role of familiarity in correcting inaccurate information. *Journal of Experimental Psychology: Learning, Memory, and Cognition, 43*(12), 1948–1961. https://doi.org/10.1037/xlm0000422

Weingarten, E., Chen, Q., McAdams, M., Yi, J., Hepler, J., & Albarracín, D. (2016). From primed concepts to action: A meta-analysis of the behavioral effects of incidentally presented words. *Psychological Bulletin, 142*(5), 472–497. https://doi.org/10.1037/bul0000030

Woodward, H. E., Taft, C. T., Gordon, R. A., & Meis, L. A. (2009). Clinician bias in the diagnosis of posttraumatic stress disorder and borderline personality disorder. *Psychological Trauma: Theory, Research, Practice, and Policy, 1*(4), 282–290. https://doi.org/10.1037/a0017944

Zeigarnik, B. (1938). On finished and unfinished tasks, in W. D. Ellis (Ed.), *A Sourcebook of Gestalt Psychology*, London: Kegan Paul, Trench, Trubner & Co.

We Can Only Be Who We Are (Self as Therapist)

"Use of self" in therapy is now a muddy kind of term that seems to encompass (at its worst) all sorts of potentially harmful things, like florid self-disclosures and reckless disregard for evidence-based practices. At its best, it's a positive therapeutic influence that can be imagined as the full, authentic engagement in the "I–Thou" relationship with clients (Buber, 1937). But Buber's philosophical and almost metaphysical description (recall this from Chapter 20) is a little hard to wrap our minds around and even more difficult to enact. So, let's run with Virginia Satir's beautiful description of use of self in therapy:

> The metaphor of a musical instrument comes to mind when I think of the therapists' use of self. How it is made, how it is cared for, its fine tuning, and the ability, experience, sensitivity, and creativity of the player will determine how the music will sound. Neither the player nor the instrument writes the music. A competent player with a fine instrument can play well almost any music designed for that instrument. An incompetent player with an out-of-tune instrument will vilify any music, indicating that the player has an insensitive, untrained ear. I think of the instrument as the self of the therapist: how complete one is as a person, how well one cares for oneself, how well one is tuned in to oneself, and how competent one is at one's craft. I think of the music as the presentation of the patient. How that music is heard and understood by the therapist is a large factor in determining the outcome of the therapy. (Satir, 1987)

These last chapters will help us "tune our instruments" by considering Rogers' concept of congruence and getting to know ourselves more deeply. Increasing our self-awareness through these thought experiments will naturally make our *presence* in every session more therapeutic.

CHAPTER 91
GETTING ROGERS (REALLY) RIGHT

Remember in Chapter 2, when we talked about congruence for clients and therapists, and I mentioned that Rogers (1957) really lets therapists off the hook because he only requires that we be congruent during the therapy hour? Now that we're at the end, let's talk about what it might look like to take that into our whole lives (the way Rogers describes it for clients), to be what he calls "fully functioning persons." Don't we want to really be the people that clients hope we are, to not have to turn our congruence on and off at the therapy door?

To do that, a little more vocabulary is in order. Rogers (1959) talks about three different selves that we have (and they are unreasonably confusing, so I apologize on his behalf): the self, the ideal self, and the real self. The *self* is our view of ourselves, the kind of conceptual gestalt of who-I-actually-am-now. It may be helpful for us to think about the self as our "self-concept." The *ideal self* is the version of ourselves that we would like to be or think we should be, and it's usually based on introjected conditions of worth from valued others (that is, all of those messages we got from parents and teachers that let us know when we were better, or more valuable, or "good.") We might think of the ideal self as our "should self." The *real self* is the self we could be, if we were free from all of those conditions of worth, and actually fully congruent and self-actualized. We might do well to think of it as our "potential self."

Do you remember from geometry what congruent triangles are? For two or more triangles to be congruent, they must have exactly the same three sides and exactly the same three angles. In the Rogerian way, being *congruent* (or integrated, genuine, or psychologically well-adjusted) means that our self, our ideal self, and our real self are all the same. That is, the person we understand ourselves to be currently is also who we want to be and is in fact our actual best self.

So, how do we do that? Simple. We just develop insane amounts of self-awareness (which includes removing all of our defenses and distortions), we learn to give ourselves positive self-regard (which also involves letting go of the conditions of worth of others), and then we just fully accept and integrate every experience we have going forward (and internalize them all accurately). Ha! Ok, maybe not *that* simple. And it's certainly not *easy*.

                           DOI: 10.4324/9781003125082-101

But it's worth it, because once this congruence is in place, the other aspects of being a fully functioning person (Rogers, 1963) come naturally. When we are *fully functioning persons* we are fully open to and unafraid of every experience, and all of our feelings and reactions (i.e., we are non-defensive). We sense the internal and external world with a fair degree of accuracy and so we can allow ourselves to listen to our bodies, our inner wisdom. We can recognize the many choices available to us in any given moment, and we can choose wisely – not because we are infallible, but because by being so open to our experiences, we will definitely recognize the consequences of our choices and incorporate that new knowing into our self-understanding, making satisfying outcomes more and more likely. This internal and external accuracy also allows us to be social in effective ways and to live safely in the present moment. Because of our awareness, we continually sense the existential nature of ourselves and our situations, and we flexibly adapt and grow in response to the environment. Sounds like something worth working toward, right?

PRACTICE TIP

Want to start working on it right now? For many of us, the most difficult part of being congruent is going to be getting over our own self-criticism. So, here's a reasonably good starting exercise. Write down everything you don't like about yourself. Flip everything to a positive. Where/from whom did you learn that was a valuable thing? Is it actually valuable? Defend it to yourself. Decide if you want to keep it. Throw out stuff that doesn't actually fit you. Add in anything that came to you during the process that fits you more. Are you in progress toward being those ways you want to be? If not, how could you be? How well are you loving the in-progress version of yourself? Simple; not easy.

Oh, therapy is a great place to work on this, too.

CHAPTER 92
REALLY PRIZING

If we are going to create growth-promoting climates in therapy, we have to be able to offer unconditional positive regard to clients and *mean it*. Remember, *unconditional positive regard* is complete, warm acceptance (not just tolerance!) of every aspect of clients and their experiences and an authentic, non-possessive caring that together allow clients the space to determine their own meaning without interference (Rogers, 1961).

Preferably, we would be able to do this all the time, but it's not always easy. It's easy to warmly accept the victims of abuse; it's not always so easy with perpetrators. It's easy to prize the wounded kids we see in session, but more difficult to prize the parents who are largely the causes of those poor kids' dysfunction. If we're being honest, it's easy to accept the clients who are basically like us, and hard to accept the ones who are different.

Considering the depth of complexity of each person, there is virtually always going to be something about each client that we at least don't like. That makes unconditional positive regard an outrageously difficult thing to do, but one way to make it a bit easier to apply broadly and faithfully is to figure out our *philosophy* about people's inherent value. I've heard a few examples of such philosophies, but we each have to determine one that really fits for us, deeply.

For example, some clinicians who have a Judeo-Christian background are able to use the concept of each person being "made in God's image" (e.g., Genesis 1:26–28) to help them to recognize the ultimate value of every human, regardless of their traits, behaviors, or likeability. Other spiritual traditions incorporate a similar idea, such as the Hindu salutation "Namaste" (which is definitely as philosophical and metaphysical as Buber's I–Thou and along the same lines!); this is often described as meaning something like "that which is divine in me recognizes and honors that which is divine in you." (As a side note, some specific faith traditions, including some within the larger Judeo-Christian system, emphasize the opposite – the "fallenness," sinfulness, and/or basic wretchedness of all people, none of whom has inherent value or deserves positive regard. It may be that this is compatible with a Rogerian UPR because everyone is equally, desperately in need of care?)

Some clinicians have a more secular or biological understanding of humanity that emphasizes environmentally determined change in the

 DOI: 10.4324/9781003125082-102

direction of higher states of organization. They may have to be a little more creative in how they apply value-laden concepts (such as prizing) to inherently value-free natural processes (Vandenberg & O'Conner, 2005). For example, valuing *consciousness* allows there to be a hierarchy of value in which humans occupy the top (or near top) position, and thus may be treated as "inherently" valuable.

There is also a kind of middle ground based in the realm of our responsibilities to one another. There's no question that meaning is strongly associated with relationships for theists and atheists alike (Nelson et al., 2019). Because we are the (divinely created or evolutionarily developed) highly complex and self-aware beings that we are, we may have a (divinely ordained or evolutionarily demanded) responsibility to care for ourselves and each other. As the limited beings we are, it's difficult for us to care well for things that we don't value. So perhaps it can go either way – we care for each other because of each person's inherent value or we imbue each other with value in order to manage the necessary task of caring.

Of course, these are not the only options. It's important that we sort this out in a way that fits our individual understandings of life, the universe, and everything!

PRACTICE TIP

If you think that unconditional positive regard is really easy, chances are that you aren't really fully engaging with the complete experience of humanity that clients bring in. We are built, neurologically, to notice differences in others and to automatically not like those differences (Sapolsky, 2017). So, the first thing is to make sure you're being honest with yourself (congruence!) about this being difficult.

Then, really take the time to articulate this philosophy in words. You'll probably be surprised by how difficult it is to truly explain it, but you'll be on firmer ground once you're able to. If you're at a loss, reading some philosophers or some holy writings might help.

CHAPTER 93
FREEDOM & RESPONSIBILITY

The English language is kind of a mess sometimes. For example, why do we use the same word to mean something we feel externally (like the silkiness of sheets) and something we feel internally (like a muscle ache) and something else we feel internally (like an emotion)? Why do we use the word "my" to mean something that we own (e.g., my flip flops, my phone), something that we created (e.g., my book, my child), and something that we belong to (e.g., my organization, my country)? It's weird.

Another overly general English word is *freedom*. We use it to mean both "freedom from ..." (e.g., oppression, want) and "freedom to ..." (e.g., vote, retire). In the existential sense, which is what I'd like to address here, freedom is definitely *freedom to* – to respond to our circumstances, to create meaning, to choose from the always myriad choices present for us (and there *are* always choices, even if we don't like them). It is the freedom to "answer the questions [we are] asked by life," as Viktor Frankl says. He goes on to say, "This freedom must not be confounded with arbitrariness. It must be interpreted in terms of responsibleness" (Frankl, 1969).

Responsibility is inextricably linked to freedom because if we have a choice (and we always do) then we are choosing (and we always are). And, being the sentient, self-aware, marvelous creatures that we are, we also bear the burden of knowing that we are responsible, no matter how we try to deny it. And, oh boy, do we try to deny it!

We deny this freedom (because we are understandably terrified of the responsibility that comes with it) in many ways (Yalom & Josselson, 2014): We may boldly denounce our choices and refuse to act, we might create self-defeating beliefs that convince us we can't be responsible, we could develop pathological symptoms that excuse us from our responsibilities, or we may even indulge the "lust for submission" (Fromm, 1941) that leads us to enlist bosses, partners, dictators, and gods as an escape from our freedom. But mostly, I'd say, we do it with language. So often, in fact, that we've become numb to the phrases "There was no other choice" and "I had to ... " But what we usually mean is "That's what was expected of me," "I felt socially or morally obligated," or "I was scared to do anything different." (Remember Chapter 29, when we talked about the difference between "can't" and "don't"?)

DOI: 10.4324/9781003125082-103

Some people say that Existential Therapy doesn't take into account external factors that are legitimately out of our control, like systemic racism and poverty (the things we aren't free *from*). And it can sound like that. But remember, Viktor Frankl wrote *Man's Search for Meaning* (1959) when he was in a concentration camp. The existentialists do *not* say that we should be able to change our circumstances or limitations, only that we are responsible for how we choose to act *within* our circumstances and limitations. This is what is meant when they say that life and the world put their questions to us, and we are only responsible, but fully responsible, for our answer (Frankl, 1969).

PRACTICE TIP

If you're in a situation (e.g., a job, a relationship) in which you do the best you can with the circumstances and limitations that are put on you, and you are still miserable because there are no options that align with your values, *get out*. I don't mean if you have to make suboptimal choices sometimes, or if you can act according to your values but that makes things unpleasant for you, or if you simply don't like things or they're just not fair, or if you can act with integrity but then you have to work harder than other people. That's just life asking you the hard questions.

I mean if there are legitimately no options that don't compromise your human dignity, get out. (Chances are they're going to fire you or break up with you soon anyway, if you keep having all that integrity.) If you don't have the power to get out, ask for help. If you still don't have the power to get out, read *Man's Search for Meaning* again.

CHAPTER 94
PRACTICING WHAT WE PREACH

So, that last chapter was heavy, I know. Take a deep breath, because this one isn't much lighter – it's about *hypocrisy*. Which means it answers a similar, difficult question: How can we be authentic if we're "acting discordantly with our values?" Answer: We can't. So, let's not.

Another thing that's easier said than done.

Here are just a few common examples of how we do this, at least in the realm of therapy. (I'm not saying *you* do this, or that if you do any of these it means you're a hypocrite, or anything else you might object to. I'm just saying some people somewhere do these kinds of things, and if it hits you in the belly, well … read on.)

- We extol the efficacy and virtue of sleep hygiene (or sitting with anxiety, or exercise) and then we take sleep meds (or benzos, or SSRIs) instead of doing the work.
- Same goes for journaling regularly (but browsing Netflix instead), and practicing mindfulness (but hitting snooze instead), and setting boundaries for toxic relationships (but replaying our same old over-involved patterns instead).
- We teach clients assertiveness and then lack assertiveness when they are chronically late, don't pay, don't do homework, etc.
- We say that our clients are more than a diagnosis but then use convenient and unjustified diagnoses for insurance reimbursement (Adjustment Disorder, anyone?).
- We avoid going to therapy ourselves.

We damage our authenticity when we act in ways that are contrary to what we believe or the values we hold. And there can be damage in session because sometimes clients see us modeling things we caution against ("Do as I say, not as I do."). But possibly the greatest risk in hypocritical behavior comes from the fact that these things we call "selves" very much want to be internally consistent. When we don't act, think, and feel in compatible ways, we experience an unpleasant psychological state called *cognitive dissonance*, and we have an inborn drive to reduce it (Festinger, 1957; VandenBos, 2007).

Here's a fun study (Festinger & Carlsmith, 1959): Participants are asked to do *really* boring, *really* inconsequential stuff (e.g., turn 48 pegs in a

DOI: 10.4324/9781003125082-104

pegboard a quarter turn, one at a time, and then turn them all back, one at a time). Some are given one dollar; some are given 20 dollars. Then, they're asked how interesting and enjoyable the activities were. Results? Getting only $1 predicted much higher ratings of enjoyability and those participants were much more likely to say they'd be happy to participate again! WHAT?! That's cognitive dissonance at work. If we got paid $20 (that's about $180 today), we wouldn't have any problem living with ourselves if all we did during that hour was turn pegs. But if we only got paid $1, it *must have been* enjoyable or worthwhile in some way, right?

Here's the not-fun real-life consequence: Because of cognitive dissonance, it's often easier for us to change in the direction of believing what we have done is right and good, rather than changing our behavior to what we know is right and good.

CBT therapists know this – it's why we sometimes start with changes to behavior and then see the attendant changes in thoughts and feelings occur naturally. That's when we're using it mindfully and intentionally toward valued ends. But we need to remember that cognitive dissonance is working all the time and keep a keen watch on our own behavior.

PRACTICE TIP

It's safe to say that we've all acted hypocritically. But it turns out the least effective thing we can do about that is get together in a group and admit it, because then everyone admits it, we all feel less guilty,[1] and we go on with our inauthentic living, feeling morally justified in our conformity (McKimmie et al., 2003). It's probably much more helpful to recognize the natural tendency toward self-deception (Batson et al., 1999) and regularly invite yourself (and your consultation partner) to have a good look in the mirror.

NOTE

1   Note I said "guilty" and not "ashamed." If you're struggling with shame, ignore most of what I said and read some Brené Brown before coming back to this chapter.

CHAPTER 95
KNOWING WHO (AND WHERE AND WHEN) WE ARE

Our culture is indelibly *who we are*. Not even "part of" who we are, if we are defining it broadly. My favorite way of thinking about culture comes from Karen Horney (1937), who describes culture in a way that I now think of as our "space–time."[1] This is my favorite way because she emphasizes our embeddedness in culture and how we are fundamentally unknowable without knowledge of the space (which includes all the layers of geography) and time (which includes all the layers of history) in which we are located, along with all the people who populate our world. And I especially love it because she was a Neo-Freudian, so her thinking this way in her own space–time was *so* progressive!

Without attempting to cover the whole discipline of multicultural competence, I'd like to point us in some useful directions for managing and capitalizing on the cultural richness that is in every therapy session.

First, let's know our own culture deeply and well, in all the ways we can think of. We can think about it like the intersection of all of the multiple, specific populations to which we belong. This is the way that it's usually talked about in our counseling textbooks, with lists of different dimensions of culture like ethnicity, age, gender identity, sexual orientation, ability status, veteran status, etc. (e.g., Sue et al., 2019). We can also think about it in sociological ways, like how our cultural milieu is more or less uncertainty avoidant, has more or less power distance, is more indulgent or restrained (e.g., Hofstede, 2011). Or we can think about it in anthropological ways, examining the "useful tyranny of the normal" in the cultures of our upbringing and how we have "elastically adjusted" (Sapir, 1932). We can even think about it in developmental ways, like how the combination and interaction of our different environments, from our families to our communities to our state, nation, world, and time all create a particular growth field that no one else shares (e.g., Bronfenbrenner, 1979). We are endlessly rich, so this can be a rich and endless journey.

Second, we should intentionally expose ourselves as widely as possible – books, podcasts, documentaries, history, biographies, etc. in every imaginable area. Yes, we need to choose wisely and keep a wary eye to everything, because there are at least as many poor sources as there are good ones. But we do have a tendency to limit ourselves to areas, ideas, and people that

235 DOI: 10.4324/9781003125082-105

we're already somewhat familiar with or that resonate with the way that we already think and feel. And that can make us insulated and contribute to our ignorance almost as much as not exposing ourselves at all! So, let's intentionally get outside our comfort zones and emphasize breadth in this kind of learning.

Third, let's meet people. Unless we are lucky enough to work and live in one of the few really diverse space–times (like in a large city with a great transportation system in a sliding-scale practice), we probably experience a limited array of major cultural differences in our practices. That's ok – we can't learn everything about everyone, so this is a way to narrow our focus for in-depth learning in a really practical way, because it's most important to be fluent in the cultures of the people we serve. Better than learning just from books and such, these are people groups that we have the opportunity to learn from *in vivo*. We can make an effort to build relationships and support communities in our area with people who are different from us outside of therapy, to enrich us *as people*, not just to "improve our cultural competence."

PRACTICE TIP

Don't be afraid to read what non-you people write about you. It's not that they're always right, or even right at all, but they can still help us see things we never noticed before. For example, I had no idea that "punctuality" had a cultural component until I was in college (e.g., van Eerde & Azar, 2020). It was *obvious* to me that "being on time" was a thing everyone just did (recall the false consensus effect from Chapter 81). We are all fish in our own water, to varying degrees, no matter how long or well we've worked on our cultural competence. So, even if we wholeheartedly disagree about an area we hadn't thought about before, there's still value in recognizing it.

NOTE

1   This is a great example of the verbatim effect that we discussed in Chapter 88. I was 100% certain that Horney actually used this exact term, and re-reread two books and spent six hours searching online to find it, but apparently, that was just how I internalized the "gist" of what she said!

CHAPTER 96
SELF CARE THAT LASTS

Keeping our bodies in good condition is important for doing good work (as we discussed in Chapters 46 and 90) – eating well, sleeping well, being moderate with substances, etc. This also goes for keeping our relationships in good condition so that we have good social support, getting therapy when we need it, and maybe cultivating our spiritual lives. None of that is controversial.

But (and I know *this* will be controversial), I don't think self-care ever really needs to involve pedicures. Let me explain. Sometimes, when we talk about self-care, it's more like we let ourselves get way overstressed and then think that dropping off the planet in withdrawal or going on a self-indulgent binge is somehow the way to repair this. This chronic bounce between over-stress at work and attempts at under-stress during our time off is *not* a good recipe for longevity in the field.

I'd like to propose a way of thinking about self-care that is grounded in the concept of flow (Csikszentmihalyi, 2008, which we mentioned being useful for clients in Chapter 42). As a reminder, *flow* is that "zone" we get into when we're involved in something that's just the right balance of challenge with our skills, that we can be enjoyably immersed in with an energized focus. It's a balance, because if we try to engage in things that are too easy, we get bored. If we try to engage in things that are too difficult, we get stressed/anxious. So, if we can create flow in our work, we can leave the roller coaster of over- and under-stress behind, because we won't be running ourselves ragged during the workday and we won't feel the need to compensate with too much Netflix or too much booze. As a bonus, it will probably improve our performance in session, too!

In our clinical work, we often find ourselves out of balance. Sometimes, we take on too much – too many clients, too long of days, clients who are outside our boundaries of competence but we don't want to admit it – and still expect ourselves to have Olympic levels of therapy-stamina. Sometimes, we take on too little – get into a rut, don't challenge ourselves to build new skills, take an overly systematized job and function as technicians rather than clinicians – and still expect ourselves to have Olympic levels of therapy-enthusiasm. Other factors can pull us out of the flow zone, too. It might be that we feel we have no control – we've given up our autonomy to a harsh internship director for the sake of getting hours (oh, how you'll regret this!)

DOI: 10.4324/9781003125082-106

or we're so burdened by rules and paperwork that our actual clinical work is only a handful of minutes per hour. Sometimes, it's that we know the work isn't meaningful – we can see that clients aren't improving, our setting won't allow for the care clients need, etc.

So, how do we create flow in our work? Here are some things that help set the stage for a flow experience:

- The right level of challenge: There are two ways to work on this – one is to engage with your employer/supervisor (about making adjustments to your work tasks, clients assigned, etc.) and the other is to change things *in session* – increase the challenge or simplify as fits best for you. Therapy will improve in your flow level of challenge, not deteriorate, regardless of whether you entertain additional complexity or keep things simple.
- Intense, focused concentration on the present moment: This is partly an intention that we set with ourselves. We can also help by establishing focusing rituals that we can use in our offices and we might be able to work on the physical environment to reduce distraction and create a comfortable, concentration-friendly space.
- Sense of personal agency: I know that in some of our positions, we don't have much agency at the level of client choice, daily schedule, etc. But we probably *do* have some agency in how our actual therapy sessions go.

One caveat: We can't *make* flow happen. All we can do is set the stage and then take advantage of it when it appears!

PRACTICE TIP

When you are in flow, you *will* lose track of time. So, make sure you have a clock that you can see and that clients have a clock that they can see, to help avoid running every session over time! I know that some people don't like their clients to have a clock that they can see, but I do. To me, it's not about giving them the responsibility to keep us on time, but rather a way of respecting their autonomy – if they can monitor the session time, it lets them make important choices about what they bring up and when.

CHAPTER 97
WOUNDED HEALERS

Though wounded healers have gotten a fair amount of press lately, this is a very old idea (and, like most old ideas, has gone through some "artful revamping" over the years). The concept is probably based in the Greek myth of Chiron – a centaur raised to learn the art of medicine (after being abandoned by his birth parents), who is injured by a mystically poisoned arrow that creates a wound that will never heal. He commits his entire immortal life to healing others and advancing the practice of medicine while in continual misery. Yikes!

Jung (1957) applied the archetype of the wounded healer to psychotherapy, by suggesting that our personal wounds, defenses, and dysfunctions are the precise reason that we may want to go into the field of psychotherapy and the exact reason that we ought to complete our own therapy before we start practicing – because our wounds (and our responses to them) can hurt clients. Also yikes!

Today, we are much more likely to celebrate the virtues of having suffered from the basic human maladies of the spirit as well as particular traumas (e.g., Farber, 2017). And there is plenty to celebrate, especially if our traumas follow one of the two trajectories with happy endings: predictable recovery over time or post-traumatic growth (Zerubavel & Wright, 2012). With both of these trajectories, we may still need a break from our work, or certain parts of our work, while we work through our recovery process. (Side note: This probably needs to happen in the context of professional support. Ironically, in one version of the myth, Chiron dies from an arrow wound that he *couldn't heal himself*, despite knowing all of the medical arts!) If we're resilient enough to experience post-traumatic growth, we may be able to authentically integrate many excellent qualities into our selves-as-therapists, including viewing the self as simultaneously vulnerable and strong, discovering new potential in ourselves, enhancing our appreciation for life, developing a deeper sense of purpose and meaning, and having deeper interpersonal connections and greater empathy (Calhoun & Tedeschi, 2006). Wonderful!

But you don't need to have serious wounds in order to be a great therapist. In fact, there are a few ways that some wounds really don't work in our favor.

239

DOI: 10.4324/9781003125082-107

- First, Chiron was a god, (or at least the child of a Titan), so the fact that he could suffer day in and day out and still do excellent work is literally a myth. We are not built that way. If our wounds aren't sufficiently healed, we won't be very effective. It is crucial that a therapist's wounds are mostly healed or, at minimum, understood and processed sufficiently, to prevent them from interfering with therapy and the therapeutic relationship (Gelso & Hayes, 2007).

- Second, growing up in a really troubled family environment can have unfortunate effects on our overall relational development. Early family dysfunction that leads to insecure attachment styles as an adult predicts poorer therapeutic relationship development, empathic responding, and therapy outcomes (Strauss & Petrowski, 2017). It's worth noting that Chiron's success is often attributed to his (most un-centaur-like) temperament – peaceful, intelligent, kind, wise, gentle – which was inculcated by the attentive and loving care of his adoptive parents, Apollo and Artemis. If our wounds are of this kind, we can expect to need therapy work of our own to maximize our therapeutic potential.

- Third, the other two potential post-trauma paths are a relapse trajectory with periodic setbacks and a chronic dysfunction trajectory with continuous struggle (Zerubavel & Wright, 2012). If we fall into one of these trajectories, we need to recognize it and, with a good dollop of self-compassion, consider a career adjustment to place ourselves and our clients out of the way of additional harm. There are a thousand niches in the mental health field; there's definitely one that can accommodate our needs.

PRACTICE TIP

Do tell someone in your professional realm about your wounds, past and present, even though I know there is stigma, and you might be afraid that you will say "wound" and that person will hear "impairment." But please, at least tell your amazing consultation partner. We need someone else to help us navigate the potential perils of being wounded healers, and occasionally to call us out because the wound *is* impairing our work.

Don't tell your clients. Sure, acknowledge that you have had difficult times or suffering in your history if they ask. But detailing your wounds will almost invariably "make therapy about you." Even if it doesn't, why is it important for your client to know? How will it help them? We can find other ways to instill hope, find directions for growth, and demonstrate *true* empathy by understanding *their pain as they experience it,* rather than offering them the specious substitute of our own pain.

CHAPTER 98
KNOWING OUR SECRET NEEDS
(AND OWNING THEM)

In the last chapter, I mentioned how Jung suggested that our own personal wounds may be one impetus for deciding on therapy as a career. Of course, if we're being really psychodynamic about it, there's no way any of us chose this career for fully known reasons. Discovering and acknowledging a "behind the scenes" reason that we're in this career can not only deepen our self-understanding but improve our work. (Stop worrying ... there's no reason for us to think that just because we have a secret need that it's necessarily a bad thing!)

There are many ways to conceptualize this (e.g., Freudian defense mechanisms, Perls' introjects, Jungian archetypal journeys), but I've found that Horney's (1942) discussion of the main neurotic needs tends to hit a good balance between being deep enough that they really matter, being easy enough to get a handle on, and being relatively less threatening to imagine (because everyone experiences at least some of them a little bit). To what degree can you resonate with the need to:

- Have affection, approval, to please others, to be liked
- Follow the lead, let someone else take responsibility
- Live narrowly, safely, inconspicuously
- Control self/others through reason, foresight, wisdom, or intelligence
- Be powerful or exercise control, especially over others
- Be better than others and be able to manipulate or exploit them
- Have recognition or prestige
- Be admired and valued for personal qualities
- Achieve greatly or be the best, in important areas
- Live independently, self-sufficiently
- Perform perfectly or excellently

Read them over again. Feel free to be honest with yourself – no one is reading this but you, and you don't have to tell anyone what you discover. Pay special attention to any that were an easy "Oh, that's me!" and also any that were a definite, quick "No way!" Also, don't feel the need to go too deep right now. Horney says there are multiple layers of these, but any awareness and work will be useful.

DOI: 10.4324/9781003125082-108

A fun way to go about seeing how these operate in our lives is to start with small things. Think about the one that resonated most with you. Can you see how this impacts you when you drive to work? Are you a kind, cautious driver (because you have the need to please)? Always leave five minutes early (because you need to control your self and environment through foresight)? Do you mentally trash talk other drivers (because they are reckless idiots?! I mean, because you have a need to be better than they are)?

What about when you argue with a family member? Go to the bathroom? Think about your day? Have sex? Shop for clothes? Write an email? What about when you're in the therapy room?

Remember – it's not necessarily a problem! As long as we want approval in reasonable amounts from reasonable people who have similar expectations of us, there's nothing wrong with wanting approval. Reason and intelligence aren't bad things; why not make a life based on using those to help others have a fulfilled life? Being self-sufficient may be a virtue in and of itself, based on our cultural and family background, and as long as we don't force that value on others, is there harm in being independent?

The value in knowing these secret needs is that when we *do* go off the rails a little bit, it's usually in this direction. When we want our clients' approval too much, we can make bad therapeutic decisions. It's easier to see that someone else is being domineering because they're power-hungry; it's harder for us to see that we're being domineering because we're just sharing our wisdom, which is obviously right. Independence can be marching to our own drum but losing connection with other professionals leaves us at greater risk for things like ethical missteps.

PRACTICE TIP

If, when you thought through this exercise (or when you do later), you felt a rush of relief, or let out an unexpected peal of laughter, that's because these kinds of insights can break down old, sticky barriers that function to inhibit or paralyze us. That rush of "aliveness" is the energy freed up to move more authentically ... so use it! Start small.

If you didn't feel a rush of vibrancy or insight, don't sweat it. It might not be the right time, and as Horney says, "Evasive tactics will inevitably occur." Accept that you may be protecting yourself and that might be the right move for now. Or maybe you're actually so free of neurosis that there really is no insight in there for you. (wink)

CHAPTER 99
KNOWING OUR SHADOWS
(AND OWNING THEM)

Generally, when the Jungian shadow gets mentioned, there are either blank looks or terrified looks, and I want to change that! Though this is vastly oversimplified, two of Jung's concepts that are important for this discussion are (1) everyone has certain parts of self and (2) balance can be created through the development and tension of opposites. For example, most of us are at least vaguely familiar with the *anima* and *animus*, which are the feminine and masculine parts of self. Jung says we function better, and in a more fully authentic way, when we have explored and integrated both our anima and animus (regardless of which comes more easily to us). Likewise, he says we all have a *persona,* which is the most intentionally cultivated part of self and the part that interacts with the outside world. The opposite of the persona is the *shadow,* which is the least developed, most repressed part of self (Jung, 1959).

Possibly the reason that the shadow got such a bad rap is because it is difficult to know (and we're afraid of the unknown) and it seems to have some mysterious power over us (and we don't like being out of control). Probably it's because when we cultivate our outer selves, our personas, for the world, we are aiming to make that version of ourselves acceptable to society and valued others. If the shadow is the opposite of that, if it's filled with all of the things we don't show ourselves or the world, maybe it's filled with all evil, terrible, and guilt-inducing things?!

Sure it is. I'm not saying there isn't *anything* in our shadows that we wouldn't like to see! (And plenty that might need to stay there, out of public view.) But the shadow is also the holder of normal instincts, profound insights, and creative impulses. We don't repress only legitimately awful things; we also repress things that we thought the world, our cultures, our families, and our circumstances at any given time might not fully appreciate. But, because none of us have lived in a perfect world or have had accurate perceptions for all of our lives, the shadow is actually a potential *treasure trove* of useful, valuable things that we didn't need to hide.

We might find in there the assertiveness that our family mislabeled as disrespect, the spontaneity that was scolded because Mom always had a headache, or the sexuality that was only not scolded because it was never, ever talked about at all. We might find our genuine need for affection (that

 DOI: 10.4324/9781003125082-109

was pushed out of consciousness because affection was never available) or our precious sensitivity (that was squashed when we learned to speak the family language of biting wit and sarcasm). Maybe our laziness is in there (the laziness we think we don't have because our persona is chronically, frantically busy with efforts that never seem as productive as they should be), and if we'd recognize it and invite it to be part of our lives, we might actually find a good balance of rest and activity.

It feels a little scary to visit our shadows mostly because they are *underdeveloped.* They are underdeveloped because they've been *disowned.* And we can do something about that, whether it's as mild as a tentative inward glance or as significant as going into Jungian analysis. We can work to develop our shadows, or even our "opposite parts" if we prefer to think of it like that. Any part of us that is strong and forward is connected (think like a seesaw) to the opposite part, and we will function more flexibly and in a more integrated way if we are balancing those opposites, rather than only focusing on what is already well developed. When we develop our therapy skills, we don't only work on things we're already good at, we look for the areas that are underdeveloped. Not so scary when we think about it like that, is it?

PRACTICE TIP

Want to play around with this? Make a list of at least six famous people, some who you really like (who have a positive "pull" for you) and some you really don't (who tend to "repel" you). Consider *all* kinds of famous people – including real people like politicians, actors, sports figures, and historical figures as well as fictional people like TV, comic book, or fairy tale characters. Then, give each of them the first adjective that comes to mind. Once you have that list, it will be easy to divide it into "positive" and "negative" qualities. But the work comes next – find the seed of usefulness in every negative part and the seed of destruction in every positive part (Satir, 1978).

CHAPTER 100
KNOWING OUR POTENTIAL
(AND OWNING THAT, TOO)

I've spent a lot of time in this book calling us all to *integrity*, sometimes with gentle nudges and occasionally with gut punches. And I'm not going to stop now, in the last chapter. There's something else that many of us have disowned, and because of that, we suffer from "the Jonah complex."

This comes from the Biblical story of a man (Jonah, obviously) who was called by God to do some difficult stuff he was afraid to do, so he ran away on a boat instead. There was (not coincidentally) a big storm and Jonah got swallowed by a huge fish, and after three days and some serious soul-searching, got spit out so he could, in fact, fulfill his destiny. In psychology, the Jonah complex is described using phrases like "evasion of growth," "fear of one's own greatness," and "running away from one's own best talents." It's discussed by Maslow (1971) as the opposite of self-actualization. He says that we all have unused potentialities (or at least potential we haven't fully developed), but that we sometimes "shiver with weakness, awe, and fear before these same possibilities."

What are we afraid of?

Are we afraid it will be difficult? It will be. Worthwhile things usually are.

Are we afraid to fail? We will. And that's valuable.

Are we afraid of the responsibility? We already have it, whether we deny it or not.

If we can allow ourselves to experience these possibilities for a moment with awe – a vision of who we could be, what we could do, our own untapped potential – it could inspire us, even if it's scary. And that shimmer of feeling that our brains think is terror might just be the excitement that our inner selves feel at the prospect of The Next Step.

We don't need courage. Courage isn't even a real *thing*. It's not something we have or don't have. It's not a trait or an ability or a capacity. Courage is just a word, a reification. What we call courage is actually just *willingness*. It's the willingness to engage without knowing the outcome. And we *never know the outcome*. We sometimes pretend we know the outcome and relax into the lie, but we never actually do.

We are not objects which in motion stay in motion and at rest stay at rest. We are living people, moving through time, like it or not. And The Next Step – personal and professional – is there, waiting. Holding ourselves back

DOI: 10.4324/9781003125082-110

from it, staying in the same place, *not growing*, is an effort of will just as much as moving forward is. Often, staying in the same place is just as risky, too.

So, what's your Next Step?

PRACTICE TIP

Please, don't just close this book. Go and do *something*. I don't know if it's a training you need to attend, an apology you need to offer, a therapy appointment you need to book, a talk you need to have, a walk you need to go on, an inner child you need to comfort, a job you need to quit, a gift you need to give, a project you need to start, a nap you need to take, or a consultation partner you need to find. But do it. Be in the process of becoming the authentic you, ~~even if~~ especially if it's a little scary.

REFERENCES

Batson, C. D., Thompson, E. R., Seuferling, G., Whitney, H., & Strongman, J. A. (1999). Moral hypocrisy: Appearing moral to oneself without being so. *Journal of Personality and Social Psychology, 77*(3), 525–537. https://doi.org/10.1037/0022-3514.77.3.525

Bronfenbrenner, U. (1979). *The ecology of human development.* Cambridge, MA: Harvard University Press.

Buber, M. (1937). *I and Thou.* Translated by Smith, Ronald Gregor. Edinburgh: T. & T. Clark.

Csikszentmihalyi, M. (2008). *Flow: The psychology of optimal experience.* Harper Perennial Modern Classics.

Farber, S. (2017). *Celebrating the wounded healer psychotherapist: Pain, post-traumatic growth, and self-disclosure.* Routledge.

Festinger, L. (1957). *A theory of cognitive dissonance.* Stanford University Press.

Festinger, L., & Carlsmith, J. M. (1959). Cognitive consequences of forced compliance. *The Journal of Abnormal and Social Psychology, 58*(2), 203–210. https://doi.org/10.1037/h0041593

Frankl, V. (1959). *Man's search for meaning.* (Original title: From death-camp to existentialism). Beacon Press.

Frankl, V. (1969). *The will to meaning: Foundations and applications of logotherapy.* World Publishing Co.

Fromm, E. (1941). *Escape from freedom.* Holt.

Gelso, C. J., & Hayes, J. A. (2007). *Countertransference and the therapist's inner experience: Perils and possibilities.* Erlbaum.

Hofstede, G. (2011). Dimensionalizing Cultures: The Hofstede Model in Context. *Online Readings in Psychology and Culture, 2*(1). https://doi.org/10.9707/2307-0919.1014

Horney, K. (1937). *The neurotic personality of our time.* W. W. Norton & Company, Inc.

Horney, K. (1942). *Self-analysis.* W. W. Norton & Company, Inc.

Jung, C. G. (1957). *Practice of Psychotherapy.* (R. F. C. Hull, Trans.) (H. Read et al., Eds.) *The Collected Works of C. G. Jung (Vol.16).* Princeton University Press.

Jung, C. G. (1959). *The archetypes and the collective unconscious.* (R. F. C. Hull, Trans.) (H. Read et al., Eds.) *The Collected Works of C. G. Jung (Vol. 9i).* Princeton University Press. Patheon.

Maslow, A. (1971). *The farther reaches of human nature.* The Viking Press.

McKimmie, B. M., Terry, D. J., Hogg, M. A., Manstead, A. S. R., Spears, R., & Doosje, B. (2003). I'm a hypocrite, but so is everyone else: Group support and the reduction of cognitive dissonance. *Group Dynamics: Theory, Research, and Practice, 7*(3), 214–224. https://doi.org/10.1037/1089-2699.7.3.214

Nelson, T. A., Abeyta, A. A., & Routledge, C. (2019). What makes life meaningful for theists and atheists? *Psychology of Religion and Spirituality.* Advance online publication. https://doi.org/10.1037/rel0000282

Rogers, C. R. (1957). The necessary and sufficient conditions of therapeutic personality change. *Journal of Consulting Psychology, 21*(2), 95–103. https://doi.org/10.1037/h0045357

Rogers, C. R. (1959). A theory of therapy, personality, and interpersonal relationships as developed in the client-centered framework. In S. Koch (Ed.), *Psychology: A study of a science, Formulations of the person and the social context* (Vol. 3, pp. 184–256). New York: McGraw-Hill.

Rogers, C.R. (1961). *On becoming a person.* Houghton Mifflin.

Rogers, C. R. (1963). The concept of the fully functioning person. *Psychotherapy: Theory, Research & Practice, 1*(1), 17–26. https://doi.org/10.1037/h0088567

Sapir, E. (1932). Cultural anthropology and psychiatry. *The Journal of Abnormal and Social Psychology, 27*(3), 229–242. https://doi.org/10.1037/h0076025

Sapolsky, R. (2017). *Behave: The biology of humans at our best and worst.* Penguin Press.

Satir, V. (1978). *Your many faces: The first step to being loved.* Celestial Arts.

Satir, V. (1987). The therapist story. *Journal of Psychotherapy & the Family, 3*(1), 17–25. https://doi.org/10.1300/J287v03n01_04

Strauss, B. M., & Petrowski, K. (2017). The role of the therapist's attachment in the process and outcome of psychotherapy. In L. G. Castonguay & C. E. Hill (Eds.), *How and why are some therapists better than others? Understanding therapist effects* (pp. 117–138). American Psychological Association. https://doi.org/10.1037/0000034-008

Sue, D. W., Sue, D., Neville, H. A., & Smith, L. (2019). *Counseling the culturally diverse: Theory and practice* (8th ed.) Wiley.

van Eerde, W., & Azar, S. (2020). Too late? What do you mean? Cultural norms regarding lateness for meetings and appointments. *Cross-Cultural Research, 54*(2–3), 111–129. https://doi.org/10.1177/1069397119866132

Vandenberg, B., & O'Connor, S. P. (2005). Developmental psychology and the death of God. In B. D. Slife, J. S. Reber, & F. C. Richardson (Eds.), *Critical thinking about psychology: Hidden assumptions and plausible alternatives* (pp. 189–206). American Psychological Association.

VandenBos, G. R. (Ed.). (2007). *APA dictionary of psychology.* American Psychological Association.

Yalom, I., & Josselson, R. (2014). Existential psychotherapy. In R. J. Corsini & D. Wedding (Eds.), *Current psychotherapies* (pp. 265–298). Thomson Brooks/Cole Publishing Co.

Zerubavel, N., & Wright, M. O. (2012). The dilemma of the wounded healer. *Psychotherapy, 49*(4), 482–491. https://doi.org/10.1037/a0027824

Parting Words

I'd like to leave you with a wish.

May we each one day have the gift of Rogers' empathy, Adler's integration, Freud's confidence, Jung's depth, Frankl's tranquility, Gendlin's focus, Ellis' straightforwardness, Wolpe's specificity, Haley's perception, Madanes' astuteness, Horney's insight, Vygotsky's delicacy, Erickson's voice, Satir's authenticity, Skinner's clarity, Yalom's wisdom, Beck's perspective, Maslow's optimism, Glasser's pragmatism, May's courage, and Perls' creativity.

Too much? In that case, let me wish you bookshelves full of inspiration, at the least.

Index

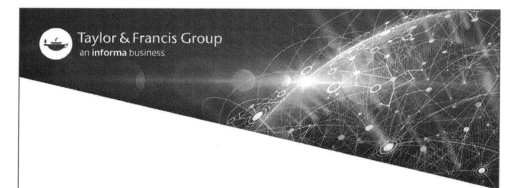